A Popular Guide to

MINORITY RIGHTS

edited by

Y. N. KLY

Published with the support of
The European Human Rights Foundation

ISBN: 0-932863-19-1

In-house Editor: Diana G. Collier

Cataloguing in Publication Data:

Main entry under title:

A Popular guide to minority rights

Includes bibliographical references.
ISBN 0-932863-19-1

1. Minorities - Legal status, laws, etc.
2. Afro-Americans - Legal status, laws, etc.
3. Afro-Americans - Civil rights. I. Kly, Y.N. (Yussuf Naim), 1935- II. International Human Rights Association of American Minorities.

K3242.Z9P6 1995 342'.087 C94-920255-X

A co-publication of:

International Human Rights Association of American Minorities (IHRAAM)
Ste. 253, 919C Albert St.
Regina, SK. S4R 2P6
Canada

and

Clarity Press, Inc.
Ste. 469, 3277 Roswell Rd. N.E.
Atlanta, GA. 30305

Table of Contents

The end of the Cold War has brought about profound changes in both Eastern and Western Europe. In the West, the end of the Communist threat has reduced the impetus towards European unification. In the East, the end of the Cold War has 'unfrozen' ethnic cleavages and fanned nationalist aspirations. In both East and West, intolerance towards minorities and refugees has appeared and racism and extremist violence have increased again, nearly half a century after what many thought was their ultimate demise with the defeat of fascism...

...[T]he fit between nation and state — which has rarely been a perfect one — is bound to get worse. A look at demographic data is revealing. Of the 132 major states with more than one million inhabitants, only 12 can be described as ethnically homogeneous. Another 25 states have a single ethnic group constituting 90% of the population. In 31 states the dominant ethnic group accounts for between 50% and 74% of all people. There are 39 major states where no single ethnic group accounts for half of the population. In other words, the homogeneous nation-state is an exception in this world and any attempt to make nation and state one is bound to lead to catastrophe. The shortest definition of genocide is, after all, 'the destruction of a nation by the state.' [On the other hand, i]f each ethnic group were given a nation-state of its own, we would have several thousand states. The economic viability of most of these mini-nations would be illusory. With the world economy rapidly becoming one global market, political disintegration is likely to reduce the competitiveness of small states. Yet in what other manner than through statehood can the apparently growing desire for group identity be accommodated? Should not the very concept of the sovereign centralized state be re-thought as the number and mobility of people increases, and as territory and its use and preservation are becoming a common concern for all mankind? What are the solutions? Is minority rights, as understood in international law, the most feasible framework for an appropriate nation vs.state compromise?

Global Issues
1994

Often, the majority sees
the minority's politico-cultural demands
as unrealistic and a deviation from society's norms.
However, if the society's norms were put in place
by the political dominance of the majority
and were never acceptable to the minority
although it was constrained to recognize them,
then this reality, too, is one of that society's norms.
Thus calls from the minorities
for what appear to be radical politico-cultural changes
do not necessarily represent deviations
from the actual societal cultural norms,
but rather reflect a lessening of controls
which permit part of the societal cultural norms
which were heretofore hidden and repressed
to be expressed:
greater cultural and political freedom from domestication and a
demand for meaningful democracy.

All disproportionalities in the problems facing minorities,
whether in health care, social welfare, criminal justice or education,
can be traced to their being successfully held
within institutions, policies, and procedures
designed by the majority for the majority
and prevented from being able to create or establish
institutions, policies and other collective arrangements
that suit their historical development and actual situation.
This raises the important moral question:
is there a sufficient reason why a minority should necessarily
accept anything that was forced on their parents through terror
and is maintained undemocratically by force?

All attempts at solutions which do not contemplate changes
in political institutions or the creation of new institutions
must necessarily ignore the minority's existence
other than as the lowest sector or caste of the majority
or amount to nothing more than the animation of new strategies
to maintain the same old inequalities

Y. N. Kly

Introduction

Minority Rights: Utopian Realism

When we speak of human rights, it is often assumed that we are referring to a set of rules and principles put together by some utopian international organization far from the realm of real problems and practical policies, with no hope of effective implementation. However, while utopian concepts of human rights do exist, the human rights instrumentation emerging from the present international system results not from wishful thinking but from real life human tragedies, from the necessity to seek peace, law and order to ensure human survival.

A cursory glance at the history of human rights subsequent to World War II, the Holocaust, and the economic destruction of Europe[1] suggests that human rights emerged from the nearly universal international recognition of the potential of humankind, in the form of sovereign states, nations and individuals, for self-destruction through their creation of situations of chaos, economic collapse, injustice, environmental disaster, appalling human misery and genocide. Statesmen were forced to recognize that an international system consisting of sovereign states which subordinated their citizens' rights as human beings to governing elites'efforts to maintain power, national supremacy and privileges, was anarchic and dangerous. Perhaps the only rational short and long range response to this challenge could be none other than the establishment of the UN and the further development of international law, in recognition of what a history of wars of conquest had taught: that the rule of law is a necessary ordering principle in the world system as much as it is in states, that violent conflicts which threaten world peace frequently entail issues of justice and rights, and that there are some rights which all need and demand, regardless of nationality, race, gender or economic situation.

In the ensuing five decades since its establishment, the UN has succeeded in the monumental task of providing for the legal-structural togetherness (in one forum) of states: large and small, rich and poor, developed and underdeveloped, and of diverse cultures, philosophies, races, ethnicities, and religions which in their entirety represent the present world system. These states, operating under the umbrella of the UN and representing, however inadequately, the people of the global village, decided it was in their collective interest, to accept limitations on their own authority vis-a-vis the human rights of their citizens. The formulation and acceptance of the Universal Declaration of Human Rights was the geo-political miracle of the 20th century.

In the United Nations Charter, minority rights received no special mention, but rather was seen as likely to result from the implementation by states of non-discrimination and equality before the law. Soon it was discovered, however, that these general principles and the policies by which they were implemented were not enough to end discrimination against minorities, and that ensuring non-discrimination as it relates to minorities required the implementation by states of special rights, similar to those known in international customary law. This history is reflected in the evolution of the focus of the UN Sub-Commission[2] from non-discrimination to its 1979 Special Report on Article 27 of the *International Covenant on Civil and Political Rights*.[3]

The Civil Rights "Everybody's the same so why can't we all just get along" Model

Following World War II, there appeared to be a widespread desire to submerge the minorities issue. Europe was still suffering from the effects of a war initiated partly on the grounds of alleged violation of the rights of German minorities, a pretext used by Hitler for invasion of neighboring states. In Asia and Africa, territories rather than peoples were accorded self-determination, thus obliging new states to engage in a process of nation-building by welding together the diverse ethnies/tribes living on the previously colonial territory. Newly-acknowledged as a superpower and seeking to proceed towards the unicultural/universalist Communist ideal (which in practical and less principled terms meant the facilitation of Russian socio-cultural domination of the U.S.S.R.), the Soviet Union was desirous of rescinding its minorities' or nationalities' originally high degree of constitutional recognition,[4] an ideological program which may have been given added practical imperatives by the pro-German behavior of certain Soviet nationalities during the war.

However, the factor most usually credited for submergence of minority rights, counter to trends manifested in the earlier League of Nations, is the emergence of the U.S. as a major world power. The U.S.' economic, social and political system enjoyed significant popularity in the major capitals across the globe, due to its comparative economic and military power, its image of ongoing opportunity in a war-devastated world, and to the apparent individual freedom and economic opportunity offered to elites, or individual citizens seeking to join the elites. Competition for world leadership with the U.S.S.R. led the U.S. to seek to attract the emerging Third World states to the American model of liberal capitalist democracy— an effort hampered by the existence within the U.S. of a minority of non-European descent which had previously been enslaved and at the time was still enduring systemic discrimination through an official policy of segregation (apartheid). The U.S. sought to resolve the dilemma on the domestic front by extending civil rights to the formerly segregated minority population, and on the international front by propelling the focus of the emerging UN human rights movement from policies or concepts of minority rights towards policies of non-discrimination and equality before the law, in keeping with the new U.S. civil rights model. This U.S. solution reflected its historically-established use of policies of non-discrimination and assimilation to assure that disparate European settler populations would be welded into a new Anglo-Saxon (white) ethny on British-dominated colonial territory, animated by the desire to consolidate hold on land taken from indigenous populations and to effectively exploit African slave labor.[5]

The U.S.-promoted assimilationist model for dealing with its European minorities harmonized with a European ethno-nationalist trend of creating "nation-states" which in essence sought to deny the existence of minorities by means of the romantic presumption that the state was the organic construct of one nationality/ethnicity, with all others to be subsumed within that national culture. However, while in Europe the desire of dominant nationalities in one state to protect the religious or cultural existence of their ethnic kin residing as minorities in the territories of neighboring states spawned a series of agreements on minority rights and the beginning of Europe's re-orientation to minority rights, no sufficient counter-pressure to the Anglo-Saxonizing assimilationist process existed in the U.S.. Western European states neither had the power nor the interest to protect their nationals — primarily an impoverished surplus population — who immigrated to the U.S..

While the U.S. civil rights/assimilationist example strongly influenced the early inattention of the United Nations to questions of minority rights, such questions could not be submerged within the world system as a whole. Despite efforts of elites worldwide to imitate the U.S. system, the issue of minority rights emerged with renewed vigour in the international system, due to the struggles for collective cultural survival of the Quebecois in Canada, the Scottish and Welsh in the United Kingdom, the Bretons in France, the Flemings in Belgium, the Basques and Catalans in Spain, the Ibo in Nigeria, the nationalities in the U.S.S.R., the Tibetans in China, the indigenous peoples, worldwide, and so on. It has increasingly become apparent that the melting pot concept, when adopted in most non-American cultures, amounted to nothing more than forced assimilation, ethnic cleansing or ethnocide, which has been vigorously resisted by most minorities concerned. Increasingly, statesmen and scholars concluded that, regardless of whatever success coerced assimilationist policies may have had in the U.S., they have proved disastrous elsewhere. This realization encouraged a shift in international law and the UN away from idealization of the U.S. civil rights model as sufficient for minority protection.

The U.S. Melting Pot: A Unique Success?

Insofar as forced assimilationist policies have largely proved inadequate globally, it seems reasonable to enquire further whether they have in fact succeeded in the U.S., thereby making it a rather unique case in the world. While it is true that in the U.S., the assimilation process managed to produce a new "white ethny," the American was in fact an Anglo-American, insofar as Anglo-Saxon culture and history became the vessel by which this new "white race" was formed and expressed. The U.S. civil rights/melting pot approach served the interest of almost everyone except the national minorities, identified not as a part of the dominant Anglo-American ethny, but rather as a devalued unassimilable sector of the population. Indeed, it can generally be argued that it was and remains the necessity to control and contain weaker less-valued minorities that energizes the successful operation of the melting pot in relation to stronger minorities allied with the desired and valued sectors of the dominant group.

The U.S. civil rights/melting pot concept was facilitated by the following factors:

1. As the most powerful, influential and perhaps most loved area by the dominant world powers due to its aura of material success and championship of notions of individual freedom and (more implicitly) unbridled economic opportunity, the U.S. has always managed to successfully subdue African, Native and Chicano-American resistance to socio-political domination

without meaningful international interference or assistance to these minorities. As an instance — whatever international criticism of the U.S. there may have been in the wake of the insurrection or riots of the1960's and Wounded Knee, the UN itself took no action comparable to that taken with regard to the Canadian/Mohawk conflict at Oka.

2) However distressing the Anglo-Saxonization process may have been to the other immigrant European populations, it did not outweigh the perceived benefits that they accrued thereby. As a whole, the European immigrant population saw the need and was willing to put aside their racial differences in order to survive and adjust in a new world to which none held ancestral claim. Their elites were handsomely rewarded economically, socially, politically and psychologically for accepting to be a part of the new white race with free land and cheap slave labor.

While the above factors might lead to the supposition that, contrary to others' historical experience, the processes of assimilation were relatively successful in the U.S. in relation to European minorities, the statistics suggest otherwise in relation to non-European national minorities. There is no want of statistics which indicate the failure of the U.S. civil rights model for protection of these minorities:

- In 1984, the net worth of holdings for black households was $4,397 as compared with $39,135 for white households.[6]

- The proportion of whites in the work force who have college degrees remains more than twice that of black workers. In 1959, the ratio was 10% white, 4% black; in 1979, it was 18% white and 9% black.[7]

- In 1992, the percentage of white families earning $50,000 or more was 34.1; for blacks, it was 14.9. On the other hand, the percentage of families earning less than $10,000, for whites was 7.3%, and for blacks, 26.4%.[8]

- In 1991, 16.1% of white children were under the poverty level, compared with 45.6% of black children; this represented a negligible proportionate change from 1970, when 10.5% of white children and 41.5% of black children were below the poverty level.[9] For only one year in the intervening 20 years, did the percentage of black children living below the poverty level drop below 40% — to 39.6% in 1974.

• According to UN statistics, there are approximately 1,500 African-Americans per 100,000 in prison, compared with approximately 400 Anglo-Americans per 100,000.[10]

• In 1989, 12.8% of whites, and 20.2% of blacks were without health insurance coverage.[11]

• In 1989, 30,705 white juveniles were held in public custody, compared with 24,003 black juveniles; 25,696 whites and 11,076 blacks were held in private custody.[12]

• In 1993, there were 94 white senators, and 1 black senator.[13]

• As at December 31, 1991, there were 1,464 whites, compared with 982 blacks, under sentence of death.[14] The number of African-Americans is nearly 40% of the total, again vastly disproportionate to their 10% of the population.

While the level of discrimination against minorities in multinational majoritarian states can be gauged by statistical means, such as measuring disproportionalities between majority and minority in an array of indicators of social wellbeing, it is also possible to gauge the extent of discrimination by a more amorphous psychological/attitudinal measurement, as suggested by Ervin Staub in *The Roots of Evil: The Origins of Genocide and Other Group Violence.*[15] The majority's orientation towards the minority, which might range from discriminatory to potentially genocidal, Smith suggested, can be ascertained by the extent to which the following 20 questions can be answered in the affirmative:

1. Has historical devaluation of the minority by the majority ethny occurred?

2. Has there been historical discrimination against the minority?

3. Has the majority developed a self-concept of superiority in relation to the minority?

4. Can hostility to the minority be found in elements of the culture, institutions or personalities of the majority?

5. Has the majority historically developed the concept that the minority treatment is justified because of a "right cause,"

i.e. melting pot/need to build a "new man" in a "new nation"

6. Is the society concerned in a state of rapid technological and social change?
7. Does acceptance of the equal status of the minority threaten the world view of the majority?
8. Does the majority culture have a strong respect for authority and a significant degree of cultural rigidity?
9. Is there a strong and purposeful differentiation of ingroup and outgroup, particularly as it relates to higher ideal concepts, scapegoating or blaming others for one's problems, or cultural stereotyping of others?
10. Is there a tendency towards just-world thinking — that people who are suffering must deserve their suffering?
11. Is the majority ethny capable of accepting difference as equal?
12. Is there, in the majority ethny, a sense of having the right to rule over the minority?
13. Is racism usually tolerated by those in power?
14. Is there effective socialization of the young in racist institutions, customs, etc.?
15. Is aggression or racism a cultural ideal of the majority ethny?
16. Is there strong bureaucratization of function in the state (each person focuses only on his job)?
17. Is there the use of euphemistic language to refer to the minority that veils the reality of the minority's existence (e.g. underclass, street people, etc.)?
18. Are victims said to play a part in their own victimization, denying reality to defend themselves which encourages their victimization?
19. Is there an absence of a genuine effort to identify elements of culture that are hostile and reduce them?
20. Have the perpetrators of discrimination against the minority come to believe either the victims have something they want or stand in the way of something they want?

In the case of a multi-national state where a largely positive response to the above questions combines with statistical evidence of inequalities, if existing policies for achieving minority equal-status or equality do not address these issues, they will likely fail.

Another indication of this failure may be a state's level of social unrest. U.S. rates, measured in relation to a wide range of factors, have been found to be above all other states in relation to social unrest,[16] which might be more openly manifest, were it not for its effective containment by an enormous police force disproportionately directed at control of minorities, as evident by the overwhelmingly disproportionate number of minority individuals (particularly African and Native Americans) incarcerated.

Even a casual consideration of the above indices, apart from our historical knowledge of the destructive effects of enslavement, segregation and ethnocide, must inevitably lead to the conclusion that all does not go well for minorities in the land where once upon a time, in a land far away, non-discrimination and equality before the law freely united peoples of many different cultures and races into *one, yearning to be free.*

Human Nature or Government Policy?

In suggesting the inability of the U.S. civil rights model to protect minorities — as is amply evidenced by the quantitative and qualitative indicators of inequality elaborated above — we do not wish to suggest that the U.S. civil rights model has no value. Of course, this model is one of the U.S.'s strongest democratic attributes as far as protection of individuals and the majority is concerned, but while absolutely necessary, it falls short of what is required to provide minority equal status and equal developmental opportunity. *In short, the U.S. has an excellent civil rights model but really has no minority protection policy of consequence.* Rather, those historically-evolved policies which relate to its chief national minority, the African-Americans, can be seen to reflect a continuing process of minority domination and exploitation, from which the new U.S. policy of civil rights does not depart.

In 1968, the National Advisory Commission on Civil Disorders concluded that: "Our nation is moving toward two societies, one Black, one white* — separate and unequal" and attributed this inequality to "racial attitudes" rather than to

* The capitalization of "Black" but not of "white" suggests that while official sectors readily define African-American identity by color, they find such a notion inapplicable in relation to Anglo-Americans.

government policy or the lack thereof. This analysis chose to ignore the fact that separation and inequality had been maintained since the nation's inception by official policies of enslavement and segregation. It in essence reflected a public analysis which blamed human nature for the problem and admitted that despite the dismantling of segregation, the extension of civil rights/non-discrimination had had little effect in either improving the socio-economic status of African-Americans or in "integrating" them into the white nation.

The Commission's identification of the conditions which led to the minority insurrections throughout major American cities in the 1960's led to a series of programs adopted by President Johnson which slightly improved the material conditions of some minority individuals, but did not redress the history of systemically-enforced political inequalities which consistently led to the relative benefiting of the majority *vis-a-vis* the minority. As analysed by J. Owens Smith, Mitchell F. Rice and Woodrow Jones, Jr. in *Blacks and American Government: Politics, Policy and Social Change*,[17] the post-slavery prolongation of inequality resulted from a further set of official systemic policies: 1) the dismantling of reconstruction programs, 2) the enactment of the Black Codes, 3) the institutionalization of the doctrine of separate but equal, 4) the National Labor Laws:

> *The Dismantling of Reconstruction Programs*
>
> To further augment the quest of Blacks for self-reliance, Congress passed a law which authorized the establishment of the Freedmen's Saving and Trust Company. The bank was established by a group of philanthropists who took care to ensure that the bank was established on sound principles...Because it was chartered and backed by the federal government, the Freedmen's Saving Bank emerged, perhaps, as one of the most financially solvent banks in the United States, if not the world. It was the only bank of its kind to have branches throughout the nation...Attracted by its vast assets, the board of trustees of the bank introduced a bill in Congress to have the law changed so that the bank deposits could be invested in other notes and real estate mortgages. This law opened the bank's vault to predators. Within a period of three years the hard earned savings of the newly freed men were lost. The whites who were running it started making numerous loans on speculative ventures which went sour. Such loans eventually drained the assets of the bank, and it was forced to close its doors.
>
> The next factor which significantly undermined the effort of Blacks to acquire self-reliance was the refusal of the federal government to assist them in acquiring land as it did white

groups. Before the Civil War, the government had a long-standing policy of helping immigrant groups to acquire land upon their arrival. For example, during the colonial period, the government gave immigrants 150 acres of land under the "headright" system. After the Revolutionary War, Congress passed the Land Act of 1800. This act allowed immigrants to buy a minimum of 160 acres of land at $2.00 an acre over a period of four years. A farmer was required to deposit only $80. In 1820, Congress amended this act to make it easier for farmers to purchase land on the frontier... Hence, these land policies aided whites to acquire their inalienable rights...But when Blacks demanded the same treatment as whites, the government flatly refused. For example, shortly after the Civil War, there were rumors that the government was going to give each Black family forty acres and a mule. The concept of giving ex-slaves land after Emancipation was nothing new. This was a concept that emanated from the European tradition. The British, for example, had enacted several servant codes which governed the relationship between servants and masters. Briefly, these codes required that masters provide servants with "freedom dues" upon their emancipation. During the colonial period, such dues consisted of 50 acres of land and other provisions to assist a servant to become self-reliant. But the American government refused to apply the same principle to Blacks upon their emancipation.

Enactment of the Black Codes

These codes operated to foreclose Black freedom to pursue a wide range of economic opportunities. Although the stated purpose of the Black Codes was to regulate labor, their operative effect was to subordinate the status of Blacks to that of whites psychologically, economically, and socially. In fact, these codes re-enslaved Blacks and made the value of their lives worse than they were during slavery. For example, the life of a slave had an economic value ranging from $400 to $1,400. After Emancipation, this value was removed; the life of the average Black was placed on the goodwill of the plantation owners who had the legal authority to hang him or violate his civil rights at will.

The Black Codes ... made it extremely hard for Blacks to accumulate any wealth. They stipulated that all laborers must sign a contract with an employer by the first day of January. Once the contract had been signed and rations issued, the laborer could not leave the plantation, for any reason, without permission from the plantation owner. Furthermore, the contract could not be terminated until all debts were cleared. The question as to whether or not such debts were cleared was left solely up to the discretion of the plantation owners...These debts became tools by which plantation owners could re-enslave Blacks.

The Black Codes were different from any other laws governing the relationship between workers and masters in the history of mankind *[thereby stepping out of western tradition, and reflecting an emerging Anglo-American tradition, ed.]*.

The Doctrine of Separate but Equal

The public policy which served as a catalyst to maintain social inequality was the *doctrine of separate but equal.* It was institutionalized into [the American] system of laws by the United States Supreme Court in *Plessy v. Ferguson* in 1895. In this case, the Court held that it was not repugnant to the equal protection clause of the 14th Amendment for the states to maintain separate public accommodations and other social facilities as long as the states provided the same facilities for both races.

The separate but equal doctrine provided the framework for the authoritative allocation of values and resources in society, i.e. the values of education, jobs, housing, and the ownership of property. [It] became a policy whereby whites were politicized to accept the notion that they have a higher social status in society than Blacks; this was a natural right.

National Labor Laws

Before the passage of the various national labor laws, the restriction placed on Black job mobility can be characterized as a product of race prejudice or *de facto* discrimination...The passage of the various national labor laws brought some labor union activities under government purview.

The political significance of the various national labor laws is that they took white employees' civil rights to employment opportunities off the good will of management and placed them on a principle of law. These laws offered white workers job security, protection against arbitrary layoffs and dismissals, protection against job demotions and arbitrary transfers...

National labor laws have always had a negative repercussion on the economic status of Blacks. These laws gave whites legal tools to displace Black workers by encroaching upon their jobs. For example, before the passage of the various labor laws, Black workers were preferred over whites by employers. Migrating from the agrarian South, Blacks were hard workers who did not have experience in labor organization. Therefore, the decision concerning hiring, firing, and other conditions of employment was left solely up to the discretion of management. Blacks were paid less than whites who were doing the same job. But the labor laws took the decisions for hiring and promotion away from management and made them a joint venture between the two.

> ...[T]he National [Railroad] Labor Act of 1926 ... provided unions for the first time with a mechanism for enforcing collective bargaining. It threw the weight of the federal government behind workers' attempt to improve their standards of living. Since unions had a long standing policy of racial discrimination, the National Railroad Labor Act also conferred upon the unions the legal right to discriminate against Blacks. The unions used the labor laws to push Blacks out of the skilled and high-paying jobs...
>
> Although the [Wagner Act] was designed to improve the conditions of workers, it had an adverse effect on the economic status of Blacks. For Blacks, [it] was a job displacement law. For example, from the 1930's to the implementation of affirmative action, unions used their collective bargaining power to foreclose the freedom of Blacks to enter skilled jobs. The decision as to who could enter apprenticeship programs was controlled by the unions and sanctioned by the federal government.

Resisting Minority Rights: Fear of Secession or Protection of Dominance?

Most contemporary UN experts on minority rights[18] tell us that the chief obstacle to the implementation of minority rights is the reluctance or unwillingness of states to cooperate. It is further explained that this is caused by states' fear that in so doing, it may lead to the splintering of the multi-national state into smaller and perhaps less viable politically independent units. This of course would not only be counterproductive for the nations involved, but also for the global village itself, by placing additional strains on the economic, political and social mechanisms of the international system (the UN), strains which it may not be able to sustain.

While this orientation to the problematic permits us to understand the difficulties faced by the UN in its efforts to promote minority rights at the international level, it falls far short of clarifying why the call for secession arises, why minority demands occasioning the call for secession are resisted, and how to approach reconciliation. To appropriately conceptualize the problematic of secession, it must be recognized that in those multi-national states faced with secessionist demands, the constitutional-legal apparatus of the state is likely under the absolute (or at minimum, disproportionate) control of the dominant nation or group in that state, which frequently seeks to maintain a centralized and politically unified state while avoiding the implementation of minority rights for reasons other than the maintenance of the unified state for the betterment of the global village, etc. The maintenance and reinforcement of the dominant majority's self-interest, indeed of its dominance, has frequently led it to seek:

1) To maintain historically acquired privilege and advantages vis-à-vis the minority by maintaining systemically-ensured economic, social and psychological domination of the minority through systems of political, economic and social dependency. These systems yield gratification and satisfaction as well as more tangible benefits.

2) To eliminate the existence of the minority either physically by policies of genocide, or in effect by policies of ethnocide, thus disguising the historical process whereby the hierarchy of privilege has been established and maintained.

3) To support systems implicitly based on racial superiority and inferiority, insofar as the assimilation process of (inferior) ethnies into the lowest sector or class of the (superior) ethny is projected rather as an educational process into a "higher level" of civic functioning and behavior, as practised by the mainstream (everybody), etc.

4) To provide conditions favorable to uncompensated acquisition of land and cultural products belonging to a minority.

5) To use the democratic process itself as a tool to facilitate and disguise majority domination even over territories where the minority is numerically dominant.

International law, concurrent with its willingness to reiterate states' fears concerning secession, appears to have addressed the problematic concerning conditions under which secession is not acceptable as well as the conditions under which it serves the interests of the peoples, the state and the international system. While most legal documents[19] discourage all attempts at secession based on ethno-nationalism or ethno-imperialism, it is clear that the denial of human rights and self-defense are internationally accepted as reasons justifying secession.[20]

However, insofar as the possibility of fragmentation of multinational states into smaller political units is a potential threat to the stability of the international system, international law instead encourages the implementation of minority rights to meet those minority demands and human rights needs which otherwise usually lead to a call for secession, hoping thereby to reconcile them to peaceful integration within a single state. The re-emergence of minority rights must be viewed as a way of encouraging states to act in ways that do not compel or justify secession, but rather provide the political, economic and social basis upon which minorities can enjoy their human rights.

As you will see in the section to follow, minority rights result from the examination of minority needs and demands for equal status, pluralist democracy, socio-economic development, the right to be different, and an appropriate degree of political power. The existence of pronounced inequalities between majority and minority, accompanied by a state's denial of those measures necessary to achieve equal status is concomitant to encouraging minority resistance to the right of the majority to rule.

This denial by states often takes place under the cover of some grand design of patriotic symbols that unjustly appeals to the emotional and national value system of the majority: the final solution (Germany), ethnic purity (Serbia), the final steps towards communism (U.S.S.R.), the melting pot and individual equality (U.S. and Latin America), the white man's burden (white-dominated South Africa), to name only the best-known instances. In all such cases, national ideals and myths are called upon to evoke an emotional and subjective basis upon which to deny the minority its human rights. *The real and not so complicated issue of the minority right or demand to share political power with the majority is conveniently lost in the struggle over "why shouldn't we all just get along"* and achieve our national goals within the idealized historically established framework (which just happens to be weighted to favor the domination of the majority ethny). Thus, the question of *secession* is inevitably linked to the question of *cessation* of violations of minority rights. To ignore this linkage is like hoping to sleep comfortably on a bed of nails.

Sleeping on Nails

It is highly unrealistic to expect that a minority should remain blind and passive in the face of its prolonged inequality and exploitation. Inevitably, there arises leadership in the minority community which is capable not only of systemically formulating the minority's grievances, but of galvanizing its resistance. Often such leaders are either imprisoned, exiled or assassinated by states wishing to close their eyes to minority needs. However, along with the majority of the minority population, they tend not to share the majority ethny's idealization of the politico-legal structures in place. They do not find the bed on which the society rests to be comfortable. While the majority dreams they awaken.

In the U.S., one such leader was Al Hajj Malik Al Shabazz (Malcolm X). In his O.A.A.U. meetings,[21] the late African-American radical ended discussions with the suggestion that the majority, through the state which they control (the U.S.), had no moral right to govern the national minorities without their explicitly expressed collective consent, and that, despite their superior force, the majority's laws should have no moral compulsion whatsoever for the minorities. He claimed that the U.S. law that sanctioned the minority's capture was no more morally acceptable than contemporary laws which he viewed as permitting the majority to virtually enslave the minority by locking them into a permanent "hind-start" in the American rat race, or the laws that continue to imprison the minorities in numbers vastly disproportionate to their population, that lead to the criminalization of their cultural difference and/or their reaction to cultural domination and political and economic oppression. Like most radical minorities spokesmen worldwide, he asked: at what historical point did the minority agree to give the right to govern to the majority, and under what circumstances did they acquire this right? If they got this right by brute force, and maintained it by brute force, he explained in the spirit of the philosopher, Jean-Jacques Rousseau, "then it is only their brute force that (the minority) African-Americans should respect. But brute force does not make moral law nor establish the moral right to rule."

Al Hajj Malik insisted that the state law represents only the will of the majority ethny (white American), written, elaborated and backed up by superior force, that historically the minority was conditioned not to break the law only for negative incentives — they may be beaten, killed, put in jail, injured, executed, or otherwise harmed — not because the application of the law to *them* (insofar as it is the codification of the will, interest, vision and priorities of the majority) is right, just or morally acceptable. Al Hajj Malik reminded his audiences that the Constitution used today was written during the period of enslavement, and at no point had the state attempted to negotiate the national minorities' permission to be governed. At no had the state seen fit to restructure its system so as to accommodate the unique economic, social, psychological, cultural and developmental needs of the minority nations within it. The majority race or nation, in short, had never entered into a social contract with minority races or nations. Malcolm also suggested that the U.S. socio-economic and politico-military institutions (evolved from the period of enslavement into modern day forms) continued to place the minorities in the diabolical position wherein the inability or refusal to assimilate meant a life of poverty (unemployment or underpaid employment), exile, or adjustment through resistance).

He concluded, therefore, that being poor or going to prison, in most cases involving national minorities, amounted in the final analysis to nothing more than the price these minorities risked for the exercise of free will under conditions of objective oppression, and collective and institutionalized discrimination, racism and hatred. While Malcolm's assertions may be seen as necessarily partisan, going to prison for minorities is often seen by the minority population itself as resulting from institutionalized discrimination and oppression and not from behavior that is anti-social or criminal. Minority prisoners are often seen by the minority essentially as victims. *This follows since it is the only non-racist explanation* for the disproportionality of minorities in prison in relation to population. Al Hajj also claimed that often minority members were acting out of the frustration not only of immediate personal need, but also of the more collective historical resentment of having endured historic and ongoing exploitation without compensation or even an official apology. He also felt that the majority's government's unwilling-ness to listen to minority's real complaints often made their unlawful actions the only method available to make a statement against their condition of oppression.[22]

Criminality or Illegal Civil Disobedience

In supporting the moral rights of minorities to resist laws which are constituted with what radical minority leaders see as the expressed intent of exploitation and oppression, such minority leaders push the limits of the political power which they feel they do not adequately share. They assume not only that power depends on obedience, but also that it can be measured by the obedience it evokes. Thus, when minorities stop recognizing laws and institutions empowered by the dominant majority which they feel lead to minority exploitation, when they stop following the minority leadership which serves as intermediary for the majority ruling class, they start to seek restructuring and re-institutionalization of the state — to seek what might be expressed in contemporary terms as a new social contract, the underlying assumption of which is that no one has the right to make laws for minorities without their full consent and participation as a people. The fact that the state may have effectively, by force, claimed this right seems to lead minorities first to ask for what has come to be understood and expressed in contemporary terminology as minority rights or the right to self-determination (aboriginal peoples). When such rights are not granted, they are often demanded. When they cannot be appropriated, they are often assumed (the Quebecois). When they cannot be collectively assumed, then they are often individually assumed (U.S. minorities). The result of the latter option usually means the creation of dysfunctional socio-economic internal conditions in the state by politicization of acts that would otherwise be seen as criminal or morally unacceptable.

Illegal acts which are seen as essentially political responses to cultural, socio-political and economic oppression are often decriminalized in minority societal values and thus represent its refusal to the majority of the moral right to govern. This leads to a redefinition of the minority's struggle, insofar as it denies the right of the majority to govern by broadening the concept of political struggle to include as political those acts which previously might simply have been viewed as contrary to existing law and authority (i.e. criminal). Acts which previously were defined negatively in terms of riots, civil disobedience or social breakdown, come to be defined positively in terms of resistance to majority domination, breakdown of the majority's political and social control systems, etc. What is important to note here is that the minority population comes to see such acts as a logical riposte to the majority's criminalization of just minority resistance against violation of minority rights and its establishment of institutionalized oppression, domination, humiliation and exploitation. At this point, the only way to achieve minority popular condemnation of such acts becomes to first end the violation of minority rights (the oppression). Ironically, the very conditions that the state feared would occur if minority rights were recognized are instead provoked by their denial, and the resulting perception by the minority that it is being oppressed by the majority ethny.

No Minority Rights, No Justice, No Peace, No Social Development

In a later chapter of this book, we have critiqued Arthur M. Schlesinger's *The Disuniting of America* as a means of illustrating how dominant ethnies often doubletalk to avoid the implementation of minority rights. In light of such persistent tendency to what we call double talk (rationalizations for the status quo), it is appropriate to ask the question: what happens when the political will for change is not present, at a historical point when the minority having no social contract is unable or unwilling to tolerate further refusal of their group rights, and the power of the government, as well as the national minority's hopes for national unity, remains such as to make successful armed resistance unthinkable?

Again, the situation of minorities in the U.S. may be providing an object lesson. Today, the U.S. secondary educational system and other socio-economic institutions operate not on the basis of common consent between the minority and the government, but by majoritarian democratic principles coupled with socio-economic and police coercion. The security in the secondary school and institutions frequented by African-Americans and other minorities resembles that in the prisons, which are grossly disproportionately filled with members of minorities. Even the security in libraries, grocery and 5 and 10¢ stores in minority neighborhoods resembles that in large banks when money is being transferred. Large areas of the most important U.S. cities look like war zones (areas of occupation). To maintain sufficient appearance of law and order so as not to interfere with the majority elites' dream, armies of minority civil servants, police, and politicians are employed or engaged to manage these areas and institutions. Indeed, the larger portion of minority employment may result from this need. New laws ("three strikes and you're out," the execution of children [juvenile offenders], the aggressive menace of the death penalty etc.) are created by the majority elites through the guise of the state, often seen by the minorities, particularly the poor, as a Frankenstein monster which the majority controls to terrorize and to punish disobedience. While it is true that this street view is far from the complete picture, it symbolizes the price that must be paid to maintain the life force of a majority elite's dream contrary to the reality of the national minorities.

The maintenance of this dream of being the most free, the best, the biggest, the richest, and as Schlesinger has put it, the new race of men weighs heavily on all. It does not accord with global democratic requirements, peace and development needs for less inequality, greater distributive justice, and human-centered development. This state model for minority treatment so attractive to other states in the past is becoming increasingly to resemble a socio-pathological delusion, having its root cause in the psychological need to justify the majority-instituted slavery, apartheid, ethnocide, greed and what would today be considered criminal behavior. While western European civilization benefited from colonial exploitation of others, the colonists' disorientation towards the rights and equality of others can only be fully shared by the actors themselves, and the resulting culture and institu-tions. Perhaps the best indication that what we refer to as a collective socio-pathology (for lack of a better word) influences the orientation of a majority towards its minorities is if or when the majority is unable or unwilling to extend an official apology to the minorities for the behavior of past governments, if or when they are unable or unwilling to compensate their minorities for the damage to the degree that it is possible, and instead, as so clearly demonstrated in the writing of Mr. Schlesinger, refuse to recognize the unavoidable consequences of previous systemic policies which militate against the continued dream or delusion of the majority or to admit the historical failure of their civil rights models to provide adequate minority protection.

We do not suggest that the need for minority rights denies the reality of the America's contribution to the cause of freedom, human rights and democracy. Rather, we suggest that this state model is insufficient for minority protection, and should be informed by international minority rights concepts. American future contributions will not come by the traditional denial of minority rights or any attempt to reimpose an anti-social contract, but through the acceptance of its minority's efforts to rescue its past and present.

---

1 See Preamble to the *Universal Declaration of Human Rights*, 1945.

2 The UN Sub-Commission on Prevention of Discrimination and Protection of Minorities.

3 Francesco Capotorti, *Study of the Rights of Persons Belonging to Ethnic, Religious and Linguistic Minorities*, United Nations, 1979.

4 See Asbjørn Eide "Minority Situations: In Search of Peaceful and Constructive Solutions," *Notre Dame Law Review*, Vol. 66, 1991, p. 1328.

5 See Y. N. Kly, *The Anti-Social Contract*, (1987).

6 The disparities listed hereunder are among only a few to be found in Perry A. Plooskie and James Williams, eds., *The Negro Almanac: A Reference Work on the African-American, 5th Edition*, 1989.

7 *Id.*

8 *Statistical Abstract of the United States, 1993, 113th Edition*, U.S. Department of Commerce, Economics and Statistics Administration, Bureau of the Census, 1993, Table 49, "Social and Economic Characteristics of White and Black Population," p. 46.

9 *Id.*, Table 736, "Children Below the Poverty Level," p. 469.

10 See UN Dept. of Public Information document DPI/1553/SOC/CON/93537/Aug. 1994/SM.

11 *Id.*, Table 167, "Persons Without Health Insurance Coverage," p. 116.

12 *Id.*, Table 339, p. 208.

13 *Id.*, Table 443, p. 227.

14 *Id.*, Table 349, "Movement of Prisoners Under Sentence of Death," p. 213.

15 Ervin Staub, *The Roots of Evil: The Origins of Genocide and Other Group Violence*, 1989.

16 The U.S. is registered as the country with the highest level of

social unrest in a chart on civil unrest , published in *Handbook of Foreign Policy Analysis*, UNIDR, 1992.

17 J. Owens Smith, Mitchell F. Rice, and Woodrow Jones, Jr., *Blacks and American Government: Politics, Policy and Social Change*, 1987.

18 See van Boven, A. Eide, Calle, Martinez, etc.

19 See reports by Capotorti, Eide, van Boven, Martinez, etc.

20 See United Nations, *Declaration on Principles of International Law Concerning Friendly Relations and Cooperation Among States* (1970), reprinted in Albert P. Blaustein et al, *Human Rights Sourcebook* 97 (1987).

21 The Organization of African-American Unity, organized by Al Hajj Malik Al Shabazz.

22 Speeches available on cassette tape: "The Ballot or the Bullet," and "Malcolm X Speaks."

Non-Discrimination in U.S. Courts: A Non-Solution?*

Aviam Soifer

There have been times, such as during the civil rights struggles of the 1870s and the 1960s, when minority groups attempted to force the United States and its courts to deliver on glittering historical promises. However, today a majority of the Justices of the United States Supreme Court seem willfully blind to the burdens of the past. We note the profoundly ahistorical approach of judges today to precisely those groups who most obviously warrant special judicial concern if there is to be any special judicial solicitude on the basis of past wrongs. Today, leading judges opt for a static abstract ideal over what is complex, contextual, and more real historically.

The pleasant judicial assumption that all citizens of the United States have reached parity now extends even to racial matters. Garbed in purported neutrality, a majority of the Justices has gone so far as to suggest that the Federal Constitution, and their judicial oaths, actually compel them to reject special solicitude for dispossessed and victimized groups.

Only eighteen years after the formal abolition of slavery, at the moment when Jim Crow began to dominate the South, the United States Supreme Court declared it high time that the former slave "takes the rank of mere citizen and ceases to be the special favorite of the law."[1] Again today, and again for the sake of presumed equality, the Court cuts off consideration of past racial wrongs. The Court's own complicity in legitimating segregation has been expunged.[2] Now everyone is presumed formally equal, unencumbered by the past. All groups — voluntary and

* Excerpted and abridged from Aviam Soifer, "On Being Overly Discrete and Insular: Involuntary Groups and the Anglo-American Judicial Tradition," in Yoram A. Dinstein and Mala Tabory, The Protection of Minorities and Human Rights, 1992. Aviam Soifer is Dean of Law, Boston College.

involuntary, white and black, corporations and Indian tribes — compete fairly in the political marketplace. Indeed, it would violate judicial neutrality to show special concern even for a group with a long history of being victimized. Special concern, in fact, may be invalid, since it denies equality in the great race of life.

We begin with a brief sketch of the origins and historical context of the idea that arose in the late 1930s that certain "discrete and insular minorities" ought to receive special judicial scrutiny. The idea that the Federal Constitution might compel judges to play a special, activist role when they review discrimination against "discrete and insular minorities" appeared only in footnote four to an otherwise obscure opinion written by Justice Harlan Fiske Stone in *United States v. Carolene Products,*[3] yet the approach suggested by the footnote's three paragraphs was to prove crucial in the treatment of minorities in American law.[4] The *Carolene Products* holding was part of a trend toward a new, limited role for federal courts. In contrast to the rash of decisions that had invalidated important elements of the New Deal and triggered Franklin Delano Roosevelt's court-packing scheme in 1937, the new judicial outlook proclaimed extreme judicial deference to the social and economic policies of the popularly-elected branches. Justice Stone's majority opinion sought to consolidate developing restraints on judicial intervention in economic matters.[5] It suggested virtually an ironclad presumption in favor of the constitutionality of all social and economic legislation. In footnote four, however, Stone went on to suggest the categories of constitutional claims that might deprive government action of the extreme deference it should otherwise enjoy. Most pertinently, in the third and final paragraph, Stone said that government action directed at particular religious, national or racial minorities might merit special judicial scrutiny. He summarized the problem as "prejudice against discrete and insular minorities," and asserted that such prejudice "may be a special condition, which tends seriously to curtail the operation of those political processes ordinarily to be relied upon to protect minorities, and which may call for a correspondingly more searching judicial inquiry."[6]

Judicial and scholarly disagreement has continued and intensified about when and if any special, activist role is appropriate for judges confronting claims by "discrete and insular" groups; the Court neither immediately nor fully adopted the activist, strict scrutiny approach suggested by footnote four. "Discrete and insular minorities" seemed to designate long-standing outgroups, groups in which membership itself often became a cause for mistrust, hostility, or worse. These unmeltable groups experienced "special vulnerability to predictable perversions by the majoritarian process."[7] In other words, these minorities repeatedly have been made scapegoats. Majoritarian politics obviously long has been — and still is — manipulated through explicit or encoded racism. African-Americans seemed the paradigmatic "footnote four" minority. Past discrimination and present membership yield current injury. Moreover, this is a special injury, to which attention must be paid. The injury is uniquely prone to be exacerbated, either by invidious legislation or by the absence of legislation. This renders judicial neutrality not neutrality, but rather complicity in perpetuating past wrongs. It suggests the need for judicial limits on permissible democratic action, and even certain inaction, that perpetuates the burdens of past victimization of special groups.

A majority of the Justices today seems to share a pervasive national nostalgia for a simpler, freer, and happier time-that-never-was. Only a smoking gun — i.e. incontrovertible proof of a specific racially discriminatory motive that an individual plaintiff can tie directly to his or her own plight — will move the Court to acknowledge that discrimination, even against African-Americans, may still be legally relevant.[8] Judges thus simplify their work by deferring to whatever results emerge from a Hobbesian social struggle. Even better, each citizen has only himself to blame if he loses in life's great struggle. The sobering history of different groups has been called off. The dream of equality for all individuals has been achieved. It is everyone for his future self.

In *Patterson v. McLean Credit Union,*[9] a case involving alleged racial harassment, we saw the Justices taking the initiative to ask: Should the Court overrule a 1976 decision, *Runyon v. McCrary*, that held that the 1966 Civil Rights Act prohibited private schools from excluding qualified children solely because of their race? Responding to dissenting opinions stating that the Court should be particularly loath to upset an important statutory precedent that favors civil rights plaintiffs, the majority answered:

> We do not believe that the Court may recognize any such exception to the abiding rule that it treat all litigants equally: that is, that the claim of any litigant for the application of a rule to its case should not be influenced by the Court's view of the worthiness of the litigant in terms of extralegal criteria. We think this is what Congress meant when it required each Justice or judge of the United States to swear to "administer justice without respect to persons, and do equal right to the poor and to the rich..."[10]

The *per curiam* opinion expressed the notion that race — the very criterion that constitutes the basis for civil rights claims — is fungible with other "external criteria;" that a higher judicial duty requires judges to treat all litigants abstractly, and thereby, to treat them formally as equal; and that the specific judicial obligation to do "equal right to the poor and to the rich" is synonymous with the idea that all litigants should be treated as if they are exactly the same, thus requiring judges to ignore different starting places, significant encumbrances, and the weight of the past. It rejects a basic point made by John Winthrop, Ronald Reagan's favorite Puritan, in the early days of the Massachusetts Bay Colony: "If the same penalty hits a rich man, it pains him not, it is not affliction to him, but if it lights upon a poor man, it breaks his back."[11] Litigants are not interchangeable ciphers. They are defined by their histories and their group associations.

In 1948, the Court noted, as it struck down state court enforcement of restrictive covenants, "Equal protection of the laws is not achieved by indiscriminate imposition of inequalities."[12] However, in *Patterson*, the *per curiam* opinion went further than allowing the "indiscriminate imposition of inequalities." It suggested that indiscriminate treatment is obligatory. Upon close reading, the ironclad judicial oath the majority invoked hardly draws such individual/group and legal/extralegal distinctions. The oath does not define "equal right" as lack of awareness of group differences. Nor does it hint of distinguishing intrinsic from extrinsic characteristics. Finally, the meaning of "respect to persons" is considerably more complex in terms of both etymology and history than the *per curiam* opinion suggested.[13] The Court aggressively presumed, however, that no approach to justice would allow judges to protect the downtrodden.

Justice Blackmun, joined by Justices Brennan, Marshall and Stevens, objected to the majority's decision to reach out "to reconsider an interpretation of a civil rights statute that so clearly reflects our society's earnest commitment to ending racial discrimination."[14] Justice Stevens, joined by three other dissenters, wrote a separate dissent in which he decried the majority's decision because it "replace(s) what is ideally a sense of guaranteed right with the uneasiness of unsecured privilege."[15] Stevens also noted the deleterious impact of this decision not only on faith in law maintained by victims of discrimination, but also on public perceptions of the Court as impartial and restrained.

In *Patterson II,* while agreeing not to overrule *Runyon v. McCrary* — that Section 1981 prohibits racial discrimination in the making and enforcement of private contracts — the Justices disagreed about the extent of the prohibition. The majority held that "the right to make contracts does not extend, as a matter of either logic or semantics, to conduct by the employer after the contract relation has been established, including breach of the terms of the contract or imposition of discriminatory working conditions."[16] On this formalistic view of contract law, the Court ignored both the substance and the historical context of the 1866 Civil Rights Act, passed primarily to protect newly-freed slaves. This is bizarre against the historic backdrop. Congress premised the 1866 Civil Rights Act on its new power under the Thirteenth Amendment. The newly-freed slaves hardly came to their initial opportunities to make and enforce contracts with equal bargaining power. Lengthy congressional hearings and debates articulated concern to guarantee equality, particularly because of extensive evidence of virulent, racially-based harassments of free contractual relationships in the South.

Writing for the majority, Justice Kennedy not only failed to heed this historic context, he belittled it. Kennedy protested too much when he proclaimed, at the conclusion of his majority opinion, that the Court was not "signaling one inch of retreat from Congress's policy to forbid discrimination in the private, as well as the public, sphere." "Nevertheless," he added, "in the areas of private discrimination, to which the ordinance of the Constitution does not directly extend," the Court must play a role "limited to interpreting what Congress may do and has done." By diminishing the Amendment that abolished *private* slavery and involuntary servitude throughout the nation, and by somehow rendering the Amendment not a direct part of the Constitution's "ordinance" (whatever that means), the majority proclaimed not a retreat but a rout.

This bleak view of the result in *Patterson* is underscored by several other civil rights decision by the Supreme Court that soon followed. *City of Richmond v. J.A. Croson* [17] is most revealing. In invalidating a minority set-aside provision which established a racial preference in the awarding of government construction contracts in the City of Richmond, the majority noted: "The dream of a Nation of equal citizens in a society where race is irrelevant to personal opportunity and achievement would be lost in a mosaic of shifting preferences based on inherently unmeasurable claims of past wrongs." To avoid mosaic law, therefore, the majority found it necessary to restrict remedial efforts by state and local entities to situations where the effects of identified discrimination within the relevant jurisdiction can be specifically demonstrated. Otherwise, "racial politics" would prevail. Thus, the history of Richmond, the capital of the Confederacy and a leading site in resistance to school integration, was quarantined, then ignored.

The majority, by adopting strict scrutiny for the first time in the context of an equal protection challenge to race-conscious remedial measures, ignored the profound difference between, in Justice Marshall's words, "governmental actions that are themselves racist and governmental actions that seek to remedy the effects of prior racism or to prevent neutral governmental activity from perpetuating the effects of such racism."[18]

In emphasizing the need for specific proof and individualism, in denigrating group identity as a relevant factor, and in rushing to jettison racial history as relevant to current reality, *Patterson* and *Croson* illustrate the complete rejection of the "footnote four" approach. The majority aggressively employed what it claimed were neutral equal protection principles to invalidate reform measures not to the liking of a particular majority of the Justices. Gone was concern for "discrete and insular minorities." In its place, a white-owned business may now trigger strict judicial scrutiny of a remedial government contracting scheme.

The two other most notable decisions sharply restricting civil rights claims the same term were *Wards Packing Co. V. Antonio,*[19] (civil rights plaintiff has burden of proving employer has no business reason for practice even if it has dramatic discriminatory effects) and *Martin v. Wilks,*[20] (new group of white firefighters allowed to intervene to challenge Birmingham, Alabama consent decree alleged to be reverse discrimination). Such decisions led Justice Marshall to suggest "a deliberate retrenchment of the civil rights agenda" by the Court which put the nation "back where we started" at the time of *Brown v. Board of Education.*[21]

The United States Supreme Court, in decisions ranging from who may enter court to who leaves it with a death sentence, repeatedly has emphasized the need to demonstrate particularized individual harm even to initiate any civil rights claim. To have standing, for example, "at an irreducible minimum, Art. III requires the party who invokes the court's authority to 'show that he personally has suffered some actual or threatened injury.'"[22] And to make out an equal protection claim of discrimination in the imposition of the death penalty, statistics will not suffice, since the condemned person must "prove that the decisionmakers in *his* case acted with discriminatory purpose."[23]

In view of the above trends, it appears legitimate to question whether the U.S. judicial system presently can be regarded as a promising avenue of recourse by which an historically oppressed group, such as the African-American minority, might seek to successfully ameliorate the effects of a history of systemic discrimination. In light of U.S. obligations to protect the human rights of all its citizens, including African-Americans, to equality and non-discrimination under the recently ratified International Covenant on Civil and Political Rights, are we prepared for what might be considered as necessary, if non-discrimination through U.S. Courts is a non-solution?

---

1 Civil Rights Cases, 109 *U.S.* 3, 25 (1983) (invalidating Civil Rights Act of 1875 that prohibited racial discrimination in public accommodations).

2 Constitutional decisions legitimating the entire apparatus of racism are legion. The classic survey is L. Miller, *The Petitioners: The Story of the Supreme Court of the United States and the Negro* (1966). Helpful recent accounts of specific decisions that upheld and even required segregation, such as in *Berea College v. Kentucky*, 211 *U.S.* 45 (1908), include C. Lofgren, *The Plessy Case: A Legal Historical Interpretation* (1987); R. Kennedy, "Race Relations Law and the Tradition of Celebration: The Case of Professor Schmidt," 86 *Columbia Law Review* 1622 (1986).

3 304 *U.S.* 144 (1938).

4 Even the former Justice Lewis F. Powell, who helped lead the recent retrenchment from the footnote four approach, acknowledged that this footnote contained "perhaps the most far-sighted dictum in our modern judicial heritage." L.F. Powell, "*Carolene Products* Revisited," 82 *Columbia Law Review* 1087 (1982). Numerous other commentators, most notably John Hart Ely in his influential book, *Democracy and Distrust* (1980), have celebrated and elaborated constitutional norms as extrapolations from the famous footnote. For further discussion, see I. Lusky, "Footnote Redux: A *Carolene Products* Reminiscence," 82 *Columbia Law Review* 1093 (1987).

5 *West Coast Hotel v. Parrish*, 300 *U.S.* 379 (1937) symbolized the new trend. In this decision upholding state minimum wage legislation, the Court reversed itself dramatically and abandoned the individualistic, substantive due process approach generally connected to *Lochner v. New York*, 1987 *U.S.* 45 (1905) and its progeny. See generally B.A. Ackerman, "Discovering the Constitution," 93 *Yale Law Journal* 1013 (1984) (identifying self-government on a national level during three "constitutional moments").

6 For this crucial proposition, Stone cited two commerce clause decisions, as well as First Amendment decisions that invalidated laws held to be discriminatory based on religion and national origin and the racial discrimination in voting cases he also cited in the previous paragraph.

7 R. Cover, "The Origins of Judicial Activism in the Protection of Minorities," 91 *Yale Law Journal* 1287, 1292 n. 14 (1982).

8 There has been considerable discussion of this trend. For criticism of its beginnings, see, e.g. Soifer, "Complacency and Constitutional Law,"41 *Ohio State Law Journal* 383 (1981); a careful dissection of the crucial middle stage is available in K.M. Sullivan, "Sins of Discrimination: Last Term's Affirmative Action Cases," 100 *Harvard Law Review* 78 (1986); recent aspects were unpacked skillfully in A. Rosenfeld, "Decoding *Richmond:* Affirmative Action and the Elusive Meaning of Constitutional Equality," 87 *Michigan Law Review* 1729 (1969).

9 485 *U.S.* 617 (1988) and 109 *S. Ct.* 2363 (1989).

10 485 *U.S.* 619, quoting 28 *U.S.C.* sec. 453 (1948).

11 *4 Winthrop Papers* 349, 351-52 (Mass. Hist. Soc. 1929-1947).

12 *Shelley v. Kraemer,* 334 *U.S.* 1, 22 (1948).

13 For a cogent explanation of the origins of the oath, and a discussion of how "the exact contours of impartiality vary with customs, law and experience," see J. Noonan, "Judicial Impartiality and The Judiciary Act of 1789," 14 *Nova Law Review* 123 (1989).

14 485 *U.S.* at 621.

15 *bid.,* 622.

16 109 *S. Ct.* at 2373.

17 57 *U.S.L.W.* 4132 (1989).

18 Marshall, dissenting, 57 *U.S.L.W.* at 4155.

19 109 *S. Ct.* 2115 (1989).

20 109 *S. Ct.* 2180 (1989).

21 L. Greenhouse, "Marshall Says Court's Rulings Imperil Rights," *N.Y. Times*, 9 September, 1989.

22 *Valley Forge College v. Americans United,* 454 *U.S.* 464, 472 (1982); see also *Allen v. Wright,* 488 *U.S.* 737, 753-56 (1984).

23 *McClaskey v. Kemp,* 481 *U.S.* 279, 292 (1987).

White Racial Nationalism in the United States*

Ronald Walters

Because it can be contended that white racial nationalism has played a major role in the formation of America,[1] *Ronald Walters' article concerning the rise of white racial nationalism as the hidden impetus behind a neo-conservative revolution which commenced during the Reagan era to counter gains made by minorities in the earlier "civil rights" period, is of particular interest. His substantial documentation (unfortunately much abridged here) of the widespread majority reaction against civil rights (to the extent of creating the seeds of an Anglo-American political revolution within the U.S.) raises the typical problematic of majority resistance to minorities' purported gains . If the dominant ethny is so resistant to the notion of affirmative action for national minorities that it is willing to change the entire social agenda in order to counteract this — even, it might be argued, against its own real interests — how might it ever be convinced to agree to the application of minority rights, which entails the allocation of a considerably greater extent of socio-political power to national minorities?*

In attempting to resolve this dilemma, it may be useful to analyse the components of majority resistance: resistance to the process of forced assimilation, fear of loss of personal economic well-being, and resistance to minority equal status. While forced assimilation may well have served elite geopolitical and domestic interests, it was imposed without consultation with either majority or minority masses or public consideration of other politico-structural options, such as minority rights, which includes, as may be required for minority equal-status development, the right to separate institutions under minority control. Neither the majority nor the national minorities appear to have favored assimilation, but rather have had it forced upon them. The minority rights approach, however, addresses the fears aroused in both majority and minority ethnies concerning disruption of their cultures,

---

* Abridged from *Without Prejudice*, Vol. 1, Issue 1, 1987. Ronald Walters is Professor of Political Science at Howard University, Washington, D.C.

removing the issue of assimilation by calling for the establishment of equal-status minority-controlled institutions.

Concerning fear of loss of personal economic wellbeing, it might be argued that the civil rights model facilitates elite control of the majority through the maintenance and manipulation of inter-ethnic rivalry. As Walters clearly indicates, the linkage of majority resistance to minority gains to a right-wing agenda clearly permits elite institution of social policies which may in reality be counter to the economic interests of the majority masses. On the other hand, the establishment of minority rights / minority institutions provides a framework for ending the high costs of handling minority malaise.

However, insofar as majority resistance may also include a simple psychological need to retain a habitual dominance and hierarchical relation to the minorities, this attitudinal need is completely incompatible with the human right of minorities to equal status with the majority. Perhaps it is only in this sense that the issue of minority gains (as instituted through minority rights as opposed to civil rights policies) can be regarded as zero / sum. While the majority would neither be required to assimilate the national minorities, nor necessarily to suffer economic deprivation because of their gains, it would nonetheless have to surrender its notions of dominance and hierarchical supremacy.

At this time, however, as Ronald Walters' article suggests, the Anglo-American majority may have taken a course toward an unavoidable spiral of despair and ultimately, chaos.

An inescapable feature of the past six years of the "Reagan Revolution" has been the extent to which the conservative ideology that fueled it has congealed into a nationalism in the United States, the breathtaking sweep of which has pervaded many aspects of domestic and foreign policy. Ultimately, it has affected the normative character of the American psyche and, thereby, influenced the quality of life and behavior within institutions and neighborhoods. Yet a search reveals few writers who have characterized this phenomenon in its nationalistic dimensions. Perhaps it is easier to see a domestic brand of nationalism when its proponents wield such slogans as "Black Power," causing a flood of articles about "Black nationalism" to pour out into the landscape as in the 1960s. However, when one is a part of a nationalistic syndrome, it is perhaps more difficult to reveal its manifestations, because people who ostensibly support civil rather than radical processes of social change may be reluctant to admit their support of it. In any case, one cannot understand many aspects of modern American political behavior without taking this resurgent nationalism into serious consideration.

The Reagan Administration has attempted to employ the current strain of U.S. nationalism, for example, to contribute to the viability of U.S. corporations in their struggle with foreign competition, and to destroy the restraints on private capital in an effort to make unbridled capitalism the engine of domestic growth. Moreover, the supporters of this nationalism have sounded a number of moral, social themes, such as the preservation of the family, respect for law and order, anti-abortion, prayer in the schools, and others as a basis for restoring a pre-1960s social structure as the substance of "Americanness." They have also attempted to repress public attention to and concern for the disadvantaged classes — Blacks, other minorities, women and others, in order to restore white dominance of the social order through the resurrection of the status of white men.

It is instructive to note that the current wave of American nationalism is chauvinistic not only because it is American, but also because it is white. The domestic indication of this fact is that in attempting to resurrect the primacy of economics and military policy, the Reaganites have led the charge for the destruction of the national social agenda aimed at disadvantaged Blacks and others — including Black immigrants, such as the Haitians and Cubans. By posing the domestic dilemma as a problem of government hegemony which required "getting government off your back, to loose you and let you be independent again," Ronald Reagan has shaped a vision of restructuring society, using the framework of a time which not only elevated the interest of the wealthy over the poor, but which also contained white hegemonic dominance. That is to say, whites were not only dominant in an objective sense, there was an explicit ideology and style of such racial dominance.

It has been unnecessary for those supporting the resurrection of white hegemonic dominance to shout "white power"! This crude manifestation of white nationalism has been left to the Ku Klux Klan, the Aryan Nations and other such groups. Writers such as Murray Edelman and others have identified a far more sophisticated process which occurs in the transmission of social values through public policy, either as a reflection of a pre-existing movement or as the will of an existing regime in power — or both.[2] Yet the unmistakable symbolism that the arrival of radical white nationalism has pervaded the culture may be found in such patriotic sounding slogans as "America is back" and "Born in America again," slogans which have both foreign and domestic implications.

If white supremacy is dead, then shouldn't the idea have seriously eroded that America should be ruled by whites, with non-white groups kept in a subordinate position in the social structure? And shouldn't the enlightened view of American pluralism with all groups sharing political, economic and social power equitably have become the new norm of social practice? The history of current events would appear to speak more loudly in answer to this point, since the practice of racial equality has been dangerously derailed by whites who perceive (I would argue inaccurately) the threatened loss of their social status. This is a powerful motivating factor in generating a conservative ideology and social movement.

Therefore, I want to assert in this paper that the current political culture contains a pervasive strain of white nationalism as one of its dynamic features. The origin of this nationalism was the reaction to movements for social change by Blacks, other disadvantaged groups and youthful whites since World War II, which caused feelings of disempowerment by a segment of the white population devoted to the preservation of the *status quo.* White, conservative populists coalesced with other conservative elements into a nationalist movement dedicated to acquiring social and political power as the instruments of returning the United States to the *status quo ante.* At the grassroots level, this conservative movement led to the emergence of an authoritarian populism which facilitated the rise of racially-motivated violence. And at the national level, it provided the impetus for a coalition which elected Ronald Reagan to the presidency. One characterizes this movement as "white" in the literal sense that there was a marked absence of substantial Black participation in its activities or support for its values. Moreover, Black progress itself has become one of the primary targets of this movement in the attempt by the Reagan Administration to rearticulate the racial problem in society in a way which subordinates Black and minority interests and restores and preserves white supremacy.

To suggest that white power was ever surrendered (and therefore needed resurrecting) may seem confusing to many, especially since it is obvious that whites as a group have never lost status in America, a majority white country. However, there is within any society a "balance of attention" to certain issues in a given historical era which defines social power in a public way that both symbolizes and influences the extant distribution of benefit. This determines the relative material condition of groups and shapes their psyche as well.

Whites, although the dominant socio-cultural group, are hardly homogeneous ideologically. This context, the outcome of struggles for the distribution of benefit among groups of white Americans, defines the national power equation existing within society relative to the dominant political formations of whites *and* the status of others — Blacks among them. To the extent that whites differ among themselves over issues, the political system can appear to alter the balance of power by the significance it gives to status and distributive issues. Black demands, on the other hand, have destabilized the system itself, having been portrayed as insatiable. For example, the Civil Rights Movement appeared to favor Blacks in that the balance of attention focused on what Blacks considered to be the *marginal* alleviation of their grievances due to past oppression. To whites, however, it appeared to be a *substantial* change, and therefore, threatened a serious alteration in the *status quo.*

Thus it may be that, for neo-conservatives such as writer Clyde Wilson,[3] "well-being" for whites may also have to contain the public assurance that, relative to other groups in society, they are firmly in charge and have not lost — and are not in danger of losing — status due to public policies such as school of neighborhood integration, affirmative action, Black business mobility or political control.

The competition and resulting social conflict over an ever-tightening job market contributed to heightening tensions over the legacy of the Civil Rights Movement policies such as Title VII of the 1964 act.[4]

The revolt of Southern populist conservatives over civil rights and the economic conservatives of the early-1970's, together with the patriotic counter-reaction to the anti-Vietnam War movement, all made possible what Omi and Winant have called the convergence of the New Right with conservative populism to produce an anti-statist "authoritarian populism."[5] Since Democrats had been in charge of running the state, the dissatisfaction with the course of the nation came to be lodged at the presidential level of government. Public opinion between 1964 and 1978, for example, exhibited a clear shift in direction toward a negative view of the power of the federal government. While Blacks agree with this somewhat, this concept is more strongly held by whites.[6] One source of this alienation is the issue of busing. In fact, one New Right spokesman says: "nothing has contributed more to white populist disillusionment than the breathtaking hypocrisy and condescending arrogance shown by the establishment over the race issue." Citing the activities of some liberal politicians on the issue of busing as a key to this attitude, he continues: "No wonder vast numbers of white working-class Americans have come to believe that the federal government holds them and their children in something approaching contempt."[7] This attitude is supported by the data which show a significant drop in popular support for busing and a striking decline in support for government efforts to ensure school integration (from 52% in 1962 to 27% in 1978).[8]

By 1978, the extent of the alienation of the white working class had reached such proportions that "roughly one-third of white Americans feel that violence against the federal government will eventually prove necessary to save 'our true American way of life'," and that "these people who love America because they are America" feel "betrayed by a system they see as growing more alien."[9] In 1976, Professor Donald Warren identified Middle American Radicals (MARs) as constituting 31% of the white American population.[10] In agreement with George Wallace, MARs identified the government, the president, radicals and big business as enemies of the traditional American values. Intellectual justification proceeded to fuel this movement as several other works of consequence emerged in 1975, such a Robert Whitaker's *A Plague on Both Your Houses* (Robert B. Luce, 1975) and William Rusher's *The Making of the New Majority Party* (Green Hill, 1975). The concepts these authors espoused helped to legitimize the growth of white populist conservatism. The movement began to build at the grassroots, and the mood of alienation which it embodied often stimulated acts of physical violence against Blacks, minorities and religious groups.

In addition to these populist stirrings, the orthodox white nationalist came to life in semi-rehabilitated form, as some officials of the Ku Klux Klan began to shed their white robes for three-piece suits to run for election. Outbreaks of violence by the old Klan abated somewhat in the early 1970's, then rose again in the mid-to-late 1970's. As is customary of political movements, this period of the late 1970's was marked by the rapid growth and reorganization of highly ideological, leading-edge, orthodox, white, nationalist groups such as the White Patriot Party of North Carolina, the Posse Comitatus, and the Aryan Nations Church, which was started in the late 1970's to "eliminate the members of the Jewish faith and the Black race from society."[11] Linkages were found to exist among the KKK and the various Neo-Nazi groups at the World Aryan Congress in July of 1986 involving such groups as The Order, the National States Rights Part, the White Patriot Party, the Aryan Student Union, etc.

The Ku Klux Klan has been the most visible manifestation of a trend toward racial harassment and violence which has had wide participation by other whites. With respect to national trends in racially motivated violence, Justice Department data shows a 450% increase of incidents in racial violence attributed to the Klan between 1978 and 1979, and a 550% increase in the period 1978-1980. Considering the fact that, from all sources, incidents of racially motivated violence increased by 42% between 1985 and 1986, with a smaller percent attributed to Klan-type groups, this is an indication that the phenomenon was diffusing into the general population.[12]

The large increases between 1977 and 1978 conform to the perspective of this paper, that a white nationalist, populist attitude within neighborhoods was responsible for the generation of violence. This point is supported by the Justice Department's 1980 Report:

> A factor for much of the racial and ethnic hostility was the perception by many White [*sic*]] Americans that minorities, mainly Blacks and Hispanics, were getting a better deal than anyone else, and that *attention and continued effort to bring them into the mainstream threatened their welfare*. Minorities, on the other hand, perceived a creeping indifference and decreasing emphasis on efforts to improve their plight, and cited as justification an increasing number of reverse discrimination suits and charges, and a marked resurgence in the activities of the Ku Klux Klan. [Emphasis added.][13]

There is other empirical evidence which supports this point of view in surveys taken in 1978 and 1981. In 1978, two years after major Black revolts abated that had destroyed parts of northern and mid-western cities, a replication of the 1968 Kerner Commission survey in those areas revealed that 10% fewer whites (1968, 39%; 1978, 49%) thought that Blacks were missing out on employment and promotions because of racial discrimination.[14] By 1981, the ABC/*Washington Post* Poll revealed that 65% of whites disagreed with the statement that Blacks were discriminated against in securing managerial jobs, and there was strong disagreement (71%) that Blacks should receive assistance from the government "that white people in similar circumstances don't get" because of past discrimination.[15]

Finally, because of the often close relationship between the local police forces and fascist or Klan-type organizations and activities historically, especially in the South, police officers are often suspected to exercise deadly force against Blacks in a manner which highly suggests racial motivation. For example, figures from the Police Foundation for 1978 indicate that 78% of those killed and 80% of those non-fatally shot by police were minorities (and most of these were Black).[16]

The white nationalist movement was cresting in the late 1970's, and Reagan was able to find the right symbols to unlock its electoral power which accounted for his election, not — as commonly suggested — that the charisma of Reagan alone was responsible. In posing the question of what were the residual rights of white people in reaction to the demands for Black rights, the ideology of "white rights" developed. The strategy of achieving full fruition of white rights, however, required the advancement of racial politics which would overturn not just the "gains" of the 1960s for Blacks, but the racial frame of reference as well. Hence it was to rearticulate the very notion of racial inequality in a way which did not continue to threaten white interests.

The Reagan Administration proceeded to follow the advice of the emergent conservative policy establishment. Reagan rightly felt that he had a mandate from whites to pursue a policy of rearticulating race through the coded strategy of the budget, the Justice Department and other civil rights agencies, and by the attempted isolation of Black leadership. By such actions, Reagan went a long way toward legitimizing what Omi and Winant have considered to be the ultimate objective of authoritarian populism.

Measures under Reagan to roll back legislated checks on white hegemony have prejudiced some of the most fundamental civil rights initiatives. These include the reinstatement of tax exemptions to segregated educational institutions, as in the case of the Bob Jones Academy in 1981-82. The promotion of a strategy known as "New Federalism" seeks to remove from national responsibility some forty-five social programs to the jurisdiction of states. This is in light of the demonstrable fact that, when the balance of power between the states and the federal government has shifted in favor of the former, Blacks have historically suffered.[17] In addition, Reagan's procrastinating on the renewal of the Voting Rights Act also sought to absolve certain southern states of special compliance with the Act, an area of the country noted as a traditional stronghold of conservative, white hegemony. Other noteworthy efforts include the debilitation of the U.S. Civil Rights Commission, contributing to the restoration in the Justice Department of a pro-white, male agenda with attempts, by 1985, to reverse some fifty affirmative action decisions taken by lower courts.[18]

The Reagan phenomenon should be more correctly understood as a direct by-product of the conservative movement of white populist nationalism. In this sense, it matters less that the President is personally racist than that he conceives of his political mandate as having racial implications and proceeds to carry them into his policy program through institutions which affect the quality of life for millions of Americans. It may be possible to change the course of policy if the problem is merely personal, but it is extremely difficult to do so where there is a movement which undergirds a political consensus binding individuals of various racial, religious and political persuasions to a common point of view in a given historical moment.

It is of course no secret that older nationalist movements have undergone transformations whereby nationalism turns into fascism in the desperate pursuit of rearticulating those aspects of society perceived to stand in the way of the reassumption of power by one disparate group or another. There should be little illusion that, within the current white nationalist movement, there are, indeed, possibilities for the achievement of what Bertram Gross has called "Friendly Fascism" — a nameless, faceless brand of racial (and class) subjugation that would be administered through the major institutions of society.[19] Once the framework has been set, all that is left is for the natural consequence of institutional racism to work its will in the many fields of society.

This is indeed a formidable problem. Even in the 1960s when there was the greatest admission that America was a racist society, there was an equal optimism that racism could be eliminated through a process that the nation was willing to undergo. This version of institutional racism might be regarded as a benign form, where (it was possible to make the case) racism is insinuated into institutional processes. Then there is the genuine search to root it out which takes into consideration the reprocessing of individual and group behavior and, thus, institutional structures and functions. However, now there is at least the pretense of unconsciousness about racism's presence and effects.

The Kerner Commission Report of 1968, which was written in the throes of a Black violent revolt, set out a vision of American society which could be achieved through the amelioration of the social ills of Blacks. By overturning this vision — and the possibilities of its achievement — what vision of the social order is being put in its place, and (more importantly) if it is not viewed by a major segment of the population as just, how will social harmony be maintained?

The stakes for the elimination of white racism are as urgent as they have ever been, yet society appears to be going in the other direction. What is there to be said for an era when institutions are busily implementing racist policies knowingly and with rationalizations? What is being destroyed now is not only the lives of some Blacks, but the hope that impressive change in the society is possible. It has formerly been this hope which has prevented the descent into an unavoidable spiral of despair which leads in the direction of chaos rather than community.

---

1 See Y.N. Kly, *The Anti-Social Contract,* 1987.
2 Murray Edelman, *Politics as Symbolic Action,* 1971.
3 Clyde Wilson, "Citizens or Subjects" in Robert Whitaker, ed., *The New Right Papers,* 1982.
4 Until the passage of Title VII of the 1964 Civil Rights Act, blacks had no effective legal mechanism for confronting discrimination practiced in employment, since most disputes were handled either by labor unions or federal agencies whose only power was to mediate disputes. Article VII established the Equal Employment Opportunity Commission (EEOC), an executive agency with the authority to receive, file and investigate complaints of employment discrimination. Title VII barred discrimination by private employers or unions with more than twenty-five workers or members if the employers or unions "fail or refuse to hire or to discharge any individual, or otherwise to discriminate against any individual with respect to his compensation, terms, conditions or privileges of employment, because of such individual's race, color, religion, sex or national origin." (P.L. 88-352, 88th Congress, H.R. 7152 (2 July 1964): U.S. Senate at Large, 241.
5 Michael Omi and Howard Winant, *Racial Formation in the United States,* 1986, p. 120.
6 See Table 2, Attitudes toward the Power of the Federal Government, 1964-1978, in unabridged version of this paper, p. 13.
7 Robert Hoy, "Lid on a Boiling Pot," in Whitaker, ed., *supra.,* p. 99.
8 Survey Research Center, Institute for Social Research, University of Michigan, *National Election Study Data Sourcebook, 1952-1978,* 1978, pp. 181, 277.
9 Robert Hoy, *supra.,* p. 91.
10 Donald Warren, *The Radical Center,* 1976.
11 *The Washington Post,* 18 December 1984, p. A3.
12 Community Relations Service. U.S. Department of Justice, *Annual Report,* 1979, 1980, 1985, 1986.
13 *Id.,* p. 3.
14 Survey Research Center, *National Election Study, supra.;* CBS/ *New York Times* Poll, *The New York Times,* 26 February 1978, p. A2.
15 *The Washington Post,* 25 March 1981, p. A2.
16 Thomas Johnson, "U.S. Agency Moves to Head Off Racial Conflict over Allegations of Police Misuse of Force.," *The New York Times,* 11 August 1979, p. 1.
17 Ronald Walters, "Federalism, 'Civil Rights' and Black Progress," *Black Law Journal,* Vol. 8, No. 2, 1983, pp. 220-234.
18 *The Monitor,* December 1986.
19 Bertram Gross, *Friendly Fascism: The New Face of Power in America,* 1980.

Proceedings of the Conference on *African-Americans and the Right to Self-determination*

Hamline University

May 14, 1993

PREFACE TO THE CONFERENCE

Clarence Davis[1]

The following materials represent the *Proceedings of the Conference on African-Americans and the Right to Self-Determination* held at Hamline University School of Law on May 14, 1993. The conference was sponsored jointly by the Hamline University School of Law and the International Human Rights Association of American Minorities (IHRAAM).[2] Co-sponsors included a number of concerned local, national and international human rights organizations, professional legal associations, and academic organizations.[3]

This conference marked an historic initiative in exploring the rights and equal status needs of African-Americans. Historically, the rights of African-Americans in the United States have been discussed almost entirely in terms of United States constitutional law (U.S. civil rights), rather than in the broader international legal framework of human and collective rights. However, important recent developments and perspectives raise new questions. In September 1992, the United States ratified the *International Covenant on Civil and Political Rights* developed under the auspices of the United Nations. This covenant protects the right to self-determination, the right to non-discrimination, the right to remedy, and the rights of minorities. Yet, in that same month, the *Human Rights Monitor*, a Swiss-based publication of the international service for human rights, revealed that the United States was among three nations that narrowly escaped condemnation in 1992 by the United Nations Sub-

Commission on Prevention of Discrimination and Protection of Minorities for a pattern of gross human rights violations. The complaint, submitted by IHRAAM to UN Secretary-General Boutros Boutros-Ghali on April 30, 1992, was based on the continuing pattern of gross human rights violations suffered by African-Americans in the United States, as typified by the case of Los Angeles motorist, Rodney King.

What is the context for such a complaint? What is the legal vocabulary for a discussion of these issues? Do African-Americans have a right to self-determination under international human rights law? These are the issues addressed by the keynote speaker, Dr. Yussuf N. Kly and the distinguished groups of scholars assembled for the conference. Dr. Kly's address, along with the comments of the conference panelists, are published here[4] as the Proceedings of this Conference.

KEYNOTE ADDRESS

African-Americans and the Right to Self-Determination

Dr. Y. N. Kly

I. *Introduction*

The purpose of this presentation is to provide the perimeter and international framework from which can emerge a socio-politically meaningful and legally-functional response to the question: "Do African-Americans have a right to self-determination?" To do so, we will briefly discuss U.S. democratic traditions in relation to this question and in relation to the international human rights approach. Then we shall proceed to note the current state of law, then discuss the need for a balance between international law sources in relation to the right to self-determination. In the guise of concluding, a response will emerge to the question: "Do African-Americans have a right to self-determination?"

At decisive points in the American past, events occurred that had the effect of arresting African-American socio-political and intellectual development, subjecting it to an orbit governed by the "strange attraction" of historically-enforced paradigms, such as: no matter what actual effect majority decisions may have on the African-American, accepting these decisions represents not only what is best for African-Americans, but also the only possible way in which U.S. democracy can be expressed or maintained; to prove and confirm that the U.S. system, as is, is best for everyone, is the guideline for all legitimate African-American analysis, leadership decisions and studies; to speak of the unique needs of the African-American community within the framework of government policy formation is racist or promoting segregation or racial isolationism; special rights, self-government, segregation and separation are all to be considered the same thing.

The original conditions that brought these paradigms into force and which locked the direction of African-American socio-political development to them is, of course, too complex to be analyzed in this paper. However, suffice it to say that they are the conditions emanating from the shock and resulting tumult of enslavement, the lost recognition of rights as human beings, and all subsequent acts, terror, political control techniques and policies to which this particular community was subject during its movement through legal enslavement, Jim Crow, and apartheid (segregation). From the vantage point of the intelligentsia of the dominant group, these same paradigms are encouraged and validated as a consequence of fears, privileges, customs and orientations growing out of having experienced the advantageous side of this historical development. In short, historically, a situation of Anglo-American domination has been viewed as both natural and desirable.

We feel it would be fair to assume that the patterns of African-American leadership and the framework for decision-making that we see emerging from the chaos of what is called the African-American or black community, results from "sensitive dependence" on these original historical circumstances.

If so, then our gathering here today is historic because it represents the first effort of African-American and indeed American thinkers to free their minds (in relation to the African-American question in the context of American development) from the intellectually crushing and oppressive paradigms that have served only to loop back toward the past, thus assuring that in relation to American pluralistic societal development, we shall continue to turn in purposeless circles around our original "strange attraction" to various forms of enslavement and/or servitude, domestication and consequent materialism and dehumanization.

Our attempt today to begin the process of reorienting intellectual thought around the right to self-determination is first of all an act toward intellectual liberation, and is an historical landmark suggesting that we have finally broken free of the enslavement paradigms, and can now begin to contribute positively and meaningfully to African-American freedom and to American intellectual, political, cultural and material development. In this way, we, in our frail emergence, may rightly liken ourselves to the wings of Edward Lorenz's butterfly.

The fact that this paper will suggest the need for paradigmatic change in our thinking about democracy and minority rights automatically suggests the likelihood of unreasoned opposition. In the words of Tolstoy:

> I know that most men, including those at ease with problems of the greatest complexity, can seldom accept even the simplest and most obvious truth if it be such as would oblige them to admit the falsity of conclusions which they have delighted in explaining to colleagues, which they have proudly taught to others, and which they have woven, thread by thread, into the fabric of their lives.[5]

But both empirical and theoretical evidence suggests that in order for Americans to reasonably expect positive and manageable future ethnic relations, they must denounce much about these relations in the past and present. The shift from a domestic civil rights model to an international human rights model will be, for the professional African and Anglo-American communities, in Thomas Kuhn's words, "as if the professional community [is] suddenly transported to another planet where familiar objects are seen in a different light and are joined by unfamiliar ones as well."[6]

Thus it is only fitting, for the sake of facilitating the shift from one set of landmarks to another, that when Americans, who have seen the absence of the recognition of fundamental human rights in a state that is well known for its global contributions to these rights, shift to thinking about the right to self-determination as it concerns African-Americans, they think not only of its present provisionally legal meanings, but also of its potential contributions to democracy, minority equality, racial-ethnic conflict resolution and American socio-political and economic development. This will facilitate the discussion of the unfamiliar in the context of the more familiar norms of American thought.

II. *Self-Determination and American Democracy*

The concept of democracy has always been a cherished one in American society. With the ending of the Cold War, there has been an international expansion in the desire for democracy. As noted by Halperin and Scheffer:

> In recent years the interrelationship between human rights and democracy has become so pronounced that some scholars now speak of an "entitlement" to democracy as an emerging principle of international law that will create a right or even an obligation for the international community to act to protect or promote democracy...{T}he emerging commitment to democracy has become an important principle in the work of the Conference on Security and Cooperation in Europe, the Organization of American States, and the United Nations...
>
> The advocacy of democratic governance as an emerging principle of international law has influenced and will continue to influence both the character of self-determination movements and the international community's response to them.[7]

However, majority democracy is not necessarily successful in providing for the democratic needs of minority populations. As Halperin and Scheffer go on to note:

> The democratization process can often resolve self-determination claims by giving rise to a political system capable of protecting and accommodating groups that would otherwise be seeking changes in political arrangements or borders. But in other cases electoral democracy may not be enough. Democracy may mean little to a minority group that is constantly outvoted. It may mean little to an indigenous people whose political culture and traditions are different from those of other groups within the state. And it may mean little to a group that feels a historical claim entitles it to greater protection [or] more political power...[8]

For centuries, the dominant American ethnic group, the "Anglo-Americans," has interpreted democracy as simply establishing majority rule within the framework of electoral politics. This has developed naturally from the notion that all United States citizens have become assimilated into a single, new ethnic identity: Americans. Americans have taken pride in their concepts of achieving unity in diversity, of being composed of races from all parts of Europe who nonetheless were single-mindedly dedicated to the "melting pot," of creating one nation —a single nation-state—of assimilation, in short.[9] The paradox is that those who held this view, for whatever reason,[10] saw no contradiction in segregating both the African and the Native American outside of this "melting pot."[11] So the question arises: who was to be melted, and into which pot?

As evidenced by the existing map of racial or ethnic relations in the United States today, at least four separate pots emerged — each containing a number of diverse yet roughly similar populations, each pot interacting with the other while at the same time melting separately — out of which all Americans were molded: the Anglo-American, the African-American, the Native American, and the Spanish American. Apart from the Spanish American, perhaps, these pots developed along the fault lines of racism and are forever subject to eruption.

As a multi-national state instituting a policy of majority democracy and assimilation,[12] the United States has encountered difficulty in responding to the needs and aspirations of its minority populations. Writing on such a problem, Asbjørn Eide, technical expert on minority rights to the United Nations, has observed:

> The nation, in its most common sense, meaning the population (often composed of several ethnic groups) who cohabit within the borders ... is an association coordinated by rules and institutions. Many [minorities] consider it an ... impersonal and unfriendly entity. One [possibility] is ... ethno-nationalism... [t]he other is to transform the national society into a community at a higher level, by making the inhabitants feel that they belong together, that they identify with each other. While this is a more acceptable approach, it has its own problems, if it is pursued in a way which breaks down the lower-level communities. *Policies of assimilation tend to break down ethnic identities, and are often referred to as ethnocide.* More acceptable therefore is the road to pluralism, where the different lower-level communities can co-exist and continue to have their primary identity and yet cooperate and participate in the common domain within the larger State.[13]

A further commentary on the international community's views on forced or coercive assimilation in democracies is found in the recent Council of Europe's *Proposal for a European Convention for the Protection of Minorities.*[14] Article 13 of this Convention would require that states "refrain from pursuing or encouraging policies aimed at the assimilation of minorities or aimed at intentionally modifying the proportions of the population in the regions inhabited by minorities."[15] The Convention views democracy within the framework of protection for minorities and forbids "any activity capable of threatening their existence,"[16] while it seeks to assure "the right to freely preserve, express and develop their cultural identity in all its aspects, free of any attempts at assimilation against their will."[17] It also calls for effective remedies before national authorities for violations of minority rights.[18]

Today, after numerous ethnically-inspired insurrections or riots, and the re-emerging international and UN emphasis on minority rights, Americans have begun to move away from the single melting pot theory to one of recognizing themselves as a pluralistic society. This is reflected in the greater official acceptance in the United States of the existence of national minorities such as African-Americans, and a greater recognition of their right to be different and equal. Surely the unchallenged and routine use of the descriptive term, African-American, by President Bill Clinton is important evidence of this new potential direction. However, hinting at a new direction is far from taking steps in that direction. In a majority democracy such as the United States, pluralism has no meaning as far as providing for minority rights is concerned, unless it can be accompanied by complementary pluralistic political, socio-cultural, educational and economic institutions.

The creation of pluralistic socio-political and economic institutions where required to bring about equal status and equal opportunity demands a rethinking of the concept of democracy in a multi-national state. Majority democracy (majority rule and domination) must be refashioned in such ways as to guarantee that majority rule does not extinguish minority rights. This will mean formally and philosophically recognizing the existence of national minorities with the full and formal understanding that (1) they are expected (*infinito*) to exist, to be different and to struggle for their own interest; and (2) the solution to the minority problem is really not a grand solution but rather a framework by which inter-ethnic conflict can be peacefully and beneficially managed, wherein the dynamics of inter-ethnic competition, a state-sanctioned equal status competitiveness, will serve to keep all hands above the table and lead to the maximization of justly distributed socio-economic and political power. This may equally provoke maximum socio-economic development. As Asbjørn Eide wrote:

> The alternative to ethno-nationalism [white nationalism in the case of the United States[19]] is pluralism based on the recognition of group or minority rights, providing respect for group identity... This places democracy in a serious test, particularly when democracy is understood in its traditional but now rather dubious meaning of pure majority government. Mature democracies have learned to live with and respect diversity, through formal or informal arrangements...[20]

This theoretical orientation, as formulated by its major theoretician, Arend Lijphart, is sometimes called "consociational" democracy.[21] Seen as an alternative to the majoritarian type of democracy and more suitable for good government in plural societies divided by ethnic differences where the groups are clearly identifiable, consociational democracy is built on the principle of executive power-sharing and a certain degree of self-administration for each group, whether they live together or separately (non-territorial or territorial).

Recent international thinking on minority rights was reflected in the Conference on Security and Cooperation in Europe (CSCE) meeting on the Human Dimension, held in Copenhagen in June, 1990.[22] The Copenhagen document includes an entire section on the rights of national minorities, and it suggests that democracy and individual human rights guarantees alone may not adequately protect minorities — that it may be necessary to give a minority group certain political functions and powers in order to protect minority rights.[23]

The *Report of the CSCE Meeting of Experts on National Minorities* adopted in Geneva on July 19, 1991, goes further by fusing protection of minority rights with democratic systems and with the rule of law.[24] It states: "Issues concerning national minorities, as well as compliance with international obligations and commitments concerning the rights of persons belonging to them, are matters of legitimate international concern and consequently do not constitute exclusively an internal affair of the respective State."[25]

Such views are so widely held by scholars of democracy and minority rights, and are found in so many state actions over such a long period of time, as to merit our attention as emerging international norms in relation to democracy in multi-national states. After noting the difference between special measures and special rights, Gudmundur Alfredsson, an official of the Human Rights Center in Geneva, adds his voice to those favoring consociated democracy in multi-national states:

> Special rights for minority individuals or groups are necessary in a democratic system which guarantees individual rights. Non-discrimination in the enjoyment of general rights and freedoms does not suffice. A group does not really enjoy an equal status with the majority population unless it is accorded conditions equivalent to the majority.[26]

In view of the fact that most national institutions and policies reflect majority interests, only pluralist arrangements for power sharing through degrees of control over various jurisdictions (such as education, health, criminal justice, culture and taxes), insofar as they concern the minority, can approximate conditions naturally enjoyed by the majority. Alfredsson reminds us that "[s}pecial measures to overcome discriminatory patterns, such as preferential treatment and affirmative action, require temporary action until the problem gets solved. Special rights, however, such as the maintenance of educational and cultural institutions, call for ongoing entitlements."[27]

Most scholars agree that special rights are necessary for securing equality and dignity in political representation; for lending a meaningful content and direction to the minority's right to develop and be different; and for giving real meaning to the concept of democracy. Is it not strange that, in a country where democracy and the democratic process is considered a crowning achievement, methods for selecting African-American leadership remain undemocratic? What has the African-American's experience with democracy really been? Does democracy mean only the exercise of the right to vote in order to demonstrate good citizenship, without the legitimate expectation of ever exercising significant or effective influence on actual policy?

A survey of the legal systems in numerous multi-national states reveals that most multi-national states are aware of the possible meaninglessness of majority democracy in relation to the democratic needs of minorities. This is evidenced in the variety of legal-structural arrangements they have established, such as:

- constitutional and/or legislative recognition of the group's existence and of minority history and customs
- the duty of governments to obtain consent from or consult with minorities about matters affecting them, i.e. minority veto power
- guaranteed seats in the legislature and other political organs, including inter-governmental ones, and the appointment of officials chosen by the group to either specific positions or to a fixed minimum percentage of posts in the national legislature and other pertinent governing bodies
- minority boards to license psychiatrists, doctors and other professionals who work in the minority community
- the right to a just proportion of the taxes paid to government
- proportional representation
- special minority legislative bodies

- formal recognition of minority interests in the Cabinet
- formal advisory bodies
- local and autonomous administration of socio-cultural and economic institutions, as well as autonomy on a territorial or non-territorial basis, including the existence of consultative, legislative and executive bodies chosen through free and periodic minority elections
- self-administration by a national minority of aspects concerning its identity and social welfare in situations where autonomy on a territorial or non-territorial basis does not apply; and
- de-centralized or local forms of minority government.

Suffice it to begin a conclusion to this section by noting that the search for meaningful democracy, equality, ethnic freedom and human rights in multi-national states will involve far more in relation to structural-legal arrangements than the provision for majority democracy, non-discrimination and equal protection before the law. We suggest it calls for a consociated philosophical approach to democracy as well as a willingness to grant national minorities the right to self-determination short of the right to secession. We emphasize our belief that for the United States, the issue of self-determination should be addressed in connection with a number of existing or emerging norms in international and American thought, although some may have little to do with the right to self-determination in international law, such as representative democracy, good governance, public accountability, free and meaningful political participation, community empowerment, community-based justice, equal status non-discrimination, progressive civil rights, dignity, identity and tolerance.

Alexis Heraclides' concept of learning the ability to move apart while at the same time moving together[28] embodies the most important future need of American democracy, for it is only through this art that societal pluralism, the right to be different, and appropriate stimulants to economic and social development, can be achieved. His concept sees both future freedom and economic development in multi-national states as dependent on consociational democracy. It suggests that, when exercised collectively, self-determination is to peoples (minorities) what freedom is to individuals. It can be said to be the necessary condition for the very existence of human rights in the sense that, where it does not exist, minorities or members of minorities cannot be free, because they are not empowered to be different and to make public policy choices, i.e. establish operative guidelines for those social, legal and administrative institutions that directly impact their special or unique socio-economic and political needs. Is the principle of self-determination, as such, one of the human rights, or is it perhaps, as frequently alleged, the essential condition for all human rights in relation to minorities and peoples?[29]

III. *Self-Determination: A Historical Sketch*

We shall start at the point which seems favored by most modern scholars. It begins on January 8, 1918, when President Woodrow Wilson announced fourteen points as a proposed basis for world peace. He emphasized, *inter alia*, the principle "that in determining all such questions of sovereignty, the interests of the populations concerned must have equal weight with the equitable claims of the government whose title is to be determined."[30]

In the 1919 peace treaties, careful attention was given to the protection of ethnic minorities. At that time, implementation of the principle of self-determination included international protection of minorities, regional autonomy, nationhood within a federal state or within a commonwealth of nations, and finally, political independence or the right to secession.[31] One of the main methods of realizing the principle was plebiscites to ascertain the just social, cultural and economic claims of the inhabitants. However, this "central principle" and method was certainly not applied universally, but rather in accordance with political expediency. It was not regarded as a legally binding right, but as a mere political principle which, according to the case in question, might or might not be applied. Before the Second World War, African-Americans or aboriginal peoles living together, like the populations in the Allied colonial territories, were not regarded as "peoples."

In the aftermath of World War I, neither the external nor the internal promises of the principle of self-determination were fulfilled. None of the successor states created at Versailles were established by plebiscite. The Great Powers also did not apply the principle of self-determination to their own people. Nor did they respect ethnic boundaries beyond Europe — either as they divided Germany's vast Asian and African territories or in their own colonial empires.

From a doctrine narrowly applied after World War I when the Great Powers redrew European boundaries, self-determination in international law evolved into an enforceable right to freedom from colonial rule. In the *Declaration on the Granting of Independence to Colonial Countries and Peoples,* adopted by the UN General Assembly on December 14, 1960,[32] a first attempt was made to link the evolution of the field of human rights to the right of self-determination. This document established the first close connection between the principles of self-determination and respect for human rights. It begins with the declaration that "{t}he subjection of peoples to alien subjugation, domination and exploitation [i.e. the denial of self-determination] constitutes a denial of fundamental human rights..." Although it is emphasized that "{a}ll peoples have the right to self-determination," the effect of the preamble, where the desire to end colonization is mentioned not less than four times, is to permit the interpretation that self-determination, in terms of the right to full political independence, is a legal principle only as far as it concerns people under colonial rule. This Declaration reinforces the fundamental international legal concept of the right to rebellion against conditions of denial of fundamental rights.

The "self-determination of peoples" is mentioned twice, if somewhat cryptically, in the *United Nations Charter.* [33] It has since been elaborated by a series of UN resolutions, including the first articles of the two 1966 International Covenants on human rights,[34] the advisory opinions of the International Court of Justice on Namibia and Western Sahara, [35] and by the "Friendly Relations" Declaration of 1970.[36] While both International Covenants on human rights contain in their first articles a guarantee of the right of self-determination of peoples, neither defines either "peoples" or the content of self-determination, nor do they establish a procedure for its realization. Faced with the nearly universal resistance by states to the full right to self-determination insofar as it might include the right to secession, and yet aware of the utility of this notion as a means of conflict resolution and assuring world peace, international legal scholarship has developed a division of the concept of self-determination into two wings. The first wing entails the right to external self-determination, i.e. the right of a people to undertake external roles such as foreign policy and defense, usually reserved for States alone, and as such seemingly almost indistinguishable from secession. The second wing entails internal self-determination, i.e. the right of peoples or minorities to varying degrees of jurisdiction over affairs internal to the state. This definitional solution proposed by international legal experts appears to result from the balancing of several major yet contradictory factors: the legitimacy of state fears for territorial integrity; the central, yet unelaborated, reference to self-determination in the International Covenants; and the historical policies promoted over time by what were then called "civilized nations" to protect peoples or minorities — often minorities in another state with whom the promoting nation-state was tied by ethnicity — which by our present period have developed into a relatively substantial body of state practice illustrating a wide range of options for devolution of state powers to minority populations.[36]

Bearing in mind the widely accepted notion that the right to self-determination represents the foundation upon which all other rights can be assured, and the equally important and generally accepted notions of the equality of all peoples, and the universal right of all to democracy, it appears that the notion of self-determination excluding the right to secession, or minority rights (which may include varying degrees of internal self-determination) has become an accepted and central premise in the literature. Indeed, as Asbjørn Eide noted, the notion of majority democracy — the ongoing subjugation of the wishes and needs of a minority population to those of the majority population, which are assured expression through electoral processes — is now nearly totally discredited.

The notion of internal self-determination, as discussed in international legal writings such as those by Francesco Capotorti, Hernan Cruz, Asbjørn Eide, Claire Palley, Gudmundur Alfredsson, Irene Erica Daes, Alexis Heraclides and Richard Falk, has evolved into what seems to be an articulation of the type of rights most often demanded by national minorities. This articulation is achieved not so much by altering the scope or beneficiaries of the first articles of the International Covenants, as by looking beyond those articles to the evolution of minority rights in customary international law, which allows for an appropriate interpretation of Article 27 of the *International Covenant on Civil and Political Rights* (ICCPR). Article 27 simply states: "In those States in which ethnic, religious or linguistic minorities exist, persons belonging to such minorities shall not be denied the right, in community with the other members of their group, to enjoy their own culture, to profess and practice their own religion, or to use their own language." However, it is argued that varying degrees of self-determination short of the right to secession are often required in order to truly enable minorities to enjoy and sustain their own culture in equal status with the majority. Indeed, most of the arrangements for self-determination mentioned in the Atlantic Charter of August 14, 1941, short of the right to secession, coincide with what is now referred to as minority rights under Article 27. This would suggest that a national minority may have a legal claim to self-determination short of the right to secession or may have the right to most of the same rights as peoples under Article 1 of the ICCPR. As a point of fact, efforts are presently underway at the United Nations to have the same UN agency deal in the future with demands under both Article 27 and Article 1 of the ICCPR An obvious reason for this, overlooking the technical details that Article 1 provides for self-determination and Article 27 provides for minority rights, is that the rights in both these articles evolved through customary international law, and most groups probably state their demands for minority rights as demands for self-determination.

IV. *Notes on the Current State of Law*

We should begin by reiterating that in current law the term "people" as used in the first articles of the International Covenants, is defined as the population of a separate political unit on delimited territory with a background in colonial history or recent occupation (at least since 1945 or possibly sometime after the conclusion of the Kellogg-Briand Pact in 1928).[37]

A comprehensive definition to distinguish the term "people" from the term "minority" was sought,[38] and a compilation of definition proposals submitted to the United Nations over a forty year period was recently issued.[39] However, the only conclusions the literature permits is that minorities differ from "peoples" in that they always share a non-dominant position. They are the same as "peoples" in that they possess acquired characteristics established over a period of time. It appears to have been useful, for political reasons, to make a legal distinction between minorities and indigenous and tribal peoples, on the one hand, and the term "people," on the other. The latter needs to be more concretely defined in international instruments, as there is a tendency to get different meanings depending on the political maxim and legal source. As to external self-determination (the right to secede), the term "people" has in practice been limited to populations of fixed territorial entities, such as overseas colonies, more often than not, and until recently without regard to the ethnic and cultural characteristics of the people living within the territorial boundaries. In some Third World instruments, such as the *Declaration on the Right to Development*[40] and the *African Charter on Human and People's Rights*,[41] an attempt is made to exclude minorities from the right to any form of self-determination. However, it is never denied that a relationship exists between peoples and minorities inasmuch as some of the same claims surface, or that some groups now treated as minorities may qualify for the concept and broader rights of peoples under the law as it now stands. Also, since the end of the Cold War, we see the emergence of the recognition of national minorities as peoples, or the recognition of the right to self-determination for national minorities, e.g. Croatia and Slovenia. This indicates that the current state of conventional law is provisional and still in the process of balancing the interpretations of more recent human rights instruments with customary law for the purposes of minority protection in the political reality of the twenty-first century. The fact that the terms "people" or "minority" or "indigenous people" are not expressly defined in any of the instruments suggests that international legal opinion is likely to continue changing in relation to the evolving new world order.

Concerning the content of the right to self-determination, Article 1 of the ICCPR stipulates that "State Parties ... shall promote the right in conformity with the provisions of the Charter of the United Nations." The ICCPR stipulates that under this right, peoples "freely determine their political status and freely pursue their economic, social and cultural development."[42] Although international instruments do not provide a succinct definition of the contents of the right to self-determination of peoples, the *Declaration of Principles of International Law Concerning Friendly Relations and Co-operation Among States* stipulates that the creation of a sovereign and independent State, the free association or integration with an independent State, or the acquisition of any other freely decided political status, are all means through which a people can exercise the right to self-determination.[43] Here, it is interesting to note that Article 27 of the ICCPR has been interpreted as providing minorities with some of the same rights.[44] A large number of states such have introduced autonomy or self-government. Such regimes have a good record of fostering harmony between majority and minority. In many instances, self-determination has come to mean self-management, home rule, or merely the delegation of powers to a municipal authority with expanded functions. The title does not matter as long as the central government agrees to power sharing and leaves a sufficient and acceptable amount of control over minority affairs in the hands of group representatives. Sufficient self control by certain groups over their internal affairs is seen in human rights law as essential for protecting dignity, identity, and diverse customs, and placing groups on an equal footing with other parts of society.[45]

The United Nations' *Declaration on the Rights of Persons Belonging to National or Ethnic, Religious and Linguistic Minorities* states:

> 1. States shall protect the existence and the national or ethnic, cultural, religious and linguistic identity of minorities within their respective territories and shall encourage conditions for the promotion of that identity.
> 2. States shall adopt appropriate legislative and other measures to achieve those ends.[46]

The Declaration, which is not legally binding, gives us direction as to the interpretation of Article 27 of the ICCPR, which is legally binding on state parties ratifying the Covenant. The Declaration enumerates the rights of "persons belonging to minorities" and the obligations of states toward them, such as:

> Persons belonging to minorities have the right to participate effectively in decisions on the national and, where appropriate, regional level concerning the minority to which they belong or the regions in which they live, in a manner not incompatible with national legislation.[47] [But what if national legislation is incompatible with this right?]

> States shall take measures to create favorable conditions to enable persons belonging to minorities to express their characteristics and to develop their culture, language, religion, traditions and customs, except where specific practices are in violation of national law and contrary to international standards.[48] [But what if it is in keeping with international standards but contrary to national law?}

> States should consider appropriate measures so that persons belonging to minorities may participate fully in the economic progress and development in their country.[49][Would demand for the right to receive minority tax revenues to establish a minority bank for economic development fall under this umbrella?}

> National policies and programs shall be planned and implemented with due regard for the legitimate interests of persons belonging to minorities.[50] [Does this suggest the need for proportional representation, minority referenda, or similar special rights?]

> States should cooperate on questions relating to persons belonging to minorities, *inter alia* exchanging information and experiences, in order to promote mutual understanding and confidence.[51]

Article 8 states that nothing in the Declaration "may be construed as permitting any activity contrary to the purposes and principles of the United Nations, including sovereign equality, territorial integrity and political independence of States."[52] It describes the constant promotion and realization of minority rights in the context of "the development of society as a whole and within a democratic framework based on the rule of law..."[53]

These special minority rights do not constitute privileges; these rights are rooted in the principle of equality of treatment just as is non-discrimination. Special rights have been defined as the requirement to "ensure for the minority elements suitable means for the preservation of their own characteristics and traditions,"[54] as specified and demanded by the minority itself. Today, the most important generally accepted instruments provide for these rights and the relevant measures for the preservation and promotion of the dignity, identity, characteristics and traditions of minorities.[55]

It has been an obstacle in the past to believe that a common definition and a common set of rights should apply to all kinds of minorities. The emphasis should be on a proper analysis of the particular problem faced by the minority in a given situation and on finding a solution to that problem which is in conformity with international law in general, and human rights in particular. Each individual has the right to identify him or herself with a group of persons differing from the rest of society with distinct socio-cultural, religious, linguistic or ethnic character,[56] and this inherent right suggests that self-determination is and will remain a chief concern of what are called national minorities.[57]

The recognition of the rights of these types of minorities is bound up with the realization that there is a contradiction between affirmations of freedom and justice, on the one hand, and situations of domination and exploitation brought about by existing non-pluralistic political or economic systems in multinational states, on the other.[58] Thus, internal self-determination or, as earlier defined, self-determination short of the right to secession, is intimately linked with the notion of pluralist democracy. The key to the right to internal self-determination is partly found in the *Declaration on Principles of International Law Concerning Friendly Relations and Cooperation Among States*,[59] and partly in Article 25 of the *Universal Declaration of Human Rights*.[60] They indicate that when it is found suitable through peaceful negotiations to subdivide jurisdictions in regard to some aspects of authority, making it easier for ethnic groups or national minorities within the state to control their own fate in certain functional areas, states may have the obligation to do so.[61]

When members of minorities demand, as the traditional African-American leadership has always done, no more than equal treatment, which has been increasingly interpreted in U.S. courts to mean the same treatment, the ordinary rules concerning non-discrimination apply. However, if a national minority such as African-Americans began effectively to demand, in some respects, differential treatment for the purpose of achieving equal status, it becomes necessary to distinguish between the domain which is of common concern and that which is specific to the members of the minority. In all matters of common concern, the principle of equality and non-discrimination continues to reign supreme. The first level of obligation for the sovereign state, the United States in this case, is to respect the equality of all individuals before the law. This presents the first problem: Should the law be the same for all groups? To what extent, and in regard to which circle of persons under which circumstances, should a legal or political system for that particular group be recognized? To the extent that it is found necessary in order to allow for the preservation of the identity and equal status of the group, certain matters may have to be transferred to the area of separate concern. While this does create problems in the common domain, these are problems which can be much more easily managed than the problems that arise from the denial of minority rights. They are also problems whose general management leads to a higher quality of life as well as a higher potential for democratic and economic development.

The first level of state obligation is inextricably intertwined with the second level, which is to assist its inhabitants in enjoying their human rights through fulfilling their justified claims to minority rights as spelled out in human rights instruments. This means that equal enjoyment of human rights must be achieved through active legal regulation and its administrative and financial implementation. In some circumstances, particularly with regard to indigenous peoples, restoration of land rights can be a useful tool in this effort. In the case of African-Americans, the use of affirmative measures, non-territorial self-government, or certain forms of institutional autonomy, can help to redress past discrimination and/or inequality in the enjoyment of rights by recreating equal opportunity in fact. This requires an affirmative definition by the group itself of its wishes and of its minority or "nation" identity (the subjective factor). Self-definition for African-Americans will have the effect of defining their status for the purpose of justifying their entitlement to transitional affirmative measures, special rights or minority rights, and compensation for gross violations, depending on the democratic demands of African-Americans.

V. *Balancing Sources of Law*

It is often said that there is much confusion about the right to self-determination. At the same time, we are often reminded of the importance of this right in relation to a group's capacity to enjoy its human rights, to the maintenance of world peace, and to conflict resolution in multi-national states. Many scholars, like most groups, use the term self-determination when referring to both "peoples" and "minorities." This causes confusion because other scholars separate the terms by reminding us that the legal source for the right to self-determination is the first articles in both International Covenants, while Article 27 of the ICCPR and the recent *Declaration on the Rights of Persons Belonging to National or Ethnic, Religious and Linguistic Minorities* are the legal sources for the rights of minorities.

Why is this? It seems that an answer to this question lies in the historical evolution of group rights in customary international law, where no clear distinction between peoples, minorities and nations, as it relates to the right to self-determination, evolved. Indeed, even with what has appeared to be the United Nations' efforts to resolve this gap by creating the necessary conventional law, no universally accepted definition of minority or people has emerged. The confusion is maintained when scholars (particularly those not familiar with international legal research methodology) analyze self-determination in the first articles of the International Covenants in such a manner as to conform with group rights in international customary law, without designating the legal source (conventional or customary international law). At the same time, in the conventional law of the ICCPR, Article 1 is seen as distinct from Article 27. Even a casual examination of the "travaux preparatoires" of both Articles clearly indicates that both these rights evolved from "state practices" in customary international law. Have the customary international legal principles for deciding which groups are nations — which are to be provided with the full measure of sovereign equality, and which with only a partial measure — been divided into two parts in the ICCPR and represented in Articles 1 and 27 as a result of political necessity, that is, to limit the right to secession to groups in colonial territories while providing a lesser degree of self-determination to other groups? Does this explain the tendency to divide self-determination into internal and external?

Often scholars of international law attribute the confusion in relation to the right to self-determination as expressed in the first articles of both International Covenants to the fact that the word "peoples" remains poorly defined and that the "content" of what is meant by self-determination is not clear. Thus, it is curious and confusing that most of these same scholars do not hesitate to ascribe to the interpretation that (1) Article 1 provides this right (whatever it may be) solely to colonial territories or territories containing ethnic groups distinct from the governing country, and (2) that it is clear from the "travaux preparatoires," the *UN Charter,* as well as the practices of emerging Third World states, that Article 1 is intended to apply to territories with distinct ethnic populations, not to the "peoples" in these territories.

The fact that, for the purpose of UN recognition of the new states, colonial boundaries were to function as the boundaries for these emerging states suggests an irresistible political influence. A question is whether the use of this UN orientation in relation to self-determination was actually in keeping with customary international law or only an evidence of the possible emergence of a new norm. Do the black letter rules of the UN resolutions sometimes conflict with customary international law? Does the drafting and interpretation of UN documents in relation to the right to self-determination and the rights of minorities, as processes resulting from political struggles, sometimes reflect this conflict in their awkward attempts at politico-legal compromises, or at updating international law?

The *Declaration on the Granting of Independence to Colonial Territories and Countries* states that "[a]ll peoples have the right to self-determination; by virtue of that right they freely determine their political status and freely pursue their economic, social and cultural development."[62] But, as Halperin and Scheffer noted:

> Resolution 1541, adopted the following day, reflected both an attempt to uphold the principle of territorial integrity and to limit the "self" to whom the principle of self-determination could apply. The resolution specifies that a territory would be considered "non-self-governing" under Chapter XI of the UN Charter only if it were both "geographically separate" and "distinct ethnically and/or culturally from the country administering it."[63]

Thus, strictly read, UN Resolution 1541 rules out classifying an ethnic group on a state's territory as a "non-self-governing" entity entitled to self-determination if it means the right to secede, but not necessarily, if freely determining a group's political status and pursuing its economic, social and cultural development would mean the granting of minority rights to autonomy status, or what is often called internal self-determination. No doubt it is through the United Nations that international law feels its greatest political impact. But, given the political structure of the United Nations, does this impact always result in the creation of universal norms as reflected in customary international law?

Protection in customary law of group rights prior to the United Nations treaties is usually dated to a series of bilateral European treaties, dating back to 1606, that gave limited recognition to a minority's freedom to practice a different religion within the state. Of course, it could just as well be discovered in the thirteenth century Islamic protection of rights of Christian minorities living in Spain, and southern and eastern Europe. By the nineteenth century, the protection of groups had broadened to include guarantees of civil and political rights, as well as religious freedom. In 1815, the Congress of Vienna included factors of ethnicity and language in addressing the governance of certain groups. A legal regime for the protection of group rights did not evolve, however, until the end of World War I and the creation of the League of Nations. Even then, there was no conventional international law to protect group rights. Rather, the League entered into a series of treaties with some newly-created and some reconfigured European states to ensure the protection of the rights of certain groups defined as minorities in the Europe of the 1920s. The treaties gave minorities the right to establish and control their own charitable, religious, social and educational institutions. They also placed upon states an obligation to give equitable funding to minority schools.[64]

Such origins serve as evidence that the right to self-determination as used in the literature, including UN documents, can be divided into the right to secede and other group rights short of secession, or in the words of Asbjørn Eide and others, into "external" and "internal" rights. Keeping this in mind should help in our efforts to interpret the various meanings of self-determination and peoples as used in UN documents and other scholarly communications. As Daniel Turp noted:

> [T]he UN Charter, the Declaration on Friendly Relations and the International Human Rights Covenants do not define the

> notion of people. This has led certain authors to assimilate the notion of people to that of a State and to make the latter, rather than the peoples that make up the State, the holder of the right to self-determination. Other commentators, basing their arguments on, among other things, the *Declaration on the Granting of Independence to Colonial Countries and Peoples,* have claimed that only inhabitants of colonies qualify as peoples... and consequently are entitled to self-determination. A common language, culture and religion play a determining role in the emergence of such a process of self-definition, but the collective desire to live together helps better define a people.[65]

It strikes one as curious (given the supposedly clear intention to refer to colonial territories) that the first articles of the International Covenants should state *all "peoples"* have the right of self-determination, instead of all colonial territories have the right to self-determination, or that Article 55 of the *UN Charter* should read "with a view to the creation of conditions of stability and well-being which are necessary for peaceful and friendly relations among nations based on respect for the principles of equal rights and self-determination of peoples..."[66] Why not "equal rights and self-determination for all states, or all colonial territories"? Indeed, insofar as classical colonial self-determination could be seen to be a short term phenomena, soon to become a right without beneficiaries[67] once colonial empires had been dissolved, are we to conclude that those who included the right of peoples to self-determination in universal international human rights instruments (e.g. the International Covenants) addressing long-term human rights goals, needs and principles, intended to insert a principle which clearly could be envisaged to become obsolete in the short term? Indeed, by the time the first International Covenant came into force in 1976, most colonial territories had achieved political independence. This raises another potentially important question: To what degree were the rights of minorities separated from that of peoples in the ICCPR to avoid the confusion that would arise in relation to when a self-determining group has the right to secession, and when it has only a right to internal self-determination, and not, as usually indicated, to make a distinction between peoples and minorities? It is interesting to note that even in the *Declaration on Principles of International Law Concerning Friendly Relations and Cooperation Among States,* which scholars agree can be interpreted to provide the right to self-determination (including the right to secession under certain conditions), it was found desirable to clearly limit the right to secession even in cases of oppression and tyranny. The Declaration states:

> Nothing in the foregoing paragraphs shall be construed as authorizing or encouraging any action which could dismember or impair, totally or in part, the territorial integrity or political unity of sovereign and independent states conducting themselves in compliance with the principle of equal rights and self-determination of peoples as described above and thus possessed of a government representing the whole people without distinction as to race, creed or color.[68]

It follows from this qualification that the framers of the Declaration, while desiring to give all groups the right to resist oppression by self-determination, did not want this right to be confused with an unconditional right to secession.

Apart from the UN instigated conventional law, which is closely tied to goals of peace and stability, has a right of all nations to self-determination (including national minorities who consider themselves a nation) developed in international customary law, and is it an emerging norm in positive international law? If so, for the purposes of international law, how can the legal sources be balanced? Cancado Trindade advises of two legal principles in international human rights law that probably could be used to balance legal sources and resolve the existing confusion over the meaning of self-determination and who benefits from it: (1) the victim's right to the most favorable interpretation or legal source, and (2) the indivisibility and complementarity of co-existing human rights instrumentalities.[69] On this point, Michele Jacquart writes:

> In spite of the adoption in 1966 of two separate Covenants... which were designed to put into effect the principles set forth in the Universal Declaration ... the indivisibility and interdependence of all the rights defined in the two Covenants just mentioned have consistently been affirmed by the various international bodies responsible for putting them into effect...[70]

This same principle applies to all other human rights instruments. Some of the confusion noted may result from the failure of many scholars to properly appreciate and exercise the principles mentioned by Trindade. However, much of the confusion in identifying the beneficiaries and the content of self-determination has deep political roots. In reality, it may result from the need for adequate legal flexibility to permit the normal functioning and development of international law within the context of the actual international political environment. Before the advent of the nation-state, nations/groups interrelated on the basis of sovereign equality. The exceptions were when one nation was unable or unwilling to protect or maintain the requirement for sovereignty (whatever the reason), or where a nation, having been unable or unwilling to maintain international relations on the basis of sovereign equality, became able or willing to do so, and (by whatever means) asserted its right to sovereignty. For example, when European nations first arrived in the Americas, they signed treaties with the aboriginal nations as sovereign equals. However, as soon as the aboriginal nations were unable to maintain their position as sovereign equals, the international status of treaties made with the aboriginal nations came into question. This is true although the aboriginal nations were still provided certain group rights reminiscent of their past status as nations that had once been viewed as possible sovereign equals. In their reduced status as members, voluntarily or involuntarily, of a new state, they gradually acquired what came to be called minority rights, and more recently, the right of aboriginal peoples (a special type of minority).[71] Thus, it is obvious that the "subjective criteria" in human rights law permits a socio-political reality to play a role in determining who is a people and who is a minority, as well as the content of what is meant by self-determination.[72]

If we accept the validity of the preceding orientation, it would suggest that a more standardized, internationally legal use of the terms nation, state, minority and peoples is called for in scholarly writings, although such definitions would be unlikely to obtain international legal sanction. In addition, there is greater need for more attention to historical and political antecedents in describing the relationship between the terms nation, people, minority, self-determination and sovereign equality; between the evolution in international law from nation, people or minority to peoples and nation-state; and between the movement from sovereign equality in the past in relation to nations, peoples or minorities to the movement toward the right to self-determination in the present. Our concluding view, similar to that of Daniel Turp, is as earlier suggested: that self-determination grew out of the historical traditional "practices of states" (nations and peoples) in relation to their dealings with other nations, states and peoples. For the purposes of this group right in customary international law, minorities, ethnic groups and peoples (provided they met objective and subjective criteria to call themselves minorities or peoples) were treated as such. The first articles of both International Covenants and Article 27 of the ICCPR, as well as Article 55 of the *UN Charter,* act to codify the meanings of the right to self-determination as derived from customary international law. The essence is codified in the first articles of both Covenants and a lesser portion of this essence is codified in Article 27 of the ICCPR. Politically speaking, Article 1, which includes the right to secession, is available for legal support to those socio-politically stronger nations or groups (e.g. Bangladesh, Croatia, Lithuania, or Senegal in relation to the Mali federation) that, by whatever means or for whatever reasons, are able to effectively or credibly declare themselves "peoples" according to the requirement of Article 1, or as colonial territories. The less socio-politically powerful nations which, for whatever reasons, are unable effectively to declare themselves as meeting the ongoing criteria for "peoples" must settle for a negotiated settlement excluding the right to political independence, unless the state concerned voluntarily provides an agreement for their demands (e.g. Canada with regard to the Inuit).

Now that we have called attention to the need to balance sources of law and give appropriate consideration to international political processes in order to negotiate the confusion that bedazzles the right to self-determination, we may now proceed, in the guise of concluding this presentation, by asking the specific question: Do African-Americans have a right to self-determination?

VI. *Conclusion*

At last, we have arrived at the point wherein a summary analysis of the information presented will permit us to examine the possible status of a theoretical claim by the African-American minority for the right to self-determination. We shall not bedazzle you with the question of whether African-Americans are a people or a national minority for the purposes of a right to self-determination, since we have earlier concluded that the question is largely one of self-definition within the context of geopolitical and legal reality. Given the present geopolitical and legal reality, a self-definition by African-Americans as a national minority seems most realistic. As earlier mentioned, the right to self-determination can be subdivided into external and internal types. It is the internal type that seems, in the present politico-legal climate, to be most available to national minorities such as the African-Americans and indigenous peoples of North America. This is true because it is apparently the type governments have found most acceptable or least objectionable.

An analysis of the African-American question thus should begin with a look at what level of political authority is absolutely needed by African-Americans in order for them to manage or resolve their most pressing crises, e.g. disproportionate representation in prisons, welfare, health care, educational dropouts, drug usage, mental institutions, homelessness, single parent families, etc. First, what is required to safeguard their right to be different and equal, and to achieve equal status with the majority? Second, what international legal responsibilities does the U.S. government have toward the African-American national minority that will assist it in achieving its political and socio-economic needs? Finally, which of these minority rights or U.S. legal obligations is it feasible to expect to be fulfilled in the present political, socio-economic and international legal climate? The second and last questions are dealt with in this presentation, and it is not appropriate to attempt a response to the first within the context of this Conference. It can perhaps be most usefully answered only in an African-American conference designed for that purpose — to reach consensus agreements that may be put forward as representing the African-American democratic and collective decisions, and leading to appropriate procedures for consultation and approval by the African-American people as a whole.

However, I am pleased to suggest that a happy marriage between the responses to the last two questions is possible, and I shall go so far, and no further, as to suggest the general types of claims available to African-Americans in international human rights law. (We should note that almost any claim assumes the existence of some type of democratic assembly that could plausibly, through the mechanism of democratic elections, claim to represent the African-American people as a whole. Of course, no such institution presently exists, and there is no indication that African-Americans presently want to, intend to, or are politically prepared to create such an institution.)

(1) First, African-Americans may wish to make their claim to international protection for the right to self-determination based on an agreement between themselves and their government. This would mean first bringing their political and socio-economic grievances to the attention of the U.S. government with a plan for internal self-determination that could feasibly resolve those grievances. Any such agreement reached would be recognized in international human rights law. In relation to this legal option, note the recent split of Czechoslovakia, and the arrangement for the indigenous minority right to self-government for the Inuit, a right which is also recommended for the other indigenous nations. Also note the historical arrangements for minority protection in countries like Belgium, Denmark and Norway as well as the demand for such

rights by the Zulu and the white nation in South Africa and in the former Rhodesia (Zimbabwe). Such an option could also be accomplished within a federal state framework by voluntary accession and with constitutional provisions allowing for special rights, or on a non-territorial basis such as that suggested in the draft Constitution for Mi'kmaq self-government,[73] or the findings of self-determination committees of the non-status aboriginal Canadians in Winnipeg. The possibilities are only limited by imagination and politico-legal restraint. (Federal state examples include such minorities as the French Canadians in Quebec, the Ibo and Yoruba of Nigeria.) Even Washington, D.C. seems to be backing into such a situation along with other metropolitan areas of the United States. Here, it is interesting to note that metropolitan areas of states are the only territorial areas where African-Americans may constitute a majority. Although achieving a majority, minority populations cannot lay claim for a territorial right to autonomy, due to the economic and social disruption it would cause the state.[74]

(2) Second, African-Americans may claim systematic and institutional discrimination, present violations of human rights (including minority rights) and past gross violations of human rights (including slavery and apartheid), claiming that this has left them in an inferior political, social and economic situation in the United States, and in an underdog position in relation to other peoples in the world, from which they can only escape through the adoption of some form of autonomy, self-government, or institutional self-management, insofar as, over the past few decades, equality before the law, non-discrimination and affirmative action have proved inadequate. Thus, a demand for special rights under Article 27 of the ICCPR would appear appropriate. If the U.S. government refuses to recognize their special rights and is still unable or unwilling to provide for equal status (assuming that they have been democratically demanded by a representative African-American assembly or council), then, backed up by references to "recourse ... to rebellion against tyranny and oppression" set forth in the *Universal Declaration of Human Rights* and the language in the *Declaration on Principles of International Law Concerning Friendly Relations and Cooperation Among States*, a third legal claim becomes available.

(3) The third option would probably be the most disruptive to positive relations between groups in the United States. African-Americans could claim they have a right to self-determination as a revolt against oppression and the violation of their human rights. This would call attention to the long history of gross violations of their human rights and the

continuation of this pattern into the present. To this point, Daniel Turp wrote:

> [A} right of [self-determination] for peoples living in independent and sovereign non-colonial States may be exercised if the latter are not conducting themselves in accordance with the right of their [national minorities] to freely determine their political status within the State and to freely ensure their economic, social and cultural development therein. As certain commentators on the *Declaration on Friendly Relations* have suggested, if a people is refused the right to self-determination domestically, it can exercise its right to self-determination [internationally], which then includes a right of secession [provided the state does not correct itself]. [T]he legal validity of [the right] in the *Declaration on Friendly Relations* [cannot] be doubted and its customary character contested, particularly since the accession to sovereignty by the Baltic States and other Soviet republics, the former republics of Yugoslavia, the Czech and Slovak republics and the self-determination process under way in Eritrea point to the nonexistence of any uniform and consistent practice along the lines of a ban on self-determination... [A] democratic right to [self-determination] is now seeing the light of day and tends to confirm the universality of the right of [non-colonial] peoples to self-determination.[75]

Many scholars argue that the principle of self-determination can be accorded priority over the competing principle of territorial integrity if a state violates the rights of minorities. One author suggests that the provision "constitutes an unambiguous affirmation of the applicability of the right of self-determination to peoples inside the political boundaries of existing sovereign and independent states..."[76] Other authors, such as James Crawford, argue that a right to secession can arise when a central government engages in "internal colonization."[77] Crawford notes that Resolution 1541 states that a non-self-governing region is one that is both geographically and ethnically distinct.[78] While geographic separateness has generally been taken to mean separation across land or sea, "there is no good reason why other defining characteristics, including *de facto* boundaries established through systematic racism and [government minority policies] might not also be relevant."[79]

We believe that African-American minority rights, equality and development can be accommodated within the context of full respect for the territorial integrity of the United States, provided the United States makes use of the wide range of options for majority-minority relations which can be derived from state practice in different parts of the world. Issues concerning

African-Americans' minority rights, as well as U.S. compliance with international obligations and commitments concerning the rights of persons belonging to the African-American national minority, are matters of legitimate international concern and consequently do not constitute exclusively an internal affair of the United States. All members of the United Nations, in accordance with Article 56 of the *UN Charter,* have undertaken an obligation to cooperate with the organization in promoting universal respect for and observance of human rights. International human rights bodies can assist the United States in minority conflict resolution by providing concepts that do not find their roots in historical minority enslavement models, by monitoring the implementation of human rights and through the handling of complaints.

The lobbying of indigenous peoples at the United Nations has helped to raise the question as to whether decolonization must be limited to overseas territories, or whether it can be extended to the metropolitan state. Because indigenous peoples rely on treaties with states, they should have a better case for internal self-determination than African-Americans. As for the external type, suffice it to say that there are no cases in North America where indigenous peoples or the governments involved are giving serious consideration to the right of secession as an option.

Politically, the issue of self-determination (whether it is interpreted to mean the ability to act independently in international relations, greater local or regional autonomy, equitable participation in federative state systems, outright independence, or some other variant) is seen by political leaders around the globe as a threat to national security, and it is the fragility of a state in crisis, on the one hand, and the force of claims for self-determination on the other, which are at the heart of the problem. However, although states resist demands for implementation of self-determination (which often means the right to secession), international law (the law of states) calls for the creation of pluralistic societies (which never means secession) in multi-national states such as the United States. We repeat and underline the importance of remembering that self-determination in pluralistic societies can refer to all forms of local autonomy or pluralistic arrangements within a sovereign state. As earlier mentioned, many specific and successful autonomy arrangements have been made for minorities to enjoy self-government over time. Some typical examples are Greenland, Euzkadi (the Basques), and the Aaland islands. There are also territorial sub-divisions made which did not originally have a pluralism intent but under some circumstances can have a pluralism effect, such as the southern United States before the Civil War, or Atlanta and Washington, D.C. today. Generally, the purpose is administrative decentralization, while the effect can be that minorities living compactly together, in areas where they form the majority, are able to develop material and cultural aspects of their identity within the scope of the power delegated.[80] For this to occur, the minority concerned must consciously and openly declare this as their intent, and this intent must be officially accepted by the national government, preferably in a written law or agreement. Administrative jurisdictions can also be attached to the minority itself, in the case of non-territorial self-determination (when the group, like African-Americans, is dispersed throughout the general population).

In an economically and politically developed democracy such as the United States where democracy and freedom are bywords, the demand for consociated democracy should not mean a zero-sum game, but a victory for all and for national development. It should mean seeking the broader models and mediating experience of the United Nations to help America break free of the attachment to its historical dilemma: the white men/black men analytical framework that prevents the United States from having to deal with the real minority-majority problem, and thus from completing its march toward becoming a world orientated society — a beacon for the day after tomorrow.

While in theory we have concluded that African-Americans do have the right to self-determination in international law, we must in all reality remind ourselves that African-Americans have not made self-determination or minority rights demands. Nor are they creating the political structure required to do so. What will this mean for the influence and image of U.S. democracy? The world awaits America's democratic lessons as well as its MacDonalds, which it observes, studies, adapts and copies well. History will not repeat itself. A future of continued minority oppression will represent a descent into ignorance and chaos. Who will be to blame? Is it history? Those who understand and are well-informed should think and act free of paradigms emanating from the "strange attraction" of America's oppressive past. We must continue to flutter our wings and hope for the strong wind that clears away the stagnant air.

PANEL DISCUSSION I

African-Americans and Self-Determination[81]

Statement of Dr. Rose Brewer[82]

Earlier, Dr. Kly answered a very crucial question regarding the issue of African-Americans and self-determination. The question was, "Are African-Americans a people for the purpose of self-determination?" and his earlier answer was yes. Yet there remain a number of crucial considerations. The formal declaration as a national minority, of course, has not happened among African-Americans. Self-determination would require such a formal definition and consideration of the knotty issues of political process: who would speak for the African-American experience, and what kind of democratic process would be invoked. Would it be representative? Would it be one person, one vote? Other issues that the panel are to respond to, of course, include the issue of African-Americans' collective rights and the U.S. constitutional legal system, the problem of territoriality, the issue of foreign policy and African-American self-determination, and the issue of economic and political development.

As a sociologist, the most striking aspect of Dr. Kly's work for me is its profound calling into question of our conditioned responses regarding thinking about African-Americans in this country. Most precisely, in public policy and in the social sciences, the discussion has been dominated by what I might call a "race relations model." This dominant assumption centers on the idea that the ultimate incorporation of African-Americans will happen. Clearly, the idea that through minor tinkering with the society, such as Affirmative Action, redresses can be won, must be called into question. Raised by Dr. Kly are those deep level, structural asymmetries, regarding wealth, political power and cultural hegemony, which exclude African-Americans in this country. Dr. Kly has placed those structural asymmetries as the center of his analysis. What I have concerns about are not those issues, because I think they were quite powerfully addressed, but I do want to raise several questions. Those questions center on issues of class and gender within the African-American community.

I would raise the issue of what prevents new class cleavagesfrom arising, even as a national identity is forged. Are the possibilities of a new national minority elite there? In a capitalist society such as the United States, does the ending of one kind of oppression engender the beginning of another? Are there other existing examples of a national minority that has chosen the socialist alternative in the context of a capitalist society? Secondly, what about women's rights and the rights of children?

Statement of Keith Ellison[83]

While noble and admirable people of all colors have worked toward the realization of integration and assimilation in American society, the reality of our experience in the United States has been essentially contrary to that. If you were to look in terms of numbers, not individual cases, but in terms of most people, you will find that there is systematic state, governmental abuse of the African-American population that dates back before the civil war, certainly during slavery, which has remained constant. We must focus on the relationship of the African-American citizen to the government of the United States, and on what that relationship has been and how it has changed over the years. While sometimes African-Americans individually may achieve some greater modicum of success, and while sometimes even all African-American citizens may have ebbs and flows in our collective condition, the condition of the African-American population to the state has remained constant; so that even today, African-American citizens are only marginal citizens of the United States.

This condition of Black people, the pseudo-citizenship, gives African-American people the right to forge their own separate, independent identity, if they should choose to do that. I think what is needed is that African-American citizens should have a right to vote on that question. Should we remain with the American State, the United States, or should we opt out of that arrangement? The common estimation and legal status of African-Americans throughout American history brings African-American citizens into the modern day position where any effort to integrate with American society is rebuffed. It is not that African-Americans have, by and large, been opposed to integration and pluralism. Whites, particularly those possessing political and economic power, have resisted inclusion. What I am saying is that if a national minority is refused the right to be integrated, then the larger society should allow and assist the national minority to opt for an independent destiny.

Statement of Dr. August Nimitz[84]

I think that the paper that Dr. Kly presented makes a very powerful legal case for African-American self-determination. I want to look at this issue politically, that is, within the political realm. It strikes me in looking at the history of the quest for self-determination on the part of subordinate, subjected or oppressed peoples, that this struggle and the achievement of that goal of self-determination takes place regardless of what the legal framework actually is. The legal system, by and large, reflects political reality. Oftentimes, it lags behind political reality. But the question of self-determination and its actual achievement takes place regardless of what the legal system says. It is important to keep in mind that the demand for self-determination has existed in the past on the part of African-Americans. I think that history shows it ebbs and flows. It emerges at some stages in history as a more important demand than at other times.

The question that Dr. Kly raises at the end of the paper is why aren't there any demands at this particular time. It seems to me the reason is that there were in fact very real changes that took place in this country in the aftermath of the Civil Rights movement that led to, if not integration, then a degree of upward mobility for increasing layers within the Black community — a degree of upward mobility that reflected something else that was taking place within U.S. society, increasing class polarization within U.S. society as a whole. Within the Black community, you begin to see increasing disparities in income and wealth. In fact, there was a layer of people who benefited quite well materially from the Civil Rights movement. I would argue fundamentally that the quest for self-determination throughout history on the part of oppressed minorities has almost invariably been led by elites and intellectuals. This was the experience of Nineteenth Century Europe, and it has been the experience of Twentieth Century Africa and other third world countries. The reality is that as opportunities have become available for elites and intellectuals within the Black community to move, to become upwardly mobile, the requests and demands for self-determination have tended to abate. To the extent, to make a forecast, that those desires, those quests, are not entirely fulfilled, we may anticipate again a demand for self-determination, but as long as the hope exists, and as long as the possibilities exist for that kind of mobility, I am not convinced that we will see a demand for African-American self-determination in the immediate future.

Statement of Toni Shola Moore[85]

I think that there are a number of questions we have to ask with respect to African-American people being designated as a people for purposes of self-determination in the international arena. Does a group of individuals who were brought to this country, a group of individuals who had racial, linguistic, cultural and historical traits that were unifying, if not exactly the same, lose their status as a people by virtue of the enslavement process? Can a group of people who were kidnapped, enslaved and brought here, be forced to be citizens in the country that kidnapped them?

To me, flowing from this idea is another question: If people of African descent in the United States were denied self-determination by the original kidnapping and transporting to the Western hemisphere, and if we were then denied self-determination with respect to enslavement, and then denied self-determination with respect to whether or not we were going to be citizens of this nation that we now found ourselves in, is it *now*, hundreds of years later, legally permissible to deny us self-determination around who we should be, where we should reside, and how we should control our destiny, because historically we have been continually denied self-determination? Does that original wrong allow an ongoing wrong to exist? The ongoing wrong has continued up to this point partly because the demand for self-determination has not been made.

The other issue in this arena is that self-determination is a fundamental human right. It is an ongoing right. It is not a right that a people, in the life of a people, get only once. You do not get to decide only once what you want to do with your destiny. Self-determination is ongoing. So, African people in this country have the right to self-determination, even though it has not necessarily been asserted or enforced.

Another question is: Who determines whether or not people of African descent in this country have the right to self-determination? I think our self-definition, which has been imposed on us, has been the definition of a minority people in the United States and not in the international context. Are the perpetrators of the wrong, the perpetrators who denied self-determination to African-Americans, the ones who are going to decide whether African people in the United States have a right to self-determination? Or will it be the international and regional organs that exist? Or will it be the people themselves? I think the answer is self-evident.

Statement of Phoebe W. Williams[86]

The perspective I choose to bring to this discussion about African-Americans and the right to self-determination focuses on economic development. The international discussions acknowledge the relationship between self-determination and economic development. I propose that we expand our discussions about African-Americans and economic development to include freedom from racial discrimination operating in markets other than those traditionally addressed by human rights agendas.

Generally, domestic civil rights policy has attempted to address discrimination operating in a few select markets. On the domestic front, policy makers have enacted federal discrimination laws designed to discourage, detect and remedy race discrimination operating in markets for housing, employment, lending and public accommodations.

An examination of international human rights policy suggests that, similar to their domestic counterparts, international policy makers tend to focus on discrimination operating in a few discrete markets, i.e. housing, employment and public accommodations.

Examination of the rights enumerated in international human rights instruments suggests that policy makers assume that economic development is dependent primarily upon access to employment, just compensation for employment, and collective bargaining. The international vocabulary appears to ignore the necessity for oppressed minorities to have equal opportunities for entrepreneurial ventures and accumulation of capital.

I suggest that we expand our discussions about economic development and self-determination to include other economic transactions. We must also consider the extent race discrimination disadvantages African-Americans in markets for consumer goods and services, commercial contracting opportunities, consumer and commercial loans, and consumer and commercial insurance products. An emerging body of research suggests that race discrimination operating in these markets also significantly impedes African-American economic development.

Post civil war legislation is hardly efficient for preventing, detecting or addressing racial discrimination in consumer transactions.

We must expand our discussions about self-determination and economic development. We must consider that race discrimination disadvantages African-Americans at both ends of consumer and commercial transactions.

Statement of Hon. Edward Wilson[87]

Dr. Kly came to the conclusion that for some purposes we are a "people." I think that we obviously have quite a way to go, and for some purposes, I must say we are not yet a people. The question that is posed, I think, is an extremely important and provocative one, and it is one that we have just started to explore. The ramifications and implications of that, for both African-American society and the larger society, are enormous.

In this country, we have traditionally been viewed as a minority group, and under some models of social theory, minority groups will eventually assimilate into a larger community. Under such models, various differences will melt away or boil away or blend away in this melting pot. We can see obviously that that has not been the case throughout two hundred and some years of American history. We can see, for instance, that the tensions in the past year or so, in the wake of the Rodney King beating and the subsequent trials of the officers involved, were such as to point out what I think we already knew: that there is a tremendous tension which borders upon not just a disagreement but a fundamental distinction in world outlook and values between the African-American community and the larger white community in this society. Among European immigrants who have been in this society for a couple of generations or so, most if not all of the cultural differences have been washed away or blended together. But this obviously has not been the case with the African-American community. What I suggest, what I believe, is that we ought to begin immediately in getting away from the use of the term minority and viewing ourselves as minorities in every sense of that word. Our efforts ought to be directed toward achieving the status of peoplehood or peopleness, if that is the word, if not in numbers, then at least in spirit and in economic and political power. What is a minority after all?

The cold dictionary definition defines it as a racial, religious, or ethnic, political or national group, which is regarded as being different from the larger society of which it is a part. Again, that is a sterile dictionary definition. It does not begin to take into account the aspects of minority group status of which we are all aware, such as being underemployed, underhoused, and undereducated on the one hand, and being overpoliced, overregulated, and overlooked, on the other. Being a minority group carries with it the implicit recognition of being a victimized group. It carries with it the recognition that you are a group that deserves to be protected. For instance, our U.S. Supreme Court has developed a very complicated system of protecting the rights of persons who are viewed as being members of a minority group, and any time that we have a state or federal law that is seen as having a substantial or adverse impact on such a group, that law has to be viewed with what is called strict scrutiny, in order for it to withstand constitutional muster. The very word minority, then, seems to suggest a weakness or a need to be protected from those who would otherwise harm you.

The United Nations, as has been pointed out in this seminar, has in various contexts begun to deal with that question. In the *International Covenant on Civil and Political Rights,* we see that Article 27 talks about the fact that members of ethnic, religious, and linguistic minorities shall not be denied the right to enjoy their own culture, profess or practice their own religion, or to use their own language. I would like to add a different perspective to that. When we talk about a group as a people, we have to talk about a different set of expectations and rights that minority groups do not have. The analogy that I want to present and suggest as something to consider is that of Native American people in this society and in the state of Minnesota.

The Native American people are also traditionally considered a minority group, but they also have a unique status based on their history and unique relationship with the United States government that give them rights that other so-called minority groups do not have. We can see, for instance, that Native Americans are able to engage in certain businesses, such as casinos, which are extremely lucrative, in which other groups cannot engage. They also enjoy certain fishing rights which other groups do not have. That is a result of their unique status. So, while they are considered to be a minority group, on the one hand, they do have some very obvious and very beneficial rights, on the other, which are accorded to them. They have not yet achieved the status of a people, of course. We know that they do not have the self-determination which is given to a group which has achieved peoplehood. However we must at the same time recognize that the rights they have are far and above those of us who have not yet achieved that particular unique status. It seems, then, that clearly what we have to do, is to work toward achieving that status of being a people.

PANEL DISCUSSION II

Duties Associated with the Right to Self-Determination

Statement of Robin Magee[88]

This has been and is an urgent and necessary conversation. I have been richly fed by Dr. Kly and the prior panel. This panel has been charged with extending the inquiries of earlier this afternoon into some useful directions.

The two basic questions carried over from earlier today are: (1) Whether the African-American community has the right to self-determination, and (2) whether as a people or a national minority, if they are different, the African-American community is willing and able to exercise the right. Assuming the right to self-determination, will it, should it, and/or can it be exercised here in the United States and/or be protected by the international community generally or by the United Nations, specifically?

Towards answering these questions, the panelists will discuss the benefits and/or limitations on the various mechanisms available at the international level to advance and maintain a right to self-determination. The panelists will consider whether the mechanisms of arbitration, negotiation and conciliation are sufficient to protect or implement the right, or will the use of these mechanisms within the United States — the historical oppressor of the African-American community, within the context of an organization that is chiefly funded by that historical oppressor — the United Nations — further thrust the African-American community into a downward spiral of compromise and dissatisfaction. Related to this inquiry, the panelists are charged with examining the responsibilities attendant to the African-American community should they assert their claims to civil and human liberties at the international level. If African-Americans are required to consider the impact that securing and maintaining their right of self-determination might have on other domestic communities and the larger global community in pursuing and shaping this right, will the claim of the African-American community be diluted by these considerations and whatever calibrations that these considerations might require?

When I reflect on the interpretative trajectory of the Fourteenth Amendment, I am personally cautious. The Fourteenth Amendment has been applied fairly broadly to a host of groups that were not originally contemplated under the amendment, while at the same time it has been rather restrictively applied to the African-American community. Arguably, the Fourteenth Amendment now provides less protection to the African-American community, the group for which it was enacted, than it does other communities. In short, the right of self-determination looks good and sounds good, but may not, in fact, provide African-Americans with any long-lasting benefits.

Statement of Cheryl I. Harris[89]

I am very excited to be participating in what is an important discussion. I begin with the idea that one duty connected to the right of self-determination is the duty to recognize history. If we do so, then, we must recognize that this discussion on self-determination is an effort to internationalize the struggle and the claims of African-American people, of Black people in this country, that has a very long history. Indeed, even during the period of slavery, Black people sought to claim protection under international law. In addition to asserting that slavery was itself a blatant violation of international law, we can think of specific examples, such as the "Amistad" case, involving a ship in which the slaves mutinied, took control of the vessel, and claimed protection under international law as citizens of a foreign country who could not lawfully be delivered as slaves to the United States.[90]

Following slavery, the arrangements regarding the balance of power between the North and South broke down, leading up to the Civil War. We are aware that the Civil War was fought, not to insure the freedom of the slaves, but to determine the form and the shape of the U.S. political economy and power. Formal legal equality was conferred through the post-Civil War amendments, but those rights were usurped through decisions of the courts that stripped the amendments of any substantive meaning. The withdrawal of federal government troops from the South allowed the violent retrenchment of white supremacist power that is well-documented. So we witness a paradigm, a constant, about the dissonance between formal equality guarantees and the inequality — in effect U.S. domestic apartheid — that was legally ratified by the Court in *Plessy v. Ferguson.*[91] International law continued to have tremendous impact, however, particularly in ending the period of *de jure* segregation. In one aspect, the international balance of power was a major impulse behind the *Brown v. Board of Education* decision. In its competition with the Soviet Union for influence in Africa and Asia, the United States was taking a lot of heat over its domestic policy *vis-a-vis* Blacks. It was very difficult to convince the nations of Africa that were coming out of colonialization that the U.S. democratic capitalist system was a good one when these countries looked at what was happening domestically to U.S. Blacks. Thus, the U.S. Justice Department filed briefs in *Brown* urging the lifting of legalized segregation because it was a foreign policy disaster.

Recognizing the history of internationalizing the struggle of Black people requires that we acknowledge the contributions of advanced sectors of the Black movement itself. Both W.E.B. DuBois and Paul Robeson sought to draw out international linkages between the struggles of Blacks in the United States and the struggles of African peoples and people of color against colonialism and imperialism on a worldwide basis. During the 1960s, sectors of the Black movement like the Student Non-Violent Coordinating Committee, the Black Panthers, and the Organization of African-American Unity founded by Malcolm X, all recognized the importance of these international linkages. Malcolm X said then that we need to recognize this is a human rights struggle, not a civil rights struggle. In 1979, the National Conference of Black Lawyers (NCBL) prepared a petition charging the United States with genocide and other violations of human rights norms in connection with its treatment of Black people. This petition was filed under the United Nations Economic and Social Council Resolution 1503 procedure with the Sub-Commission on Minorities. Many organizations and individuals have sought to internationalize the human rights struggle by laying claims before international fora regarding gross violations of human rights of Blacks in the United States. It is important, then, to acknowledge and really learn the lessons of history, because we all stand on the ground that has been laid down.

I think that the other duty we have is to be democratic. This means that we are required to observe not only the process, but the substance of democracy. Other speakers have noted the need to form structures which allow for democratic consultation and articulation of basic principles through which we can lay claim to our right to self-determination. None of this is easy or obvious. I think it is going to require building durable political institutions.

A comparative kind of analysis, one that is very useful to me at times, is to look at South Africa and look at the founding and history of an organization like the African National Congress, which has been in existence since 1912. In terms of laying a claim to self-determination, over time the ANC has moved through various phases of struggle from peaceful petition to armed resistance, but basically grounded itself in a certain democratic ethic. This focus on broad consultation and participation led to the all in-Africa Congress in 1955, through which the principles guiding the movement were articulated in the Freedom Charter. The Freedom Charter is still a document that South Africans talk about, relate to, and can quote from today as a valid expression of the aspirations of the South African masses.

The democratic ethic also has to do with looking at the range of options in terms of how the right to self-determination will be realized. That means we cannot pre-empt a full discussion of all of the options. Dr. Kly has talked about the range of options, which go from integration to secession, which can be territorial or non-territorial or institutional, looking at various domains that might be placed under control. But we also have to consider the implications arising from each of these choices. What choices are going to amplify the possibilities for equitable and nonexploitative development? What form should the demand for self-determination take where the economy has moved from an agricultural to an industrial to the present post-industrial "information society" (or should it be disinformation society)?

We also have to think about what it would mean to assert the right for self-determination, for example, as a separate territory in geopolitical terms. If we consider the economic dynamic of the global village, of consolidation and the move towards the greater fluidity of international capital, what does this mean for a demand of a separate geographical nation? If we look at the role of the International Monetary Fund, World Bank, and other international capital structures, what would our relationship be to these macro structures of the international economy?

The other thing we have to consider is the question of what our claim for self-determination means in a situation where citizenship has become very fluid. We are now in a world where states are under extreme stress, and many are experiencing mammoth population influxes, increases in immigration, and floods of refugees. Typically, we have had a model that has talked about attaching rights to people based on their nationality or based on recognizing their rights vis-à-vis their nationality or even national minority status. But what does it mean to talk about national identity and nationality in this context when you have millions of people that are flowing back and forth across borders as a result of economic and political crises?

The other thing I think we have a duty to consider is what our claim of self-determination means vis-à-vis other peoples. If, for example, we take notice of demographic trends in the United States, it suggests that by the middle of the next century Blacks will no longer be the largest national minority group, being replaced by the category of Latinos, a multi-national, multi-cultural and multi-racial group, comprised of Mexican-Americans, Puerto Ricans, Guatemalans, El Salvadorans and Nicaraguans. What is it going to mean vis-à-vis those people?

Finally, we have a duty associated with any African-American claim of self-determination that has to take into account the rights of indigenous people. Particularly as it pertains to territorial claims, it is the Native American people who stand in an original position with regard to this land, and it is they who have experienced the brunt of genocide and conquest. That is not to deny African-Americans' history in connection with this country.

I think we also have a duty to recognize what I might call context and contradictions. Dr. Kly has talked about the model of consociational democracy as being one that might be available for solving these very complex questions. Of course, as many of you may know, it is the language of consociationalism that the South African government has attempted to use to beat back claims for democratic majority rule in South Africa. That has been the white minority's effort to reform apartheid. When people denounced apartheid as a violation of international law, the South African government claimed consociationalism as a model, indicating it could figure out how to recognize whites as a minority group, and Blacks as a minority group, and let everybody have their own rights in individual states or under a loose confederation arrangement.

Statement of A. Ray McCoy[92]

I want to start by saying that I am grateful to be a part of the conference. The thought that African-Americans could go through a process which would ultimately result in them sitting down as equal partners with representatives of the U.S. government and negotiating their status within this country is a very powerful concept to me. Concerning the parameters of such negotiations, we would not ask for things that would undermine the country we were negotiating with. For example, we could not ask for the government to turn over the treasury to us. There is an obligation to go to the bargaining table with some sense of good faith and an interest in trying to reach an agreement.

Could the United States, with the intervention of the United Nations' good offices, negotiate in good faith? All I have to go by to answer that question is history. When African-Americans have sought to peacefully seek redress of grievances by the government, they have been met with indifference, hostility and violence.

As we think about the duties imposed upon us as we move toward self-determination, we should reflect on the kinds of obligations we are going to have in terms of understanding the United Nations process.

AFTERWORD

Toward a New American Conversation On the Rights of African-Americans

Howard J. Vogel[93]

The Proceedings of the Conference on African-Americans and the Right to Self-Determination invites all Americans to engage each other in a new American conversation on the human rights of African-Americans informed by the language of international law. It is an invitation not to abandon the Constitution of the United States, but to open up possibilities of full participation in American life for African-Americans under the Constitution, by drawing on the resources of human rights law developed in a global context.

The Constitution itself, by its very terms, in Article VI, makes "all treaties made ... under the Authority of the United States ... the supreme law of the land." By virtue of this provision, the American ratification of the *International Covenant on Civil and Political Rights,*which took effect in September of 1992, incorporates the human rights principles of the Covenant within the Constitutional framework. The terms and conditions of the American ratification, however, attempt to prevent application of the Covenant in the domestic courts of the United States. This limits American participation under the Covenant merely to prosecution of human rights violations *outside* the territory of the United States. While the *terms* of the American ratification raise serious problems about the enforcement of the Covenant within the United States, the *fact* of the ratification invites us to undertake a new American conversation on the meaning of human rights *in* the United States.

The Proceedings of the Conference published here are the first effort to sketch out the possibilities of such a conversation that takes seriously the status of African-Americans as a national minority under principles of international law. In this way the Proceedings seek to construct a new language to address one of the oldest and most vexing problems at the heart of the American nation.

This event comes at a turning point in world history. The character of this moment illuminates what we are beckoned to undertake by the invitation. The demise of the Berlin Wall in the Fall of 1989 signalled the beginning of dramatic changes in the international order. The events of the last four years have caught the attention of people around the world. No one's attention is more riveted to the convulsive developments in Europe than those of us whose forebears emigrated from that continent. The possibilities for a new world, both wonderful and horrifying, outstrip our ability to imagine or discern.

Despite the profound and tragic ambiguity in the news from the "Old World" that we read about everyday, one clear central fact has emerged: the categories employed in the United States for the discussion of international affairs during much of this century have lost their meaning. Old enemies have become new friends, and peoples we have rarely paused to notice dominate the international pages of our newspapers. The vocabulary we have used to approach the world has faded in its usefulness as has the cold war reality that placed it on our tongues. In the midst of the breakup of the old international order, a new conversation is struggling to be born. We grope for new words and new categories without "experts" to guide us as we construct a new language for a new conversation about a "new world order."

The new conversation about human rights must take seriously the sovereign claims of national, linguistic, cultural and religious minorities upon those majorities with whom they share political territory. Distinctive cultures, long suppressed by the hegemonies of the old order, have expressed themselves in dramatic ways. Often violent, they clash with each other around the globe. The conflagration in the Balkans is perhaps the most savage expression of the tribal warfare that has gained a prominent place in the international news. Leaders of large nations armed to the teeth, who once confronted each other, stand by, wringing their hands, while the blood flows without cease in the streets of the "civilized world." In the face of such horror the need for conversation about international human rights has become urgent, and the future of the United Nations as a positive force for democracy hangs in the balance.

The agony of civil war and the threat to democracy in the violent cultural clashes occurring in many distant lands tempt Americans to look outside of their country when human rights become the topic of conversation. When we yield to this temptation, we ignore the threat to democracy that lies within our borders. Inside the United States, the commitment to democracy is called into question by the outbreak of civil strife at points of contact between the many different cultures that can be found across our land.

For many, the encounter with difference is an occasion of pain and threat rather than one of promise and opportunity. Some observers describe contemporary American life as dominated by "culture wars" rather than by efforts to build the "one nation of one people" of which Lincoln spoke. While Americans are often quick to condemn "human rights abuses" in other lands, we are too often unable to see the human rights abuses in our own history and learn the lessons embedded in our past.

One need look no further than the United States Constitution for evidence of the problem. In 1776 the Declaration of Independence charged the English King with gross violations of basic human rights. In 1787 the Framers sought to secure these human rights by establishing a Constitution "to form a more perfect union ... and secure the blessings of liberty." Yet the very text of the original Constitution provided the basis for enforcement of the slave-colonization of African people under American law. To read the slave trade and fugitive slave clauses of the Constitution is to be reminded of how human rights were honored in the breach in the very founding of the nation. To read Chief Justice Taney's opinion in *Dred Scott v. Sandford*[94] is to see the Supreme Court confirm the view that people of "African descent" were not viewed as "persons" under the Constitution, and thus were reduced to the status of chattel property excluded from the "blessings of liberty."

The Thirteenth Amendment ended slavery, but the status of African-Americans changed little in the aftermath of the Civil War. We invented apartheid, and South Africa borrowed our invention. The law of segregation denied the Fourteenth Amendment's promise of full participation in American life for African-Americans. The poll tax deprived African-Americans of the right to vote guaranteed by the Fifteenth Amendment. The legal and social successors of slavery that plague American life and politics today are a grim reminder that the full participation in society as a matter of human rights that we demand on behalf of minorities in distant lands, is still denied to African-Americans at home.

The scar of this legacy across two centuries of American history has truncated our ability to talk about human rights, except as a problem in the world at large. The status of African-Americans in American society has, at least since *Brown v. Board of Education*,[95] been dominated by the vocabulary of *civil rights* protected under the Constitution. Yet today, forty years after *Brown*, the bright hope of becoming "one nation, one people" by dismantling the formal system of legally sanctioned segregation has faded into despair in the wake of uprising after uprising. No city of any size can claim immunity from the legacy of inequality rooted in the slavery clauses of the Constitution.

If anything has changed since *Brown*, it is the realization that the legacy of slavery and segregation, and the racism that rationalized that system, is not, and never was a "Southern problem" or a "Negro problem." Yet few are willing to say what must be said — that it is an "American problem." And fewer yet are willing to explore the possibilities of a new language for a new American conversation about the rights of African-Americans by exploring the language of international human rights and the meaning of self-determination for American national minorities under international law. Instead our halting efforts at confronting this legacy today are dominated by the question: "Can we talk—about race?" Such questions are more likely to send people streaming toward the exits than toward the center of the room to engage each other in conversation. Forty years after *Brown v. Board of Education* many are not sure we *can* talk, let alone "get along." The prospect of public conversation about anything of public concern grows dimmer as diatribe replaces dialogue. As grim as this litany may sound, frank recognition of it may well be the first step we need to take if we are to accept the invitation to embark together on a new conversation on the status of African-Americans in America.

The Proceedings published here need not be read as a text for rejection of the effort to construct a community of liberty and equality under the Constitution. Rather, they may be read as an invitation to draw on the resources of international law in our constitutional quest for "a more perfect union." What the colonists claimed for themselves in the Declaration of the Eighteenth Century, and what Woodrow Wilson claimed for people in other lands in the Twentieth Century — the right to self-determination — is what we are now challenged to explore within our own land for those who were, as a matter of foundational law, denied it at the outset of our history. If we accept this invitation, the conversation we shall create will be our conversation — an American conversation about an American problem. But it will be a conversation that will be open to discovering new possibilities for the American language of constitutional justice in the vocabulary of international human rights law. From this perspective, the Proceedings published here invite us to expand our imagination and our creativity in pursuing the vision of "one nation, one people."

---

1 Mr. Davis is a human rights activist and community development specialist in the Twin Cities of Minneapolis and St. Paul. He served as organizer of the Conference on African-Americans and the Right to Self-Determination held at Hamline University School of Law on May 14, 1993.

2 IHRAAM is a nongovernmental international human rights organization (NGO) with consultative status (Roster) with the Economic and Social Council of the United Nations.

3 Co-sponsors were: Department of Afro-American Studies, University of Minnesota; National Conference of Black Lawyers, International Affairs Section; Hamline University School of Law Student Organizations [Advocates for Cultural Equality (ACE), Black Law Student Association (BLSA), and International Law Society]; Minnesota Minority Lawyers Association (MMLA); Minnesota International Center (MIC); United Nations Association of Minnesota (UNA-MN); Minnesota Advocates for Human Rights; Human Rights Center, University of Minnesota; and the Gordon B. Sanders Chair in Education, Hamline University.

4 *Hamline Law Review*, Volume 17, Number 1, Fall 1993. The following represents an abridged version of the original publication of the Proceedings.

5 James Gleick, *Chaos: Making a New Science* 38 (1987) (quoting Leo Tolstoy).

6 *Id*. at 39 (quoting Thomas Kuhn).

7 Morton H. Halperin & David J. Scheffer, *Self-Determination in the New World Order*, 60-61 (1992).

8 *Id*. at 65.

9 See Yussuf N. Kly, *The Anti-Social Contract*, 1989.

10 Perhaps to create racial nationalism. *See id*.

11 The American system of segregation that existed until the 1960s is well known. See also Immigration and Nationality Act, 8 U.S.C. §§ 1101-1525 (1988).

12 Assimilation is referred to as forced when minorities are not given a choice; where the constitution, laws or political institutions of a state do not provide for the right to be different.

13 Asbjørn Eide, "The Articulation of Human Rights and Democracy," 5 (1993) (paper presented to UNESCO's International Congress on Education for Human Rights and Democracy, Montreal, Canada, March 8-11, 1993). Emphasis added.

14 Council of Europe, European Commission for Democracy Through Law, "Proposal for a European Convention for the Protection of Minorities," Strasbourg, March 1991, reprinted in 12 *Human Rights L.J.* 270 (1991).

15 *Id*. at art. 13.

16 *Id*. at art. 3(1).

17 *Id*. at art. 6(1).

18 *Id*. at art. 11.

19 Eide, *supra* note 13, at 5.

20 *Id*.

21 Arend Lijphart, *Democracy in Plural Societies: A Comparative Exploration* (1977).

22 See Halperin & Scheffer, *supra* note 7, at 58, citing Conference on Security and Cooperation in Europe, *Document of the Copenhagen Meeting of the Conference on the Human Dimension of the CSCE* (June 29, 1990), reprinted in 29 *Int'l Legal Materials* 1318-20 (1990).

23 See Halperin & Scheffer, *supra* note 7, at 58.
24 Conference on Security and Cooperation in Europe: Report of the CSCE Meeting of Experts on National Minorities, 30 *Int'l Legal Materials* 1692 (1991).
25 *Id.* at 1695-96.
26 Gudmundur Alfredsson, "Human Rights, Fundamental Freedoms and the Rights of Minorities: Essential Components of Democracy," 12 (September, 1991) (discussion paper presented at the Strasbourg Conference on Parliamentary Democracy, September 1991) (on file with author).
27 *Id.* at 5.
28 Alexis Heraclides, *The Self-Determination of Minorities in International Politics* (1991).
29 See, e.g., Hector Gros Espiell, *The Right to Self-Determination: Implementation of United Nations Resolution* ¶59 (United Nations 1970).
30 Woodrow Wilson, The Fourteen Points Address (1918), reprinted in 45 *The Papers of Woodrow Wilson* 534 (Arthur S. Link, ed., 1984).
31 See Alfred Corban, *National Self-determination* (1948).
32 United Nations, International Covenant on Civil and Political Rights (1966), reprinted in *UNIFO, International Human Rights Instruments of the United Nations 1948-1982* 91 (1983) [hereinafter Instruments], at 62.
33 *UN Charter*, art. 1(2), and art. 55.
34 *Instruments*, *supra* note 32 at 86.
35 See Edmund Jan Osmanczyk, *The Encyclopedia of the United Nations and International Resolutions* 453 (1990).
36 United Nations, *Declaration on Principles of International Law Concerning Friendly Relations and Cooperation Among States* (1970), reprinted in Albert P. Blaustein et al., *Human Rights Sourcebook* 97 (1987).
37 See Eide, *supra* note 13.
38 This geographical rather than popular emphasis is said to be confirmed by language in the *UN Charter* on trust and non-self-governing territories, by the Organization of African Unity's insistence on unchanged boundaries, and by the title of the United Nations' 1960 *Declaration on the Granting of Independence to Colonial Countries and Peoples.* The latter is reinforced, as far as the country or territorial element goes, by procedural descriptions in UN resolution 1541 of the same year.
39 See Oldrich Andrysek, *Report on the Definition of Minorities*, SIM Newsletter Special no. 8 (The Netherlands Institute of Human Rights, 1989).
40 Alfredsson, *supra* note 26, at 39 n. 17, citing UN Doc. E/CN.4/1987/WG.5/WP.1.
41 G.A. Res. 128, UN GAOR, 41st Sess., Supp. No. 53, UN Doc. A/41/925 (1986).
42 See Richard B. Lillich, *International Human Rights Instruments* § 530.1 (1990).

43 *Instruments, supra.*note 32, at 91, Art. 1.
44 See Blaustein et al., *supra* note 36, at 97, ¶ 3; see also Daniel Turp, "Quebec's Democratic Right of Self-Determination" (1993) (paper presented to the Martin Ennals Memorial Symposium, Saskatoon, Canada 1993) (on file with author).
45 Francesco Capotorti, *Study on the Rights of Persons Belonging to Ethnic, Religious and Linguistic Minorities* 31-40 (United Nations 1979).
46 Gudmundur Alfredsson, "Speaking Notes for the Martin Ennals Memorial Symposium" (1993) (paper read to the Martin Ennals Memorial Symposium, Saskatoon, Canada 1993) (on file with author).
47 G.A. Res. 135, UN GAOR, 47th Sess., UN Doc. A/47/678/Add. 2 (1993), at art. 1, ¶¶ 1-2 [hereinafter *Linguistic Minorities*]
48 *Id.* at art. 2(3).
49 *Id.* at art. 4(2).
50 *Id.* at art. 4(5).
51 *Linguistic Minorities, supra* note 47, at art. 5(1).
52 *Linguistic Minorities, supra* note 47, at art. 6(1).
53 *Linguistic Minorities, supra* note 47, at art. 8(4).
54 *Linguistic Minorities, supra* note 47, preamble.
55 Alfredsson, *supra* note 26, at 3.
56 See Appendix II: Minority Rights: Selected Texts, hereto.
57 Asbjørn Eide, "Self-Determination and Minorities" 12 (March 1993) (outline of a paper prepared for the Martin Ennals Memorial Symposium on Self-Determination, Saskatoon, Canada, March 1993) (on file with author).
58 See UN Doc. E/CN.4/1989/MG/SM at 1.
59 See Mohammed Bedjaoui, ed., *International Law: Achievements and Prospects* 103 (1991).
60 Blaustein et al, *supra* note 36, at 97.
61 United Nations, *Universal Declaration of Human Rights* (1948), reprinted in *Instruments, supra* note 32, at 5.
62 See Eide, *supra* note 57.
63 G.A. Res. 1514 (XV), UN GAOR, 15th Sess., Supp. No. 16, at 66, UN Doc. A/4684 (1960).
63 Halperin & Scheffer, *supra* note 7, at 22 (quoting G.A. Res. 1541).
64 Halperin & Scheffer, *supra* note 7, at 54.
65 Turp, *supra* note 44, at 4.
66 *UN Charter,* art 55.
67 See Heraclides, *supra* note 28, at 29.
68 Blaustein *et al., supra* note 36, at 97.
69 Cancado Trindade, "Co-existence and Coordination of Mechanisms of International Protection of Human Rights (At Global and Regional Levels)," in *Recueil Des Cours: Collected Courses of the Hague Academy of International Law* 1 (1987).
70 Michele Jacquart, "Economic, Social and Cultural Rights," in Bedjaoui, *supra* note 59, at 1085.
71 A.C. Hamilton & C.K. Sinclair, *Report of the Aboriginal Justice*

Inquiry of Manitoba: The Justice System and Aboriginal People, Province of Manitoba (1991).

72 Georg Schwartzenberger, *The Inductive Approach to International Law,* (1965).

73 See *Constitution of the Mi'kmaq Commonwealth*, Appendix I hereto.

74 International human rights law would regard UN recognition of the right to municipal autonomy as contrary to the principle of non-interference in international affairs of the state.

75 Turp, *supra* note 44, at 6.

76 Halperin & Scheffer, *supra* note 7, at 23-24, quoting M.G. Kaldharan Nayar, "Self-Determination Beyond the Colonial Context: Biafra in Retrospect," 10 *Texas International Law Journal* 337 (1975).

77 James Crawford, "Self-Determination Outside the Colonial Context," in *Self-Determination in the Commonwealth* 13 (W.J. Allan Macartney, ed., 1988).

78 *Id.*

79 *Id.*

80 See Eide, *supra* note 57.

81 The following panelist statements are abridged from statements carried in the "Proceedings of the Conference on African-American Right to Self-Determination," *Hamline Law Journal, supra* note 4.

82 M.A., Ph.D., Indiana University; N.I.M.H. Post-doctoral Fellow University of Chicago; Associate Professor and Chair, Afro-American/African Studies Department, University of Minnesota.

83 J.D., University of Minnesota; Executive Director, Minneapolis Legal Rights Center.

84 Ph.D., Indiana University; Associate Professor of Political Science, University of Minnesota.

85 J.D., Loyola University; Deputy Director, Amnesty International USA, Midwest.

86 J.D., Marquette University Law School; Associate Professor, Marquette University Law School.

87 Judge, Ramsey County District Court. Judge Wilson previously taught law at Hamline University School of Law, and served as Staff Attorney with the Legal Aid Society of Minneapolis and the Neighborhood Justice Center in St. Paul. He currently serves as a volunteer with the Minnesota Advocates for Human Rights.

88 J.D., University of Michigan Law School; Associate Professor, Hamline University School of Law; previously served as Bigelow Fellow and Lecturer of Law, University of Chicago Law School, and Research Fellow, University of Nairobi.

89 J.D., Northwestern University Law School; Assistant Professor, Chicago-Kent College of Law, Illinois Institute of Technology; Co-Chair, National Conference of Black Lawyers.

90 See Andrew Koppelman, "Forced Labor: A Thirteenth Amendment Defense of Abortion," 84 *Nw. U.L. Rev.* 480 n. 137 (1990).

91 163 U.S. 537 (1896).

92 J.D., University of Minnesota; Attorney at Law, Gordon, Miller & O'Brien; Assistant Dean for Students at Hamline University School of Law.

93 Professor of Law, Hamline University School of Law, Faculty Liaison for the Conference on African-Americans and the Right to Self-Determination.

94 19 U.S. (1 How.) 393 (1856).

95 347 U.S. 483 (1956).

Minority Rights: Some Questions and Answers

Y. N. Kly
& Diana Kly

QUESTION: Why should African-Americans look to international human rights law for help in achieving equal status and equality in America?

International human rights law promotes norms of minority treatment that are more wide-ranging and have been more successful in practice than the limited concept of civil rights (non-discrimination and equality before the law, which in the United States is interpreted to mean the same treatment). These norms reflect the modern world's experience in trying to accommodate the problems of minorities by giving the historically evolved situation and circumstances of the minority group adequate consideration, leading often to positive state action and different treatment, in view of their different requirements.

Viewing the problem of minorities within the international context prevents the error of thinking that local minorities' problems are unique (and hence insoluble). By enabling the African-American problem to be viewed within the context of a whole range of problems which have typically arisen for minorities worldwide — by the mere fact of their being a minority[1] — we can see that African-Americans' development problems are essentially caused by the fact that they are a minority in a state that refuses to recognize or provide for their minority rights or to permit any form of community control. Segregation attempted to institute the cultural assimilation of African-Americans while maintaining their physical separation.

QUESTION: International human rights law as a model for minority rights is all well and good, but who says America will pay any attention?

The political pressure created by African-Americans demanding these rights, in conjunction with international pressure, will create circumstances that will raise the cost both domestically as well as internationally, of denial of these rights beyond the benefit of not providing for them. To maintain the credibility of its position as a leading power, the United States must provide for minority rights, should these rights be demanded. As a matter of fact, in cases where effective demands are made by Native Americans, we have seen positive action on the part of the United States government. Faced with an effective contingent of Native American lobbyists from the United States and politically forced to respond in an internationally supported forum concerning the needs of the world's indigenous peoples, the United States delegate to the United Nations Working Group on Indigenous Populations was forced to respond, according to the *UNPO Monitor*, that:

> ... although human rights of indigenous people is promoted in the United States, the promotion of the rights of dignity and "equality" are not sufficient. Expressed support of the basic goals of the draft Declaration [on the Rights of Indigenous Peoples]. Offered a working model on how the rights of indigenous people can be recognized and implemented -- on the right to self-determination, raised the issue of the recognition of tribal self-governance and autonomy over a broad range of issues as a positive development in the national level. Highlighted the uniqueness of this concept of self-governance which considers a "government-to-government relationship." Finally, expressed determination to explore how this concept of self-determination might be translated into international terms.[2]

Paradoxically, one of the strongest arguments for the effectiveness of the international human rights treaties is the general reluctance of states to ratify them and hence become subject to their jurisdiction. The United States, for example, for all its bravado about being the most powerful, most independent state, for decades was afraid to ratify more than the Genocide Convention. Y. N. Kly has argued, in *The Anti-Social Contract*,[3] that such reluctance stems from the fear that its domestic minorities, African-Americans in particular, will thereby be made aware of and given the incentive to demand this internationally-recognized right.

Only recently has the United States ratified the International Covenant on Civil and Political Rights (ICCPR) and at that, it has hedged its ratification in a forest of reservations, understandings and declarations. Most particularly, it has refrained from ratifying the first Optional Protocol, which would permit groups and individuals (as opposed to states) to take human rights grievances to the Human Rights Committee, which monitors state adherence to the ICCPR. The United States has yet to ratify the International Covenant on Economic, Social and Cultural Rights, the International Convention on the Elimination of All Forms of Racial Discrimination (CERD), the International Convention on the Suppression and Punishment of the Crime of Apartheid, the Convention against Torture and Other Cruel, Inhuman or Degrading Treatment or Punishment, or even the Convention on the Rights of the Child — to name but a few. Why such hesitancy, if there were not the fear of the obligations incurred thereby, which might be too politically expensive to resist.

A state's ratification of the human rights treaties brings along with it the obligation to report to the United Nations on its human rights practices, and to have its reports questioned by the various states' representatives of the treaties concerned. Non-governmental organizations (NGOs) have the right to submit communications concerning these State Reports, communications which may provide documented information on human rights violations by the state.[4]

Criticism by state representatives in human rights forums and tribunals becomes fodder for world public opinion and permits the exertion of constant pressure on states which don't abide by their obligation to enforce internationally protected rights.

QUESTION: It is often said that the United Nations depends heavily upon American financial support for its very existence. How, then, can the UN act effectively against the hand that feeds it?

First, a serious observation of the decisions reached by the UN over a period of the past 30 years does not support the assumption that the UN will not reach decisions contrary to the will of the United States. Indeed, the evidence against this assumption is so overwhelming that we only need to examine UN decisions in almost any area: law of the sea, decolonization, human rights, the embargo of Cuba, etc.

Most major African-American leaders have known that, in order to be successful, the African-American struggle to achieve equality within America must be internationalized. Today, there is no other mechanism in existence which permits a group to internationalize their struggle except the UN. All minority movements go there — if for no other reason than the UN is the crossroads where the world meets and makes decisions which come to represent the moral and legal authority of world opinion. As a pivotal arena of public opinion and thereby political power, the UN forces states to be concerned about its views. No state (nor indeed any serious liberation movement) questions its value — although they may attempt to devalue it because they fear its power or criticism.

IHRAAM African-American Delegates to the UN report that the UN is full of diplomats in inter-governmental and governmental capacity who harbor good will towards the African-American cause. But they can do nothing if African-Americans themselves do nothing. UN diplomats themselves understand that the credibility of their human rights program itself could be severely called into question if it should appear that they were unwilling to address the African-American plight because of the power of the United States. And United States diplomats in turn realize that their road is made harder, every time they wish to press an issue with a state, if they can be countered in turn with the issue of their treatment of African-Americans at home.

QUESTION: Haven't African-Americans tried to pursue their human rights — unsuccessfully — through the UN before?

No. The human rights machinery of the UN is a recent development. Past efforts were never processed or followed through. Since its inception, the United Nations has been viewed as a focus of appeal by numerous aggrieved nationalities who have been stymied in their attempts to achieve adequate response to their grievances through domestic legal systems. However, all too frequently, the groups concerned are unaware of the legal and political conditions and processes which will enable the United Nations to consider their complaints. Trips to Geneva are made, important contacts are spoken to, good will is expressed, and well-documented grievances exchange hands. And yet, because the necessary political and legal processes are not followed (or did not exist), it is as if nothing had been done at all — even though the minority/nationality representatives concerned may in all sincerity feel that they have taken their group's grievances to the UN.

Many African-Americans are under the misapprehension that their grievances have already been successfully submitted (maybe even numerous times) to the United Nations. But this is not so. The most noteworthy of such instances is that of the "We Charge Genocide" petitioners, a distinguished body of

African-Americans, Dr. W.E.B. DuBois among them, who addressed their complaint to the General Assembly in 1951. At the time of this petition, the UN was under the sway of the "impossibility to act" doctrine which asserted the unlimited sovereignty of states over their citizens, and states' right to non-interference in domestic affairs as it relates to gross violations of human rights, apart from a genuine threat to world peace. (This doctrine has now been overcome.) Also, as above-mentioned, short of a threat to world peace, there were no legal procedures within the UN that would have permitted it to respond to such a communication. At that time, the United States had not yet ratified the Genocide Convention, nor the International Covenant on Civil and Political Rights, with its minority protection article (27). A cardinal principle of international law is that a state is not bound by a treaty to which it is not a party. ECOSOC's Resolution 1503 (XLVIII) concerning gross violations of human rights, enacted in May, 1970, had not yet come into force.

While the National Conference of Black Lawyers submitted a complaint through the 1503 procedure in 1979, their complaint was not accepted by the Working Group of the Sub-Commission, and thus was not given to the Sub-Commission. This may be due to problems deriving from the political pressures in the Sub-Commission from the United States and its numerous allies, or the fact that the UN's minority rights law was not as fully developed as it is today (Special Rapporteur Francesco Capotorti's study had not yet been received, nor had the 1992 Declaration on Minorities been adopted, nor had the Human Rights Committee released its General Comment interpreting Article 27 as requiring positive measures of minority protection on the part of states, etc.)

Now, however, there is an extensive body of international legal instruments available in support of international legal argumentation for minority rights, and there are African-American experts in international law undertaking action on various levels, from complaint procedure to information provision to the various Committees monitoring the UN treaties, to conflict warning. Through the International Human Rights Association of American Minorities (IHRAAM), an African-American-launched international NGO awarded consultative status with the Economic and Social Council of the United Nations in 1992, United States minority issues are being presented to the UN Commission on Human Rights and other UN organs. Now, through IHRAAM, African-American groups have a means of direct and official input to the UN.

QUESTION: You know, frankly, I'm tired of being referred to as a belonging to a "minority." No matter how you shake it, the word itself makes you feel as if minority people are somehow less important than majority people.

For the purposes of international legal protection, the term minority is essentially an international legal construct, like victim, accused, plaintiff, etc., in domestic law. It need not relate directly with how peoples refer to themselves or how they are referred to in the domestic constitutional-legal documents of states. Hence in the Philippines, the term "cultural communities" has been used. Romania has used the term "co-inhabiting nationality," etc.[5] This was a way of addressing the fact that the term "minority" had itself become debased, and was synonymous with various forms of inequality between "the majority" and "the minority," because the term "minority" specified a category of citizens whose overall position in the state is less strong than that of the majority ethny.

While negotiations between minorities and states might lead to the substitution of other terms for that of "minority," at the present time it is appropriate to refer to minority when approaching the issue of minority rights in international law, because this is the international legal terminology in which international law presently frames the rights of non-dominant groups living in multi-national states.

QUESTION: What are minority rights in international law?

Minority rights are the rights of persons belonging to non-dominant nations, communities, groups, etc. living in the same state, exercised individually and in community with members of their group. While these rights include the right to non-discrimination and equality before the law, they also include the right to be different and to exercise appropriate degrees of autonomy as required for equal status.

The intent of minority rights is to protect and preserve the unique ethnic, cultural and religious identities of minorities, and to facilitate their equal status development. In order to accomplish this, most multi-national states have evolved, in addition to non-discrimination and equality before the law, a wide range of proactive practices, including politico-legal structures permitting minority autonomy in various socio-economic fields such as education, health, culture, criminal justice, welfare, etc.

QUESTION: How do minority rights differ from civil rights?

From the perspective of providing for protection from oppression by the dominant group, which usually controls the apparatus of the state in which both live, minority rights are human rights and are therefore inherently held by minorities both on an individual and a collective basis. The ultimate responsibility for their interpretation and implementation lies with the international tribunals, agencies, the UN, other states, etc. Civil rights authority resides in the legislation and case law of the state (usually controlled by the majority ethny) and they are the final judge and jury as to its interpretation and implementation. However, civil rights is often used to implement human rights domestically so that citizens need not go to the international tribunals for remedy. Where this is largely successful, for all purposes, civil rights and minority human rights are the same.

While valuable, civil rights is fundamentally a general right which functions as if all citizens were the same. It asserts the right of persons belonging to minorities to freedom from discrimination, but not to positive entitlements which promote minority equal status with the majority.

QUESTION: Why hasn't civil rights worked?

As a minority in a majoritarian democratic system (as opposed to a pluralist system), African-Americans don't have the voting power to enforce adequate consideration of their needs. American electoral procedures such as the single non-transferable vote (as opposed to proportional representation) and at large municipal voting (as opposed to the ward system) are all geared to ensure majority domination.[6]

However, even if African-Americans were to vote under a system which gave them full representation according to their voting numbers, insofar as they are a numeric minority, they could still continue to be outvoted on every issue where their interest might clash with that of the majority. There would still be no (institutionalized) way which ensured that the system would address their specific needs, or permit African-American communities to address their needs, themselves.

QUESTION: Surely, if individual African-Americans are elected to office, this should mean greater clout for the community?

While African-Americans holding elected office doubtless feel strong obligations to their community and project their concerns in whatever arenas they may be functioning in, such officials also have obligations to the other communities over whom they also have jurisdiction. Frequently, in fact, elected black leaders have operated what Cynthia Enloe, writing with regard to black Americans, terms a *sub-machine:*

> a patronage and favor-dispensing organ nominally controlled by a politician from a relatively weak ethnic group [whose]own influence and resources depend on access to the resources of the larger machine controlled by politicians of another community. In essence, the sub-machine boss is the loyal lieutenant of the machine boss; but he is permitted enough autonomy to build a personal power base of his own so long as it never rivals that of the senior patron.[7]

These representatives, while they may be African-American, cannot be seen to be speaking for the African-American communities. Their position is therefore very ambiguous where the interests of majority and minority conflict. While a number of mayors in major American cities are now African-American, in many instances it cannot be said that the African-American communities that have elected them have benefited. So the question remains: who has the legitimacy and authority, as conferred by the democratic process, to speak for African-Americans? Is there a need for an African-American election? Are African-Americans enjoying democracy in America, or have their interests and needs, insofar as they differ from that of the majority population, been consistently submerged by the interest of the majority Anglo-American ethny? Is the subordination of African-American need to majority interest even visible in the very court decisions which enforced their civil rights since, as Derrick Bell has observed, "Successful court decisions in relation to civil rights coincide with those case decisions that also serve to benefit the majority ethny even more"?[8]

QUESTION: Were we misdirected when we struggled for civil rights and against the "separate but equal" doctrine?

No. At the time, there really wasn't much understanding or discussion of the options (nor indeed, was conventional international law as developed with regard to minority rights as at present). Resistance to segregation, the American version of apartheid, and indeed, the image of apartheid and bantustans as practiced in South Africa, may have weighed against the maintenance of separate institutions, in the presumption that they would necessarily be controlled by Anglo-Americans and thus kept *unequal*. However, the African-American people may not have generally understood that what may have appeared as the only alternate process,"integration," was in reality assimilation, and would encourage the dismantling of the existing degree of African-American economic, political and educational institutions, communities, families, etc.

Most important to note is that African-Americans were neither separate nor equal. The doctrine, while using the words "separate but equal" was actually a doctrine of segregation and racism. All institutions of the African-American community were under the indirect control of the Anglo-American majority ethny through the apparatus of the state: school curricula, the justice system, the licensing system for professionals, etc. Thus, African-Americans have never fought for nor against a separate but equal system. They have fought against racist (Anglo-American) oppression and for civil rights, assuming that civil rights was the way of overcoming Anglo-American oppression, while racism was simply the tool to maintain the oppression.

While African-Americans may have brought about the end of official constitutional-legal discrimination (segregation), they have not achieved equal status (particularly as a group) in the electoral system, or indeed, in terms of general level of political and economic control in any sector. So while the struggle for civil rights (the rights of a citizen) has been valuable, it has not provided equality or equal status in law or in fact. It has provided for African-Americans to be treated the same as Anglo-Americans regardless of whether they have different circumstances and needs; regardless of whether this "same" treatment leads to greater inequality in fact or not, and regardless of whether treating African-Americans as the same legally produces greater or lesser legal equality. It provided for their cultural and political assimilation into the Anglo-American underclass, for their disappearance as a separate nation; in short, it provided for ethnocide.

QUESTION: Does non-discrimination (equality before the law) work for African-Americans?

Apart from marginal remedy for some individuals, not at all, because most discrimination is institutional, structural and systemic. The main recourse provided by equality (same treatment) before the law/non-discrimination is threat of court action. As any who have ever undertaken such legal action can testify, it is a tremendously costly and lengthy process, with the outcomes always uncertain and the proofs concerning individual situations burdened by subtleties often beyond the power of the courts to capture. While successful lawsuits likely do cause some attitudinal discrimination to abate, it is likely that attitudinal discrimination is pushed underground, while systemic discrimination remains, disguised in legitimate institutions, politico-legal mandates, prerogatives and necessities.

A further problem with attempting to solve discrimination problems through the courts is the fact that, increasingly, the United States judicial system regards equal treatment "of rich and poor alike" as before mentioned, to mean the same treatment (in the abstract, making these two unequals equal in such a way as to seem concerned rather with preventing the possibility of discrimination against the rich) and thereby discounts factors that differentiate the parties concerned, such as poverty, historic oppression, etc.[9]

Constant litigation on the part of aggrieved individuals is not the solution but remains a symptom of the problem, which is systemic and institutional.

QUESTION: If non-discrimination laws don't end discrimination, how do you end discrimination?

First we should consider some of the sources and purposes of discrimination. Discrimination does not derive from a free-floating attitude of "racism" arising spontaneously in the minds of some "bad people" who "don't like [black] people." Typically it evolves dialectically through specific historical events leading to the creation of systemically generated and ensured inequalities, whether it concerns today's third world economic refugees, victims of the neo-colonial international economic order, or the situation of the African-Americans, victims of a long history of one nation's official systemic policies devoted to ensuring the dominance of Anglo-Americans. The material and psycho-social hierarchies generated by systemic inequality in turn condition a web of attitudes, fears, distastes, and hostilities.

However, awareness of this systemic causality plays little part in most inter-group relations — not just because of the complexity of the understanding required, but also because what is really at issue is not just majority distaste for this or that trait of the discriminated group. The issue is collective power relations between the groups, and the individual power of group members that either benefits or suffers from this unequal relation. These are pocketbook issues and concern "having" (as opposed to "sharing" which can be properly viewed as "having an appropriate part of," or negatively viewed as "having less," or at minimum as "maximizing your losses," insofar as failure to share may result in a situation in which the pie itself is destroyed.) It concerns habits of interaction, customary assumptions and so on, all of which are measured on a scale of relative privilege.

Psycho-spiritual complexes deriving from the long history of official systemic discrimination and gross human rights violation to which African-Americans have been subjected, lead many in the majority culture to take it for granted that they should receive priority consideration over African-Americans in the allocation of social benefits, i.e. jobs, education, housing. Many, while refusing to admit the relevance of historical/ systemic factors to the present day African-American condition, consciously or unconsciously anticipate and fear retaliation for their disproportionate privileges. Few can be impervious to the distorted and inflammatory depictions of African-Americans in the major American media, or indeed the reality of their disproportionately negative standing in all typical Anglo-American measurements of social well-being (income,life expectancy, health, education, etc.) Such a web of motivation often leads the majority population to a reluctance to surrender any of the advantages and privileges which have been directly tied to its historical role as victimizer. Far better to blame the victim than to admit or dwell on causal factors which could lead to its recognition of both the justice, need and wisdom of surrendering its position of superiority, both material and attitudinal, which translates into the proportionate sharing of political and economic power and resources.

Equally, the remediation of such ingrained attitudes and long term abuse as has existed in the African-American case might require not merely the alleviation of material inequality, but also a form of public repentance as exemplified by an official admission of and apology/reparations for the history of systemic discrimination and gross human rights violations.

Once a measure of equal status has been established between groups, any tendency to discriminate would likely lose its deep-rooted and destructive basis, and where it remained, become similar to the milder rivalries and frictions which exist between cultures which nonetheless recognize each other's full human equality, e.g. the rivalry between the British and French, etc. It is in such cases that non-discrimination and recourse to the courts is most effective. However, in situations where the historical situation has led to deep and pervasive structural inequalities in the relationship between majority and minority, the effectiveness of policies of non-discrimination for creating equality are negligible.

So the question is one rather of establishing equal-status and interdependence between groups.

Within the American framework, the notion of how nondiscrimination policy can succeed in producing equality probably goes something like this: if every instance of discrimination is prevented, then discrimination as a whole will be ended, and thus meritorious individuals, who exist in similar proportions in all groups, will rise to their natural place in the general social order, and hence all groups, by natural process, will end up having a proportionate share of the social product, and a proportionate standing in all social indicators, i.e. equality.

This view of non-discrimination is concerned, not so much with protecting the right to be different, as with insisting that difference not be noticed or not matter, when it comes to allocating benefits, etc. In actuality, it becomes a game of "let's pretend": let's pretend that the controller (the employer, the landlord, the banker, the real estate broker, the university professor) *doesn't notice* that you are a minority member; he/she will treat you *as if he thought you were equal (the same as an Anglo-American)* although actual social conditions and prejudicial Anglo-American social criteria may lead him/her to assume (rightly or wrongly) that the schools you attended as a child were under-financed, that the community you grew up in and presently live in is beset by social problems resulting from unemployment, underemployment or low-wage employment, that your ability to excel or even function in the job may be impaired by the whole gamut of social factors which beset you as a member of a devalued group, thereby rendering you less capable, less reliable, and so on. This not only leads inescapably to hypocrisy, but is also highly insulting. Insofar as the collective identity of the minority is burdened by stigma, so is the standing of the individual, whether the attendant presumptions apply to him/her or not. There is no way for individuals to completely, or even sufficiently, escape the stigma attached to the collective identity even if they do manage to escape the material conditions. In short, the game of pretending to ignore differences is a way of suggesting that there is something wrong with being different (non-Anglo-American): a way of imposing cultural domination and ignoring your right to be who you are, with equal-status.

Non-discrimination can only be achieved by ensuring the right to be different by whatever means that may require. It may require both an attempt to put a stop to negative action, as well as taking positive action on behalf of preserving the identity and promoting the equality of discriminated-against groups through politico-legal or socio-economic policies directed specifically towards the group concerned.

QUESTION: Maybe discrimination is rooted in human nature and can't be prevented?

This is unlikely. Most research shows that the source of discrimination lies in a historical oppression or devaluation which is systemically implemented and ensured by the state. Thus, it can only be appealed against to the state that is also its creator and preserver. As far as minority rights are concerned, the key may lie in sidestepping the issue of discrimination; in getting equality through minority control of institutions, and leaving prejudice to its most natural correction: the development of respect and esteem deriving from equal-status relations and the creation of situations of interdependence among groups.

Discrimination counts most and is maintained when one group has to go to another group which is prejudiced against it for fulfillment of basic needs: shelter, housing, education, capital; that is, when one group is made dependent on another, and when the law of that group governs the life of the minority. The dominant group comes to feel that they are superior to the dominated group, and that there is something wrong with any number of aspects of the dependent group. If African-Americans run their own communities, their own socio-economic institutions, then they no longer have to try to achieve their needs in and through socio-economic institutions (etc.) controlled by the Anglo-American community. They are then able to provide for their own through initiatives enabled by access to a proportionate share of the public purse (i.e. tax revenue, etc.), thus creating conditions of interdependence between groups, enabling the marginalization of the problem of discrimination.

QUESTION: Aren't rights or measures that are just for minorities a kind of reverse discrimination?

No. The concept of reverse discrimination as used in the United States is an effective way of attempting to ignore the existence of minorities and minority rights, and psychologically prevent minorities from seeking rights outside of their control. It suggests that the historical situation of the dominant group is the same as that of the devalued minority, and that where there is no difference, no right to be different, all should be treated the same — even if the effects maintain inequality for the minority. International law specifically militates against the concept of reverse discrimination. See Article 1:4 of the *Convention on the Elimination of All Forms of Racial Discrimination* (CERD) and 8:3 of the *Declaration on the Rights of Persons Belonging to National or Ethnic, Religious and Linguistic Minorities*, in Appendix II.

QUESTION: Do special measures and special rights apply to all minorities? What about homosexuals, or the disabled? What about Greek or Irish Americans?

Minority rights are essentially collective rights as they exist for the purpose of eliminating minority oppression and inequality. Therefore in a technical sense, the word "minority" and the word "victim" in domestic law become similar when the right to international protection is evoked. It is evoked because some important aspect of the minority's rights and needs is being denied, ignored or trampled upon by the majority. Customary international law suggests that rights involved in Article 27 of the ICCPR, as far as the United States is concerned, apply particularly to the national minorities: the African-Americans, Native Americans, and Chicanos. These minorities existed collectively within the state at the time it was constituted, and are not seen as immigrants from another state within the international system.

Immigrant minorities, on the other hand, have made individual choices to leave duly constituted states in which they were citizens; there is implicit in the notion of immigration, the acceptance on the part of the immigrant of the desire to assimilate. This does not mean, however, that the state may not be willing to accord them certain resources or special rights. Canada, for instance, has such a multicultural policy which benefits its many immigrant minorities. This does not put them on the same plane, however, as Canada's national minorities, the aboriginal peoples and the French Canadians, who either enjoy or are recognized to have the right to significantly greater politico-legal control of socio-economic and cultural institutions, and who seek to be regarded in full equality as founding nations of the state.

Social minorities (gays, the disabled, women [so-defined because of their non-dominant position], etc.) do not figure within the configuration of national or ethnic, religious and linguistic minorities protected by international minority rights law. However, other human rights law applies to them.

QUESTION: What is the difference between special measures and special rights?

While special measures refer to measures taken on behalf of the group which may cease to exist once the minority achieves equal status with the majority, special rights are permanent and are accorded with a view to recognizing the minority's right to remain different, to continue to exist and develop as a minority or nationality distinct from the majority culture, while interacting with it on a basis of equality and interdependence.

Special rights may include the notion of proportionality, widely recognized as effective for reducing group conflict and ensuring equal development. It may be introduced in a limited manner (e.g. in only some sectors such as hiring in the civil service) or extensively in most public jurisdictions. In Switzerland, for example, the French, German and Italian populations share federal executive, legislative and judicial positions proportionally;[10] proportionality is even taken into account in the armed forces. In Belgium of the 1950's-60's, a near 50-50 form of proportionality was extensively used. Belgium's 1971 constitution stipulated that with the possible exception of the prime minister, the cabinet must comprise an equal number of Flemish and French ministers. The same devotion to the principle of equality is also found in the Belgian government's allocation of resources. When railway lines had to be abandoned, when industrial development projects were sited and financed, when roads were built, the decisions were made on the basis of equal shares in the benefits for each nationality or minority.[11]

In particular, special rights creates pluralist democracy in order to assure equal status of all nations or minorities in the state — minority control of institutions in various sectors, such as education, health care, the justice system, culture, welfare, tourism, etc. Control over these sectors, whether achieved through autonomy, devolution, federalism, etc. permit minority control over important elements affecting its well being and daily life. This allows the minority a measure of self-determination without threatening the territorial integrity of the state.

QUESTION: Can we talk about self-determination and not be talking about secession?

Yes. Self-determination has come to be divided in scholarly discourse between external self-determination (the right of a group to secede and become fully politically independent) and internal self-determination (where a group exercises political rights, among them the right to control over jurisdictions of social activity such as education, health, criminal justice, etc. in varying degrees, while remaining within the existing state).

QUESTION: In Article 1 of both Covenants, self-determination is said to be the right of "peoples." Is self-determination a minority right, too?

Many scholars such as Ian Brownlie argue that trying to establish differences between groups such as "peoples," "minorities" and "indigenous peoples" and their respective rights is fruitless, insofar as the issues are the same, and "the segregation of topics is an impediment to fruitful work." [12] In his keynote address to the Hamline Conference on African-Americans and the Right to Self-Determination reprinted herein, Dr. Kly further advances these arguments. In practice, varying degrees of internal self-determination have been accorded to both peoples and national minorities in order to promote harmonious inter-group relations.

When used in relation to national minorities,[13] self-determination is concerned primarily with internal jurisdictions, and does not permit the right of secession or threat to the territorial integrity of the state. The word "autonomy" is being used with greater frequency now, in this regard. While "internal self-determination" as it relates to national minorities, and "autonomy" can be regarded as functionally the same, there is no escaping the liberating connotations which continue to cling to the former term.

QUESTION: What are African-Americans? A people? A racial, ethnic or national minority?

There is no internationally agreed upon definition for either peoples or minorities. Both share many characteristics. Also states have devised solutions in domestic law to permit nationalities to exercise varying degrees of self-determination. While a common language, culture and religion may play an important determining role in the process of definition, the subjective factor — self-definition, the desire and ability of the group concerned to assert its will to exist as such, to be seen and to develop as a group, and to express its need for "autonomy" or some form of internal self-determination to achieve equal status — is a major factor in determining how a group is defined in international law.[14]

Keeping in mind the international legal relationship between the word minority and the word victim, the most important factor calling forth legitimate demands for (internal) self-determination may be their historical circumstances, and the extent to which they have been unable or unwilling to assimilate, or have been prevented from assimilating by the majority culture, and remain trapped in a condition of permanent inequality *vis-a-vis* the majority.

While there has been no internationally accepted definition of national minority (let alone minority), this term continues to appear in international legal texts. Some have argued, in fact, that this is the only type of minority that truly has rights to international protection,[15] insofar as all others are essentially immigrant or social minorities, and are covered by other human rights instruments.

While classification of African-Americans as a national minority abrogates the issue of whether they are an ethnic minority, it seems clear that their self-definition as *African-Americans*; their recognizability anywhere in the world as such; their distinctive music, dance, cuisine, dress and manner; and their sense of a shared history would clearly make the ethnic definition, too, an appropriate one.

QUESTION: Do African-Americans have a unique cultural identity?

Many factors make up a people's or a national minority's unique identity; these concern shared characteristics such as language, religion, or a common heritage. While most national minorities do to some degree share many of the same characteristics (as majorities, and indeed as the people of many independent states), it is important to remember that the African-American culture was consolidated under conditions of oppression. It would be difficult to argue that there is a common history between the enslaved and the enslaver, i.e. a shared experience of that history, a shared interpretation of that history, or a shared evaluation of its major actors.

Assuredly, African-Americans have a unique identity. Their roots go deep into Africa, not Europe. It would be nonsensical to assume that, over the passage of generations, parents transmitted to their children nothing of the practices and understandings with which they themselves had grown up — even under the hostile conditions of enslavement, which attempted to erase all prior identities. African-American culture in the southern United States still retains many direct linkages — the basket weaving women of South Carolina, the syntax and vocabulary of the Gullah language[16] which many have claimed provides the basis for what is commonly referred to, and coming to be taught as, African-American language, etc.

Despite the long history of theft and borrowing from African-American blues and jazz, there is nonetheless recognition of the distinctive cultural source of this music. Even today, the reference to "crossover" music asserts a continuing difference and distinctiveness of the African and Anglo-American musical cultures.

While African-Americans, like Mexicans, Cubans, French, etc., do to some degree share some of the same religious beliefs as Anglo-Americans, they also practice many religions not generally practiced by Anglo-Americans. Within the African-American community, we find Muslims, Holy Rollers, the Green Door Society, the Yoruba, the Black Hebrews, Daddy Grace, Father Devine, and so on. The religious culture of African-American Christian churches is strikingly different from that of Anglo-American churches, to the extent that some worship an African Christ. Most African-American Christians still belong to the African Methodist Church.

QUESTION: Why does having a unique identity matter? Why can't everybody just be the same. After all, we're all alike under the skin.

Unique cultural identities result from the historical circumstances of a people. It is not, on the collective level, what a group chooses cognitively, although it may be influenced or changed by what a group chooses. It results essentially from group historical experiences and situations. Therefore, the correct question in relation to minority rights law is not, why can't we all be the same — we are essentially the same — it's why should one people be oppressed because of its difference from another group? The minority rights answer is: they shouldn't, and therefore they must be afforded the rights required to be equal.

A group's ethnic identity is made up of the common experience of their families, their ancestors, and their communities. It concerns their social beliefs and religious practices, their values, their goals, their way of doing things. It means their music, their way of dress, their hair-styles, their marriage mores, their languages as well as their way of talking, their interests, their particular talents, their cooking, their dance, their sports and entertainment, their treatment of children and the elderly, and so on. These aren't attributes that people "put on," in the way that people are sometimes said to "become cultured." These are attributes that people take in with their mother's milk, from the historical practice and customs of their community. They provide the fabric for daily life.[17]

Frequently an ethnic identity can be impoverished by oppression. Various expressions of that identity can be devalued by another ethny which has the power to enforce its values. The instance where African-American corn-row hairstyles were once rejected as unsuitable for those working in Anglo-American-controlled banks is a case in point. The denigration and suppression of an ethnic or cultural expression previously accepted as natural can only have a negative effect on inter-cultural relations.

Groups *are* different, and they have the right to have their differences recognized and respected as much as their sameness. These differences don't go away by ignoring them. Rather, ignoring the ethnic dimension of an individual's identity (while at the same time accepting majority ethnic identity as somehow "universal") puts minority groups at a disadvantage, since it prevents the society from being able to adequately process their unique demands, needs and requirements for equal status.

QUESTION: What if the minority doesn't express the desire to maintain its culture, but sometimes seems to be trying to escape from it and assimilate into the majority?

The fact that an oppressed minority is usually afraid to express its unique culture where an environment hostile to the culture is maintained by the state, is well understood in international law, and is the chief reason for promoting minority rights.[18] African-Americans, like all nationalities, have throughout their history affirmed a strong desire to maintain their culture in every way except where it was feared that doing so would provoke retaliation from the Anglo-Americans who controlled the apparatus of the state. [19]

More often, the minority is simply forced to find means of accommodating the majority culture while at the same time rejecting it, in order to survive and function in situations where the majority has control and enforces its cultural preferences: in the workplace, in housing, in social services, in educational institutions,and other areas. For instance, many African-Americans provide an official and unofficial name to their children.

QUESTION: What if the individual minority member wants to assimilate, or join the dominant culture?

We should stress that it remains a feature of minority rights that the individual minority member should not be forced to avail him/herself of the rights he/she might bear as a minority individual, and should be regarded as free to assimilate into the dominant culture, if so desired, and to participate in it fully, without discrimination.[20] However, this decision of the individual does not affect the right of the group. The individual is simply deciding to be a part of one group and not the other, or both, if the circumstances permit. Minority rights are not to be taken as enforced ghettoization of minority members.

It should be reiterated that the desirability of assimilating into the dominant culture is often simply due to the dominant culture's power in the society, and the fact that it has refused to share power with the other nationalities (minorities) and has denigrated their culture and traditions. Were the minority to achieve equal status through the exercise of minority rights, then minority traditions, values, standards of beauty, etc. would have equal appeal to that of the majority.

QUESTION: You said earlier that minority rights can mean that minorities have the right to control socio-economic and cultural institutions. Give me an example.

Let's take education. Since *Brown vs. Board of Education* as well as during segregation, African-Americans have been integrated into the Anglo-American education system. In practice this has meant the demise, at a remarkable pace, of colleges which traditionally have served the African-American population.[21] On the other hand, African-American students have not felt at home in Anglo-American-dominated institutions. They have not felt that these institutions adequately represented their history, their interests or their needs. In short, they did not feel these institutions were "theirs," in the same way as Anglo-American students might.[22] Many felt embarrassed by the existence of affirmative action programs, the claimed intention of which was to accelerate their entrance into the Anglo-American institutions and thereby their assimilation into Anglo-American culture, but which often were administered and interpreted in such a manner as to discredit their true capabilities or to catapult them, under intense scrutiny, into a situation of hostile and unfair competition. Applying the minority rights argument, there could be African-American and Anglo-American educational institutions as well as bi-cultural institutions. All would of course be multi-racial.

QUESTION: Does self-determination mean we could control our own schools? Re-establish African-American colleges? That sounds like going back to segregation. We heard "separate but equal" before but it was never equal. Why should we believe in it now?

Yes, self-determination might entail African-American control of college curricula, programs and financing. But this wouldn't be like returning to segregation. For one thing, there would be no restrictions based on race. Those African-Americans who wished to attend Anglo-American or bi-cultural institutions would be free to do so. Anglo-Americans who wished to attend African-American or bi-cultural institutions would also be free to do so. But this time, unlike during either the segregation or the civil rights period, the control of the African-American educational situation would be *in African-American hands*. This would mean, among other things, that African-Americans could decide qualifications for teachers, hiring and firing, curricula, student eligibility and professional licensing standards, disciplinary codes, dress codes, fee scheduling, etc. (albeit with some restrictions resulting from mechanisms which might be put in place for ensuring parity, where required, with multicultural national standards.) However, in general African-American institutions would not be accountable to any other agency or administrative oversight outside of the African-American community.

During the period of segregation, while African-Americans did almost all the administration and teaching, African-Americans, in conjunction with the African-American community, did not establish the subjects or content, nor the priorities, nor were they culturally or politically free to promote their culture and vision of the world and the U.S. in equal-status with Anglo-Americans, or to affirm their cultural or political preferences, thus creating the intellectual and cultural ethos of their institutions. Also, during the period of segregation, African-American institutions did not have the funding to permit them to function on a par with Anglo-American institutions.

QUESTION: How would African-American colleges be in any better financial condition in a situation of self-determination?

Article 27 of the ICCPR, as amplified by Article 1 of the Declaration on the Rights of Persons Belonging to National or Ethnic, Religious and Linguistic Minorities, requires governments to "create conditions" favorable to the preservation and development of minority cultures. In practice this has often meant giving minorities jurisdiction over their own schools. The educational sector has historically[23] been the most common sector for minorities to exercise their cultural rights. The funding of these educational institutions has been a government responsibility, financed by a share of public moneys, i.e. transfer payments in those situations where minorities were not also given the right to raise money in the numerous ways that governments do: by power to tax, by licensing fees, etc. (See, for instance, Articles 41-43 of the Statute of Autonomy of the Basque Country, 1979, in Appendix I.) In Canada, the federal structure and provincial taxation rights thereunder has permitted French Canadians, by means of their control of the Quebec provincial government, to directly control a sector of the taxation rights accorded to Quebec and secure funding for educational institutions and the Desjardin banking movement.

QUESTION: If African-Americans controlled their own educational system, how would this make a difference?

First of all, it would enable African-Americans both to preserve and develop their unique cultural identities by accepting community practices and understandings as normative rather than (at best) "different but all right." On the higher level, this is not just a matter of teaching African-American literature or studying African art. It also permits *the expression of an African-American perspective* on all the various disciplines: history, political science, law, sociology, psychology, economics, anthropology, and so on — in the same way that this naturally occurs in, say, Canadian, Quebecois, French, and British educational institutions. It creates responsiveness not just to the needs but also to the views and practices of the African-American community, seeking to affirm, substantiate and empower these views (both intellectually and in actuality). As such, it would serve as a cornerstone and pillar establishing and ensuring the unique African-American intellectual contribution to global scholarship.

Secondly, it would mean jobs for the community — not just jobs in the present (teaching and administrative positions) but also the guarantee of jobs in the future, for the students coming up, since education as well as professional and other licensing authority could be geared towards meeting community needs.

QUESTION: Since "integration" and the significant movement of whites into traditionally black schools and colleges, many African-Americans have wanted to set up schools to preserve their own culture. But then they thought: what was the use in establishing schools, if non-discrimination meant they were obliged to open their doors to whites, who might come in and take over. Could they have a policy saying no whites were allowed to come?

It isn't a matter of the presence of the whites or any other race, it's a matter of establishing the purpose and curricula of the school in relation to the highest African-American standards and needs. All people should be invited to assist a worthwhile purpose. The curricula and policies would be dominated by universal values as understood by the African-American community, as well as courses specifically geared to meet the needs of the African-American community.

QUESTION: Does African-American control of the educational system mean that kids would be learning Afrocentrism?

What African-American control of African-American education means is just that: control of schools by the African-American community. It's not simply a question of the curriculum, it's a question of the administration, philosophy, world view, etc. It will be the democratic consensus of the community which decides those qualified to determine what goes into the African-American curriculum.

African culture inhabits African-American culture like the sap, the tree. Whether consciously rediscovered, or simply passed on as family practice from one generation to the next it is pervasive throughout African-Americans' daily habits, ways of thought and belief, modes of relating, political and lifestyle preferences, and so on. For generations it has represented their heritage and their aspirations. There is no way for the two to be torn apart. And yet, with the centuries of life in America, the African-Americans have evolved to become a new African people in North America — Africans who are also American, and whose relation with Europe is significantly different from that of African or Asian populations. Who is to say how that identity, given its freedom to develop according to its own tastes and abilities, might evolve?

If the African-American community as a whole wants Afrocentrism, then likely it would play a large role. But there are other elements in the community as well, wanting other things. Undoubtedly Afrocentrism represents yet another rich channel of African culture pouring into the African-American pot. But insofar as Afrocentrism is (self)-consciously imported, insofar as it can be sensed as representing something other than what the people presently are, then it must be recognized as being a part, not the whole of the African-American culture; as feeding into the whole, enriching it, undoubtedly, but not being it. *The whole is what the African-American people are, today, as they stand,* as they remember, as they have forgotten, as they experience subliminally, habitually, and so on. As UNESCO's World Conference on Cultural Policies in Mexico recently declared:

> [Culture] comprises the whole complex of distinctive spiritual, material, intellectual and emotional features that characterize a society or social group. It includes not only the arts and letters, but also modes of life, the fundamental rights of the human being, value systems, traditions and beliefs.[24]

It would be a mistake to assume that African-American control of their own schools would mean that they would have to go out and start behaving in a way that they were not presently behaving. Unless they wanted to. Unless they decided, as a group, to do so. It would be similar to taking all the noteworthy English writers, poets, scholars, musicians and exponents of "high culture," as comprising the whole of English culture. Where, then, would one find steak and kidney pie? Or stiff upper lips?

QUESTION: What could self-determination mean in relation to other jurisdictions such as criminal justice?

It's well known that the United States has the highest incarceration rate in the world in relation to its African-American population — in fact, four times the rate of white-dominated South Africa.[25] Much of African-Americans' disproportionately higher rates of incarceration stem not only from acts deriving from the circumstances of poverty and oppression that they endure, but also from the disproportionate tendency of law enforcement to apprehend, convict, harass, intimidate and scapegoat the African-American community. Much also stems from the exacerbated tensions between law enforcement and the community over time. The introduction of black judges and enforcement personnel has been a largely unsuccessful attempt to mitigate the poor relations existing between the African-American community and the criminal justice system, insofar as such black personnel have not themselves been in control of their working environment, but rather caught up in it like helpless cogs in a machine, forced rather to prove themselves to their working environment (the various peer groups and hierarchies within the criminal justice system) than to their community.

Dr. Roberta Sykes, eloquent spokeswoman for the Black Aboriginal minority of Australia, made the following observation pertinent to police work in her own community, which suffers similarly high rates of incarceration:

> We have to work out methods whereby Blacks can have immediate and profound influence in policy and practice. It is my contention that it does not matter very much what color a police officer is — what matters is who he or she is accountable to.[26]

If African-Americans were enabled to influence the criminal justice system or establish their own criminal justice system insofar as it concerned the African-American community — not just through personnel, hiring, firing and appointments, but through a systematized form of African-American input into criminal law content, policy, behavior codes, sentencing, parole, passage or prioritizing of laws, etc., it is likely that an entirely new relationship between the African-American communities and law enforcement would be achieved. Law enforcement would be seen as it properly should be — as an extension of the community values, needs and understandings, and responsible to it rather than to politicians, absentee property holders or Anglo-American philosophic, socio-economic and political priorities or public opinion. The community would have the freedom to find alternatives to incarceration; to give appropriate consideration to community evaluations of offenders;[27] to give due weight to mitigating socio-economic and cultural factors in relation to crimes and misdemeanors; and to stop harassment by establishing procedures to ensure enforcement responsiveness and responsibility to the community and community evaluation of service and service personnel.

QUESTION: If we want to talk about the African-American community controlling its education and criminal justice systems, etc., don't we have to talk about how we decide what the African-American community wants?

Yes. African-Americans will need to institutionalize a political and democratic means of accessing African-American demands and needs. The main question African-Americans need to politically and democratically determine is whether, as a people, they wish to assimilate, or to be empowered, collectively. Their answer to this question determines the direction that they should follow — civil rights or minority rights.

This could be done by holding some form of referendum for African-American voters only, which might draw on the good offices of the United Nations to provide the required expertise and legitimacy. There are numerous bodies in the international world concerned with the establishment of electoral procedures under a wide variety of circumstances; they would have answers to the numerous technical questions which would arise in that regard. The required expertise is there, if there is the will and desire to access it.

Also, African-Americans need to establish democratic structures or institutions which will provide arenas for policy debates, and the emergence of an African-American-elected leadership responsible to the African-American people.

This may mean establishing a National Council, an African-American Congress, an African-American Assembly or whatever, and demanding its recognition by the government as the only legitimate voice of the African-American people.

QUESTION: What are the advantages of an African-American National Council, Assembly, Congress, or what have you?

It would enable African-Americans to choose their own leadership, which would have to answer first to them. This would encourage the leadership to put forward policies that African-Americans want and need that reflect their history and circumstances. This is particularly important when the federal government puts into place policies that solely or even predominantly affect African-Americans. Rather than consulting with people whom the federal government has decided it is willing to recognize as African-American leaders, the federal government would be encouraged to confer with a body which is directly responsible to the African-American people, and hence responsive to its needs. Because the National Council, etc., would have been democratically chosen by the African-American people and legally recognized as the sole voice of African-Americans, the federal government will be less inclined to behave as if this leadership may or may not (depending on federal government whim or interest) represent the true will of the African-American people. It would be unlike the present situation where individual leaders are summoned for consultation to the White House, and remain just that: individual VIPs — any of whom might be "de-legitimized" simply by failing to receive an invitation next time.

The National Council, or whatever, would provide an apparatus for the African-American people which would enable them to make decisions and institute planning in relation to African-American philosophy and cultural paradigms as it relates to how they see their best interest, as well as how they see the best interest of all, globally as well as nationally.

Further, this authorized representation would counter the present situation where media heroes engage with world leaders on whatever issues may move them (or be mediagenic at the time), representing the authority of the African-American people without having been legitimately given it.

A National Council, once integrated within the governmental structures of the American politico-legal system, would be able to function like another layer of government, regulating and responding to its key population group within the spheres of its own jurisdictions.

QUESTION: What kind of politico-legal system can offer African-Americans these jurisdictions, bearing in mind that the African-American population is not concentrated in one area, but rather is spread out through many states?

True, the African-American population is spread out, but that may prove to be advantageous. For one thing, territorial concentration has a tendency to give rise to movements which seek to establish self-determination through taking over a specific territory, and demanding political independence. This is threatening to both the state and the local non-minority population which may be located within such territories, insofar as it may arouse fears of secession, and dismemberment of the country. No state easily countenances secession, and in any event, African-Americans may not have the relative numbers, power, or desire to move toward taking political control of a specific territory, so long as their survival needs can be better obtained as an integrated part of the country they feel they helped to build.

The international legal norm of minority rights instead suggests the establishment of politico-legal structures *within* the framework of the state, related *specifically* to the use and needs of African-Americans as a dispersed minority. While in practice and in law, territorially-concentrated minorities' needs are more easily facilitated, there are existing and historical precedents for empowering dispersed minorities which could serve as examples for African-Americans. This does not preclude the combination of local territorially-based autonomies with a national politico-legal structure geared towards a dispersed population.

Insofar as each minority situation has its own particular conditions and is advanced or constrained, according to the needs, structures and views of the state with which it is negotiating implementation of its rights, it is unlikely that the model of any other country would be adopted in the United States without substantial revision or embellishment. What is needed at this point is to use these historical models as a means of initiating a discussion of new possibilities.

QUESTION: How would African-Americans go about establishing a National Council?

What is most necessary is widespread recognition of the need and a consequent demand for such a body within the community itself. Ideally, at such time, a non-partisan entity permitting all groups, large and small, to participate, might serve the technical role of establishing the procedures and facilitating the process. While the UN might assist such an entity, and legitimize and provide expertise to the process, insofar as the process must be sufficiently self-developed, the UN, international organizations and African states must plainly see a manifestation of the demand before participating.

QUESTION: What role would the United States government play?

Since any such National Council, Assembly, or what have you, formed at the initiative of the African-American community and suing for government recognition, affects traditional power relations in the state, its recognition could entail constitutional and/or legal changes, bureaucratic changes, changes in the tax structures or transfer payments, according to the powers which might be acceded to it and/or, attendantly, to the African-American community.

At the present time, the United States government has no single, logical, constitutionally-delineated and institutionally-coordinated policy for dealing with its national minorities.[28] Indeed, with the emergence of "rainbows" and "multiculturalism" even within African-American activist organizations themselves, and the failure of the major political parties to raise, let alone deal with, African-American issues, there appears to be a desire, within both the white and black echelons of power, for the existence and problems of African-Americans to be submerged in the generalized distress of what has been termed the American "underclass."

And yet, time is running out. African-American populations dominate major metropolitan areas. Already the decay in

American cities is ominous. Something has to be done, or the good ship U.S.A., punctured by the gaping holes that are its major cities, and ravaged by a major ethnic conflict that could approach third world proportions, will sink. It is in the interest of the country as a whole to solve the problem of African-American inequality. African-American autonomy — which may indeed by the only way this community will be able to develop, insofar as four decades of civil rights have produced neither assimilation nor non-discrimination — is therefore ultimately in the interest of the USA.

Consider the similar situation of majoritarian democracy in South Africa. Will the present South Africa under majority rule be able to satisfy the desire of the Zulu — and indeed, the Afrikaner minority — for protection and maintenance of their unique cultures? Already these groups are demanding minority rights and internal self-determination. If such internationally-recognized rights are not, to some degree, accorded to them, will South Africa be able to achieve the peace required for its economic development?

QUESTION: Why should African-Americans give much value to achieving true democratic participation through democratic pluralism? In most democracies where elections are in place, people can't even be bothered to vote.

The simple attainment of democracy as it concerns African-Americans and as it is reflected in some form of a national council permitting the formulation of policy and election of leaders directly responsible to the African-American community, in and of itself represents an assertion of the right of the African-American community to existence and to socio-economic development as such. It represents a mechanism for encouraging the direction of political power and economic resources into the community. Even should the voting pattern of African-Americans in elections that concerned their community alone subsequently reflect an indifference similar to that of other communities, this would not change the immense impact the very existence of such politico-legal and socio-economic institutions would have in promoting African-American equal-status relations through creating a high degree of political and economic interdependence in place of dependence with the majority community.

QUESTION: Will it be necessary to wage a war of liberation in order for African-Americans to achieve minority rights?

This may not be necessary. We have before us the example

of the restructuring of eastern Europe, where systemic changes too vast to have been contemplated even a year earlier, once initiated, took place swiftly and with little bloodshed. Why? Because the time of these ideas had come. The old order was helpless before them. The agreement on the need for change was general and all-pervasive, and therefore unstoppable. In the case of America, it is clear that the explosive situation caused by the systemically-enforced inequality of African-Americans is reaching the end of its containment. That something *must* be done — something *new*— will become apparent to most. Once this realization becomes pervasive, sufficient numbers of the decision-makers in all communities will be enabled to facilitate the systemic shift to minority rights required to avoid catastrophe.

QUESTION: If self-determination for African-Americans is so beneficial, what can possibly hold it back?

The major questions remain the extent to which the African-American struggle will meet with the good will of the United States ruling circles, and how prepared they are to make sacrifices. The economic capability for it exists in the U.S. — inherent at minimum in the redirection of economic resources already being spent on containment of African-Americans in situations of political and social malaise. The international paradigms are there — paradigms which need not be taken as gospel, but simply as a way of introducing conceptual flexibility, of freeing the mind from the rigidities of past practice and opening up new possibilities.

Again, as Dr. Roberta Sykes noted with regard to her own Black Aboriginal community in Australia:

> Being supportive of self-determination is attitudinal and behavioral, so there is no handbook or set of commandments to make the task easier. At each point along the way, policy makers must ensure that their work is guided by determinations made in the Black community about the Black community's welfare. Anything less is not self-determination, and the principle of self-determination is non-negotiable.[29]

America stands in danger of running aground on its minority problem. If good will cannot be generated from traditional American moral values — the belief in equality, fairness, sharing and justice — then in the end it may come to be realized, willy-nilly, through another no less quintessential American belief — that of enlightened and pragmatic self interest.

1 While the UN Sub-Commission was unable to achieve a consensus on the definition of minority prepared at its request by Mr. Jules Deschênes, his definition suffices for this article: "A group of citizens of a State, constituting a numerical minority and in a non-dominant position in that State, endowed with ethnic, religious or linguistic characteristics which differ from those of the majority of the population, having a sense of solidarity with one another, motivated, if only implicitly, by a collective will to survive and whose aim is to achieve equality with the majority in fact and in law." UN Doc. E/CN.4/Sub.2/1985/Para. 181.

2 *UNPO Monitor*: Draft Summary of the Principle Points Raised at the United Nations Working Group on Indigenous Populations, Day 2, Morning Session, Tuesday, July 25, 1994.

3 Y.N. Kly, *The Anti-Social Contract,* 1987.

4 IHRAAM submitted a lengthy *Communication to the Human Rights Committee,* August 9th, 1993.

5 Cited in Francesco Capotorti, *Study on the Rights of Persons Belonging to Ethnic, Religious and Linguistic Minorities,* United Nations, 1979, p. 8.

6 Richard L. Engstrom and Michael D. Mcdonald, "The Effect of At-Large Versus District Elections on Racial Representation in U.S. Municipalities," in Bernard Grofmann and Arend Lijphart, eds., *Electoral Laws and Their Political Consequences,* 1986, p. 116.

7 Cynthia H. Enloe, "Internal Colonialism, Federalism and Alternative State Development Strategies," *Publius: The Journal of Federalism,* Vol. vii, Fall 1977, p. 150.

8 Derrick Bell, *Race, Racism and American Law,* 1969.

9 An analysis of the current U.S. judicial response to discrimination is provided in this book, in the article "Non-Discrimination in U.S. Courts: A Non-Solution?" by Aviam Soifer.

10 See Kenneth McRae, *Conflict and Compromise in Multilingual Societies: Switzerland,* 1983.

11 See Eric A. Nordlinger, *Conflict Regulation in Divided Societies,* Occasional Papers in International Affairs, Harvard University, January 1972.

12 Ian Brownlie, "The Rights of Peoples in Modern International Law," in James Crawford, ed., *The Rights of Peoples,* 1988, p. 5-6.

13 See keynote address, "African-Americans and the Right to Self-Determination, " *Proceedings of the Hamline Conference on African-Americans and the Rights to Self-Determination,* herein.

14 For an indication of the continuing importance of this view, see Final Report of the Martin Ennals Symposium on Self-Determination, March 4-6, 1993, International Alert, London, 1993.

15 See submission by the French government, drafting process of the Declaration on Minorities.

16 See Lorenzo Turner, *Africanisms in the Gullah Dialect,* 1969 reproduction of 1949 edition.

17 See UNESCO, Final Report of the World Conference on Cultural Policies, Mexico City, 26 July-6 August 1982, p. 41.

18 Cited in Francesco Capotorti, *supra,* note 5, p. 8. The Yugoslav

Government stated that it "wishes to underscore its conviction that the so-called 'subjective factor' is in many aspects dependent on the political stereotypes and the cultural and social circumstances prevailing in the individual social communities in which the members of minorities live and work. Historical experiences have shown that the 'indifference' of the members of minorities towards their national origin, position and rights are, as a rule, the consequence of the social and other circumstances in which they live. In societies with a prevailing negative attitude of the 'majority' towards the 'minority,' the members of the minorities are fearful that any declaration of one's national, ethnic, cultural and other characteristics might be interpreted as a so-called 'civil disloyalty' on the part of the minority concerned. Therefore, it would be inappropriate to ascribe too much importance to the need of a "declaration of desire" by the members of any minority in order to preserve their own national, ethnic, cultural and other features, and to manifest their awareness of their affiliation to a particular minority, especially in the case of a minority which has for decades been subjected to the pressures of systematic assimilation and de-nationalization."

19 See B.T. Warington's *Five Finger, One Hand Solution.*

20 See Article 3 of the UN Declaration on Minorities.

21 Serena L. Swaggers and H. Larry Winecoff, "Changing Profiles of Black Institutions of Higher Learning: A Study of Fourteen Private, Historically Black Institutions in the Southeast," as cited in IHRAAM Newsletter, Vol. 2, No. 3.

22 See Andrew Hacker, *Two Nations: Black and White, Separate, Hostile, Unequal,* 1992.

23 The Permanent Court of International Justice rendered an advisory opinion affirming this right as early as 1935. See Advisory Opinion of 6 April 1935 on *Minority Schools in Albania,* P.C.I.J., Ser. A/B, No. 64, 17.

24 Quoted by Anders Arfwedson, Introduction to *Information Kit on the 1994 Decade Theme: 'Culture and Development,.'* Paris, UNESCO, 1994.

25 "U.S. Imprisons Black Men at 4 Times S. Africa's Rate," *Los Angeles Times,* January 3, 1991.

26 Roberta B. Sykes, "Self-Determination: Implications for Criminal Justice Policy Makers," Kayleen M. Hazlehurst, ed., *Justice Programs for Aboriginal and Other Indigenous Communities,* Australian Institute of Criminology, Seminar Proceedings, No. 7, p. 25.

27 In this instance, reference is made to cases where offenders seeking parole (or indeed, being tried) are unable to benefit from the high standing they may enjoy within their community, as attested to by their local religious, educational or other community leaders, insofar as this testimony is not given the credence which might adhere to similar testimony given by a body of Anglo-American community figures.

28 See Y.N. Kly, *International Law and the Black Minority in the U.S.,* 1990 (third edition).

29 See Sykes, *supra,* note 14, p. 28.

*What States Can Do to Protect Minorities**

Asbjørn Eide

At the 1993 meeting of the UN Sub-Commission on the Prevention of Discrimination and Protection of Minorities, the UN's Special Rapporteur on Minorities, Asbjørn Eide, submitted a set of recommendations on the implementation of the UN Declaration on the Rights of Persons Belonging to National or Ethnic, Religious and Linguistic Minorities. *This set of comprehensive and substantial recommendations represented three years of research, including consultation with Sub-Commission members, with outside experts including IHRAAM delegates in Geneva, and with states worldwide by means of a questionnaire concerning treatment of domestic minorities.*

Mr. Eide's recommendations on state measures for resolving minorities' problems again manifests the unique capacity of those working at the UN to formulate general principles and universal goals, then provide an array of systemic policy options whereby same might be achieved, thereby, at the international level, informing, legitimizing and substantiating domestic human rights efforts.

(a) General

1 The state should be the common home for all parts of its resident populations under conditions of equality, with separate group identities being preserved for those who want it under conditions making it possible to develop those identities. Neither majorities nor minorities should be entitled to assert their identity in ways that deny the possibility for others to do the same, or that lead to

* Excerpted from Asbjørn Eide, "Possible Ways and Means of Facilitating the Peaceful and Constructive Solution of Problems Involving MInorities," UN Doc. E/CN.4/Sub. 2/1993/34.

discrimination against others in the common domain. A primary role of any state is to facilitate the equitable sharing of the economic wealth and social benefits of the nation as a whole. Priority in minority protection should be given to members of groups that are truly vulnerable and subject to discrimination and marginalization by the majority.

2 Specific guidelines for the recommendations can be derived from a combined use of the provisions of the *International Conventon on the Elimination of All Forms of Racial Discrimination* and of the *Declaration on the Rights of Persons Belonging to National or Ethnic, Religious and Linguistic Minorities*. Together, these instruments should be held to constitute minimum rules for peaceful coexistence and constructive cooperation among members of different ethnic, religious and linguistic groups inside states, to be supplemented by the provisions of the *Declaration on the Rights of Indigenous Peoples*, when the latter is adopted.

3 There is a necessity, in all states, to have a common domain where everyone is treated on a basis of equality, based on norms which are impersonal in nature and applied in an impartial way. This will unavoidably imply some degree of integration. This necessity arises from obligations undertaken by states under the international human rights conventions and is required, *inter alia*, for the state to be able to ensure equality and non-discrimination in the enjoyment of human rights. However, the integration should be developed on a basis of equality, with all groups contributing their own values and cultures to shape the common domain where their members all interact.

(b) Measures to Be Taken at the National Level

4 For the long-term prevention of ethnic or religious hatred and intolerance, measures should be taken to ensure that the substantive content of childhood and adult education is fully in line with the requirements of the *Universal Declaration of Human Rights*, Article 26.2, the *Convention on the Rights of the Child*, Article 29, (1) (b, c and d), and the *International Convention on the Elimination of All Forms of Racial Discrimination*, Article 7. Human rights education should be made a core curriculum subject in universal primary education.

5 Group conflicts often give rise to propaganda and to the emergence of organizations that attempt to justify discrimination based either on notions of racial superiority or the incompatibility of cultures or on other grounds. States should therefore take all necessary steps to implement Article 4 of the *International Convention on the Elimination of All Forms of Racial Discrimination* (ICERD), which prohibits the dissemination of ideas based on racial superiority or hatred, incitement to racial and ethnic discrimination, and all acts of violence or incitement to such acts against any race or group of people of another color or ethnic origin, and to prohibit organizations based on such ideas, as mentioned in Article 4.

6 States should take all necessary steps to ensure that perpetrators of acts of ethnic and religious violence are quickly apprehended and prosecuted under conditions of fair trial. Impunity for instigators and perpetrators of group violence, whether members of majorities or of minorities, leads to an escalation of conflict. In situations of extreme instability, however, where the state is unable to apprehend the perpetrators, the international community should therefore have a supplementary role. Outside states should, at the least, prohibit their citizens from participating in violent group conflicts inside other states or inciting violence there, and should effectively prosecute those who violate such prohibitions.

7 It is recommended that national forums (councils and commissions) be set up to propose, for the national legislature and administration, appropriate guidelines for the combined implementation of ICERD and the 1992 Declaration on Minorities, taking into account the particular situations in the country concerned. The different ethnic, religious and linguistic groups existing in the country, whether minorities or majorities, should be represented in such national forums.

Education, language and culture

8 Minorities should have the right to education in their own language. While the need is recognized for one or more official languages for state-wide communication, states should allow for, and take special measures to ensure, education in and the use of regional and minority languages,

as appropriate. Majorities and minorities in states not members of the Council of Europe might find it useful for this purpose to seek inspiration from the European Charter on Regional and Minority Languages.

9 Minorities should receive education about their own culture and also about the culture of other groups in society, majority or minority.

10 The curricula in all states should teach tolerance of all groups.

11 Majority groups should learn about the cultures of minority groups in ways which make it possible for them to appreciate those cultures as an enrichment to society as a whole.

12 Members of different groups should enjoy the right to participate, on the basis of their own culture and language, in the cultural life of the community, to produce and enjoy arts and science, to protect their cultural heritage and traditions, to own their own media and other means of communication and to have access on a basis of equality to state-owned or publicly controlled media.

Civil rights

13 The civil rights of members of minorities, as of majorities, should be given full and equal protection. Visible, impartial and effective implementation of national legislation in this field should be ensured to all. Adequate training should be given to law-enforcement officials and others who deal directly with the public.

14 Members of different groups should enjoy economic and social rights on a basis of equality. In those situations where members of particular minorities are economically in a weaker position than members of majorities, measures of affirmative action should be adopted on a transitional basis to redress the inequality. In that respect, specific policies should be formulated in cooperation with members of vulnerable groups to achieve equality of opportunity and access.

15 Ongoing, systematic monitoring of the situation of vulnerable groups should be established through periodic

sampling and collection of statistical information disaggregated by racial or ethnic group, particularly with respect to such fundamental economic and social indicators as infant mortality rates, life expectancy, literacy, level of educational attainment and average disposable income.

16 Members of the different ethnic, religious and linguistic groups should on a basis of equality participate in, contribute to and benefit from the right to development. Consequently, development policies should be conducted in ways that decrease the disparities that might exist between different groups. Groups living compactly together should always be fully consulted with regard to development projects affecting the regions in which they live.

Effective political participation

17 While it is essential that members of different groups, majority and minority, be given opportunities for effective participation in the political organs of society in ways that avoid obstructure of necessary decision-making, no single formula exists that is appropriate to all minority situations. The basic requirement is that everyone shall have the right and opportunity, without discrimination, to take part in the conduct of public affairs. To avoid this leading to majoritarian neglect of the concerns of minorities, or to a veto by minorities in areas where it would not be justified, various possibilities exist. It is recommended that states and minorities explore the following options, as appropriate to their particular situation:

(a) Advisory and decision-making bodies in which minorities are represented, in particular with regard to education, culture and religion.

(b) Elected bodies and assemblies ('parliaments') of national or ethnic, religious and linguistic minorities.

(c) Self-administration (functional autonomy, cultural autonomy) on a non-territorial basis by a minority of matters which are essential to its particular identity, such as the development of its language or its religious rites.

(d) Decentralized or local forms of government or autonomous arrangements on a territorial and democratic basis, including consultative, legislative and executive bodies chosen through free and periodic elections without discrimination.

(e) Special measures to ensure minority representation in the legislature and other elected bodies of the national society, even where their numerical strength is too small to have representation under normal conditions. In proportional electoral systems minimum thresholds for representation might be waived where minorities are concerned.

Constitutional arrangements

18 Some of the above arrangements should be incorporated into the constitution of the country concerned, in particular where autonomy or another form of pluralism on the basis of territorial subdivision is concerned.

19 It should be recognized, however, that group relations change over time and need different responses at different times. It is therefore necessary to ensure flexibility to accommodate the changing relations in the most constructive way possible.

Duties to society

20 Members of minorities should recognize and respect their duties to the society at large. The 1992 Declaration on Minorities makes it clear, in Article 8, para. 4, that it cannot be construed as permitting any activity contrary to the purposes and principles of the United Nations, including the sovereign equality, territorial integrity and political independence of states. Members of minorities should also strictly abide by the prohibition of propaganda and of organizations that seek to justify or promote racial or ethnic hatred, and abstain from incitement to acts of violence against members of other groups. No external support should be given, through states or private organizations, to

groups that engage in violence against other racial and ethnic groups.

Recourse and conciliation machineries

21 Everyone, including members of minorities, has the right of effective remedy by the competent national tribunals for acts violating their rights granted by the constitution or law. Normal legal procedures are often slow and costly, and are not always suited to conflict resolution. It is therefore recommended that states establish, in addition to courts and tribunals, other mechanisms, such as a special ombudsman against ethnic discrimination (now existing in Sweden), commissions on racial and ethnic reconciliation, which exist in several countries, or human rights committees that are required as one of their tasks to ensure equality and conditions for the promotion of separate identity.

22 In times of major political, constitutional or institutional change, pre-existing arrangements applying to nationalities and minorities, such as autonomy structures, should not be immediately demolished even if incompatible with the new structures, but a transition period should be provided to enable the adoption of confidence-building measures whereby the groups concerned can adapt to the new situation without loss of identity or acquired rights.

23 Practices of 'ethnic cleansing' must be considered illegal and should not be permitted under any circumstance. Populations which have been forced to flee during periods of ethnic conflict should be entitled to return under conditions of safety and to receive adequate compensation for losses to which they have been subjected.

24 State-sponsored mass population transfers give rise to numerous human rights problems and negatively affect group relations. Such transfers should never be undertaken except for short-term emergency purposes, and then only provided arrangements are made for an early return of the population transferred.

Democratic Pluralism, the Right to Remedy, and National Minorities

Y. N. Kly

Majoritarian Democracy in Multi-national States

Multi-national states which base their electoral processes on a simple majority / "one man, one vote" principle, and which have no official political or constitutional-legal structures established with the intent of providing for political empowerment of minorities, are commonly referred to as majoritarian democracies. Often the majoritarian form of democracy facilitates the domination of majority ethny's socio-political and economic interests by guaranteeing its control over the apparatus of the state through its numerical domination of the electoral process. Equally, it promotes the political submergence of the minorities by preventing them from exercising any effective levers (constitutionally or legally established socio-political institutions) to empower their special perspectives, needs and interests.

Where the majoritarian democratic process and structures have evolved within a historical context of minority domination, exploitation, and even gross human rights violation, they are likely to further entrench patterns of minority dominance and exploitation, rather than to provide effective political recourse to remedy past injustices and exploitation. In such a system, even though it is ostensibly democratic, a minority would be discouraged from and have no officially provided apparatus for holding elections for its own leadership and thus permitting democratic expression of its own particular interests and needs, qua minority.[1]

The United States provides a particularly striking example of this problematic, as a majoritarian democracy whose culture and politico-economic institutions evolved from and act to preserve a historical relationship wherein Anglo-American domination of the African-American minority was legally, socially, economically and culturally (through official policies of enslavement, segregation and forced assimilation) in widespread practice.[2] While the African-Americans' developmental crisis engendered by the enslavement of their ancestors has been widely discussed, in particular by popular writers such as Harold Cruise in *The Crisis of the Negro Intellectual*,[3] C. J. Woodson in *The Miseducation of the Negro*,[4] Derrick Bell in *And We Are Not Yet Saved*,[5] and Andrew Hacker in *Two Nations: Black and White, Separate, Hostile, Unequal*,[6] there is a widespread failure to examine the *post-slavery, post-segregation* politico-structural causes of the continuing socio-economic crises in African-American communities. The problem is not framed within its full context, which is: what happens to a minority when an ethnic majority, having historically dominated it through state policy (slavery, segregation) for the purpose of exploition, ostensibly transforms the state's governmental system to repudiate slavery and segregation, yet is unable or unwilling to institutionally recognize the national minority's collective existence, culture or special developmental needs, and seeks instead to force the minority to assimilate as a devalued and exploitable sector of the majority.

Insofar as the multi-national state fails to provide politico-legal structures recognizing the existence and furthering the development of national minorities, it necessarily promotes the political and cultural assimilation of national minorities into an inferior class or caste of the majority ethny. This is true if for no other reason than that the forced assimilation process itself promotes and ensures majority domination. The majority ethny is advantaged by being enabled to function naturally within its own culture, produced by its own values, circumstances, needs and history, and to promote these as universal and applicable to all.

Insofar as the system is not structurally orientated to giving equal value to minority culture, this ensures that minority differences will be devalued and negatively portrayed. Equally important is the fact that the ability of national minority individuals to function within the mainstream may be handicapped by numerous factors, such as ignorance of certain of its norms, aversion to others, apprehension of implicit disparagements which are not (consciously) apparent to members of the majority, etc. In addition, the majority culture frequently has content which may be antipathetic, exploitative and socially destructive to the minority community, insofar as this culture has evolved from a historical relation which has consistently devalued the minority and produced or permitted exploitation and gross violations of the minority's human rights.

Majority individuals are relatively advantaged by functioning in such a majoritarian democracy, and minority individuals concomitantly penalized. In the competitive process for socio-economic benefits which is governed by a wide range of implicit socio-cultural preferences, processes, nuances and attitudes, the relative advantages and privileges of majority individuals are assured. Focusing only on the results of this unequal competition, e.g. the low standing of minority members in a host of social benefit indicators, such as income levels, educational levels, professional standings, etc., and then attempting to improve the numbers ratio solely by affirmative action does not speak to the structural and systemic causes. Rather, it facilitates the operation of these politico-structural causes of minority inequality by leaving them obscure and unchallenged.

In states like the U.S., majority democracy is not only ineffective in providing the institutions required by national minorities to meet their special needs; it is actually a cause of the national minority's difficulties: disproportionate involvement with the criminal justice systems, the social welfare systems, as well as with health and family welfare services.[7] When the lack of minority political institutions suitable to meet minority special needs itself causes unequal minority economic, social and political development in relation to the majority, a vicious cycle leading to developmental retardation is created. This in turn is used to further justify and empower majoritarian democracy and its companion, forced political and cultural assimilation (ethnocide)[8] by seeming to substantiate the superiority of majority culture and the appearance of incompetence in the minority.

Forced political and cultural assimilation inescapably produces negative attitudes towards the culture which is being abandoned, insofar as that culture's (or those peoples') supposed inferiority serves as part of the justification for requiring assimilation. In a system such as that of the U.S., African-Americans are assimilated into Anglo-American culture as black Anglo-Saxonized Americans, or more perniciously, as the so-called American "underclass" without their conceptual awareness of or democratic collective consent to this process of ethnocide or involuntary non-cognitive assimilation. In the example of the U.S., we see that while some aspects of African-American culture are promoted as a valued aspect of American culture, paradoxically the status of African-Americans themselves remains economically, socially and politically devalued, and that part of their unofficial culture which is less assimilable grows increasingly hostile to that of the majority — as do those individuals who are less willing or able to assimilate, and are thereby denied access to social benefits.

Despite the lessons of history, some majority ethnies continue to hope national minorities will voluntarily accept their domination, with the good will delusion that such willing acceptance will lead to the solution of all minority problems insofar as the minority will become the same as the majority. History provides us with many examples where such delusions have led instead to our most bitter, intransigent and violent conflicts: the Dalits and Kashmiris in India, the Irish Catholics and the English, the Indonesians and East Timorese, etc. For the most powerful states, the bottom line may take longer, but it eventually arrives. The growing cancer eventually leads to effective treatment or death.

Minority Leadership in Majoritarian States

Minority leadership in majoritarian states illustrates the ramifications of a systemic structure of majority dominance, not merely through the manner in which it achieves its eminence, but also in the kind of leadership created, and the role it is expected to pursue. Successful domination requires a generalized politic of domination, and does not need creative or entrepreneurial talent from the minority side, but rather managerial talent which has the inclination to understand and the ability to implement the system's policies of assimilation, as well as assure the cooperation of the minority population. Economic and social upward mobility in such a society will be implicitly defined and instituted so that the right type of minority individuals achieve leadership roles, thereby furthering the process of ethnocide. For example, the education curricula in U.S. schools often plays the dual role of Anglo-Saxonizing as well as educating the African-American community, thus those employed in school leadership must be amenable to this mission. Unfortunately, the economic, social, psychological and political growth and wellbeing of the minority population requires just the opposite: a democratic, responsive leadership chosen through elections; a leadership that is creative, entrepreneurial, and dedicated to minority needs (albeit with appropriate consideration to the needs of the state and the global village as well.)

The majoritarian system's electoral process, however, animates a minority leadership whose primary interest and talent is in assimilating the minority by holding it in a position of political and economic dependency on the majority ethny. In the U.S., this is usually achieved by tying African-American leadership to a political party or institution whose essential principles and program is determined by the dominant (Anglo-American) group,[9] so that it will have no other democratic options but to voluntarily accept the program and objectives of the majority, hoping only to get some plank or other of its own on the majority's platform -- a hope which in many electoral years fails altogether. Granted there may be occasional reflection of a minority issue, but this only serves to enable better management of what is essentially the majority interest. Such a system fails to meet the educational, social, economic or political special needs of the minority population, not because they do not wish to be educated, to participate democratically, to enjoy political leadership, to have employment, health care, and so on, but because the hidden political priority is on assimilation, centralization of political power in the hands of the dominant group, and ethnocide. All other areas of concern (education, social welfare, crime prevention, etc.) are unhesitatingly compromised to conform socio-economic policies to this prime objective.

Today minorities in majoritarian states deeply involved in identity and developmental crises often have their (empowered) leadership selected through majority ethny-controlled institutions or political processes which feel obliged to have minorities represented and so place minority individuals in the majority-controlled systems rather than enabling those minorities to represent themselves.) In such instances, these sprinklings of minority personnel serve as conveyers and enforcers of majority interest to the minority community. Managers or "marionettes" rather than "tokens" would be an appropriate appellation for such leaders. Sometimes it is even the majority-controlled media which, by focusing on mediagenic individuals, not only chooses minority leadership, but also actually prolongs their political longevity. Such leadership therefore is naturally unable to truly work towards achieving the interests of the people it is said, when convenient, to represent, but rather is put in a position where it is required to represent majority interest and to represent minority interest only insofar as it can be made to coincide with majority interest.

Frequently elements of non-assimilationist minority leadership establish themselves by seeking to defend minority interest in terms unacceptable to the majority. Such leaders are typically exposed to public excoriation by the majority media, and cold-shouldered by that sector of minority leadership which has been accorded majority approval.[10] While this excoriation seeks to ensure such leaders' separation from acceptable minority leadership, in actuality majority hostility may enhance their credibility with the grass roots of the oppressed national minority itself. This in turn perpetuates a confrontational rather than a developmental dynamic, insofar as such a leadership tends to depend to a high degree upon charisma and rhetoric, rather than on any particular expertise related to socio-economic and cultural development. Such expertise as exists within the minority community is typically siphoned into the service of the majority institutions. Such exertise as remains available to promote minority interest in an equal-status integrationist manner rather than accepting assimilation, is handicapped by being unable to draw upon systemic resources to legitimize and finance its policies, platforms, proposed developmental initiatives, etc.

All this means that a majoritarian state creates conditions for confrontation instead of cooperation; for self-defense, rather than mutual development; for resistance, rather than peace, etc., which often is acceptable to the majority ethny due to its historically-evolved belief that its superiority over the minority race is so immense in all areas that meaningful confrontation is impossible to imagine.

The Identity Crisis of Minorities in Majoritarian Democracies

The identity and developmental crises of national minorities in majoritarian multi-national states are perpetuated by the fact that the national minority as well as the majority are educated to identify with the historically-evolved norms, values and majority rule concepts which result from the negation of minority culture and institutional needs. Insofar as the operation and premises of majority democracy as practiced in states like the U.S. discourage national minorities from developing institutions unique to their special needs, circumstances, mentality, lifestyles, values, etc. which would encourage a strong sense of their own (as opposed to the majority's) cultural identity, such systems institutionalize a rejection or devaluation of minority culture to both the majority and the minority. This further disempowers unique cultural and social controls and developmental incentives within the minority culture which would otherwise serve to provide a coherent force and framework for socio-economic equal-status development (interdependence). Systemic discrimination against minorities' cultural differences leads to a situation of institutional and individual attitudinal discrimination against the minority individuals as well.

The lack of a dialogue on the basic premises of majority democracy and lack of political empowerment as it relates to minority well-being encourages psycho-sociological explanations of socio-economic and criminal justice problems. This permits the majority to portray minority cultural differences as a pathological deviation from majority norms and the cause of its disproportionate share of economic and social problems. This diabolic method of blaming the victims while at the same time denying them the fundamental human right to be different (i.e. human dignity) is probably, in the U.S., a pathological carry-over from the institutions of the Anglo-Americans evolved during the period of enslavement, when it was necessary to assume that African-Americans were not human beings, had no dignity and no right to be anything other than what Anglo-Americans felt they were, with no right to a name different from that of their torturers, etc.

Prolonged and unmitigated exposure to the operation of majority democracy and systemic discrimination against minority differences produces a problematic of the minority's self-devaluation. Its own negation of its collective identity in relation to demands on state policies and political organization further discourages the creation of effective institutions to meet unique needs.[11] For example, until recently, even the most nationalist of African-American movements or organizations did not identify with a struggle for *African-American* self-determination — although movements of traditional "*black* nationalism" always existed. The problem was that "black nationalists" recognized and affirmed their African roots while ignoring or devaluing their American or southern roots (i.e. the initial convergence and cultural consolidation over time of the enslaved Africans in the American South). The "black nationalist" ideal was to identify with all blacks simply because they were black: Ethiopian, Ghanaian, Jamaican, Dalit, what have you, thus avoiding the necessity of having to grapple with the problematic of African-American identity and equal-status development in America.

By falling under the sway of any one group or nation, the black nationalist ended up serving its interest in much the same manner that the assimilationist was led to serve the Anglo-American interest — albeit less damaging and wastefully so, insofar as "black" interest (i.e. South African, Ghanaian, Pan-African interest) better coincides with African-American interest. Similar to those who are willing to be identified as a less valuable part of the Anglo-majority ethny, they too seemed unable to distinguish and promote the African-American nation they represented, as an entity in itself, different and separate from all others (albeit tied to Africa by history and culture). An inappropriate application of the racism paradigm borrowed from the American experience made these very real ties more affective than functional. The result was that black nationalists carried into their struggle the insupportable burden or contradiction of unconsciously reflecting majoritarian policy by devaluing themselves as an African-American collective entity, and failing, thereby, to pursue their own interest.

African-Americans subjective negation of identity adds to Anglo-American efforts at ethnocide, prolonging their entrapment (formally or institutionally) in a majoritarian state wherein they are unable to assert themselves as minority nations. It assures that their political struggle will neither appropriately address their collectiveneeds, or seek appropriate (equal status) cooperation with all other groups. Some proponents of black nationalism avoid meaningful political conflict with the imposed African-American leadership in their communities because they too are black, although such imposed leaders may represent only the program and interest of the Anglo-American majority. In so doing, they opt to fight for the black man's control of the institutions of the world, but not those in the African-American communities; to participate unequivocally in the liberation struggles of South Africans without demanding a commitment to their own self-determination in return; to be totally deprived of any possibility of systemic rewards by the majoritarian state, while nonetheless adhering to its law, its criminal justice, taxation, immigration, social service, etc. systems without demanding structural changes to meet African-American needs and world view. The saddest tragedy this poses for a resource-poor minority population is in the enormous amounts of righteous energy, material resources and goodwill wasted.

Minority Self-Recognition: Transcending Domestic Parameters

Due to the contradictions that often exist between historically evolved institutions on the one hand and minority rights on the other, minorities entrapped without recognition in multi-national states seem to have little choice but to simultaneously address their appeal for recognition not only to their governments, but also to the international community (the United Nations). The simple act of petitioning the international community by a minority which has been subjected to tactics of forced assimilation, may be its first cognitive and political conceptualization, and acceptance of itself as a people with the right to be different and also equal. It is a first declaration to the minority members themselves and to the government that, in keeping with its legal emancipation, the minority has come to fully recognize its own inherent human rights, and no longer wishes to be politically, socially or economically a subservient sub-group belonging to the majority ethny — that it now seeks a new social contract.[12] Apparently aboriginal minorities in countries like Canada have reached this stage. Canadian governmental recognition of this possibility can be seen in Meech Lake, the Manitoba Inquiry, the Innuit settlement, the Lubicon negotiations, and the numerous processes towards self-government which have continued despite the recently failed Charlottetown Accord, etc.

Today for national minorities, the use of international institutions to achieve relief from the shortcomings of majority democracy in multi-national states seems necessary, even if the United Nations or international organization is only to act as an honest broker (providing neutral conflict resolution concepts, a neutral situation analysis and frame of reference, legitimization of complaints and/or good offices) to the disputants.[13] In most cases of groups seeking minority rights, going to the UN becomes a more effective way of reaching the decision-makers (the government) of the state in which the minority lives; of giving a political voice to different social forces; of mobilizing minority, majority and other socio-political forces for change; of calling minority attention to and circumventing undemocratic and imposed tokenist systems of leadership whose chief responsibility is only to the interest of the majority ethny; and of providing the minority and the majority with a broader and more suitable conceptual framework for decision-making by exposing the society to cross-cultural and international minority rights concepts for conflict resolution. It is not without reason that the indigenous Canadians, who have recently achieved official recognition of their right to self government, or the Europeans of Zimbabwe and South Africa, found and find it desirable, if not necessary, to call upon the UN and its human rights instruments for minority rights protection.

International Law, Minority Rights and Pluralism

International law has adopted a two-pronged course in relation to assuring minority rights: that of non-discrimination, and that of positive action,[14] which may include both special measures and special rights. The concept of non-discrimination has traditionally been understood within the context of the right of individuals to equality before the law (i.e. the same treatment) while the concept of positive action emphasizes the rights of the minority as a collective to treatment that guarantees equality in fact as well as in law. It recognizes that, in order for the minority to approximate the political and socio-economic advantages taken for granted by the majority, special measures (e.g. employment or educational quotas, etc.) and special rights may be necessary in order to achieve nondiscrimination. Special rights may consist of rights such as the right to politico-legal and socio-economic institutions, taxation rights, right to proportionality in the federal civil service and other public spheres, land rights, monetary compensation, control over community social, legal or educational services, and so on. In short, this interpretation understands minority rights to be a necessary aspect of the universally accepted concept of nondiscrimination, particularly as it concerns the fundamental human right to be different.

International human rights law seeks to protect national minorities by promoting pluralism in multi-national states (the creation of legal and political instrumentality and institutions that can provide for a functional distinction between the interests of the minority and that of the majority, so that minority as well as majority needs can be appropriately addressed within the context of the democratic processes, and minority as well as majority socio-political and economic equal status development can occur). It does this with the understanding that granting the possibility for minority equal status development and need fulfillment within the structure of a single multi-national state lessens the prospects for unmanageable conflict (secession, armed liberation movements, etc.

The right of national minorities to be different and equal, to sufficient self-determination for the purpose of development, etc. may require a socio-political and economic restructuring of majoritarian states that will permit the minorities a proportionate control over appropriate state resources necessary for their material, intellectual and cultural development, thereby enabling them to vie in fair competition with the majority ethny in the private sector. In situations where state policies of nondiscrimination have proved to be inadequate to redress the destruction and arrested development within minority communities caused by historic policies of systemic discrimination, such as the past official policies of slavery, segregation, ethnocide or genocide, the existing reality necessitates that *the right to be different and equal become a prerequisite for equal status development.*

Many international legal scholars have called attention to the complex problematic of national minorities in multi-national states who wish to achieve recognition as an equal partner to the majority ethny by exercising some degree of autonomy.[15]

Also, many have referred to conflict resolution in the multinational state in the context of the need for consociated democracy[16] — a system whereby all national minorities in a state are guaranteed a reasonable degree of influence in the political system to ensure the fairest possible distribution of resources. Toward this goal, appropriate forms of autonomy should be considered as forms of consociated democracy as well as measures to end discrimination. Consociated democracy is viewed as an alternative to majoritarian democracy wherein the individual citizens operating in political coalitions are alone the most important political unit, and political legitimacy is won from the support of the majority of individual citizens. *A consociated democratic system guarantees that political decisions receive an appropriate input from representatives of the different national minorities through the institutionalization of appropriate special rights. It requires that political leaders of the majority and minorities collaborate and recognize the right of each group to work for its own interests as well as that of the state and society as a whole. It may include varying degrees of internal self-determination (i.e. short of secession), wherein minority groups are empowered to respond to issues and make decisions which affect their lives in a variety of jurisdictions, such as education, the criminal justice system, the social services, and culture, to name only a few.* This collective empowerment may be based on some form of territorial or local autonomy, or in the case of dispersed minorities, control over appropriate institutions may provide the minority with the ability to process group interests, needs and demands.

International human rights law, by promoting institutions that would preclude minorities' exploitation and domination, encourages the operation of natural law towards multi-cultural unity, peace and equality by removing the politico-legal structures that necessitate confrontation. History demonstrates that national minorities are much more likely to integrate — i.e. be incorporated into the structures of the state if by so doing they are not forced to surrender their identity, and if they feel it is in their interest to do so. In effect, through the implementation of appropriate special rights, natural law is given free rein to create conditions of real and natural forms of consociated or pluralistic socio-political and economic unity through increased interdependence within multi-national states.

However, minority rights only provides a feasible conceptual framework for minority problem solving; the framework alone does not solve these problems. The bottom line is good will, mutual acceptance of differences (that is, the realization that one can be both different and equal, both appropriately autonomous and politically united, both culturally distinct and culturally similar or the same, etc.), institutionalization and acceptance of equal status, and willingness to share power and resources. The absence of any of these attributes means the maintenance by force or coercion of a contradictory, destructive and eventually dysfunctional system which animates unmanageable conflict, and may lead to the eventual break-up of the multi-national state and decades of bitter inter-group relations. The pluralistic or consociated approach applies social contract theory to the collective or ethnic level, by reminding us that the multi-national state should exist for the well-being of the nations composing it, just as Rousseau's nation-state existed for the well-being of its individual citizens.

International Law and the Right to Remedy

Varying degrees of special measures and special rights granted to national minorities can be viewed in appropriate cases as mandated by the right to remedy in international law, and as being or including reparation for past damages. In international law, the right to remedy is well established.[17] As noted by UN Special Rapporteur Theo van Boven, "Under international law, the violation of any human right gives rise to a right of reparation for the victim."[18] Concerning this fundamental international legal principle of the special right to remedy for victims of breaches of international obligation, the Permanent Court of Inter-national Justice ruled in the Chorzow Factory (indemnity) Case:

> It is a principle of international law, and even a general conception of law, that any breach of an engagement invokes an obligation to make reparation... reparation is the indispensable complement of a failure to apply a convention, and there is no necessity for this to be stated in the convention itself.[19]

Commenting on state responsibility, UN Special Rapporteur Theo van Boven writes:

> In international law State responsibility arises from an internationally wrongful act of a State. The elements of such internationally wrongful act are: (a) conduct consisting of an action or omission that is attributable to the State under international law, and (b) conduct that constitutes a breach of an international obligation of the State... With regard to

> the international law of human rights, the issue of State responsibility comes into play when a State is in breach of the obligation to respect internationally recognized human rights. Such obligation has its legal basis in international agreements, in particular international human rights treaties, and/or in customary international law, in particular those norms of customary international law which have a peremptory character (*jus cogens*). It is generally accepted by authoritative opinion that States do not only have the duty to *respect* internationally recognized human rights but also the duty to *ensure* these rights...[20]

On the question of whether the internationally accepted obligation to remedy is applicable to damages suffered by minorities due to past gross violation of human rights, Theo van Boven notes:

> It cannot be denied that both individuals and collectivities are often victimized as a result of gross violations of human rights... it is therefore necessary that, in addition to individual means of reparation, adequate provision be made to entitle groups of victims or victimized communities to present collective claims for damages and to receive collective reparation accordingly.[21]

Sub-Commission resolution 1988/11 of 1 September 1988, supports Theo van Boven's conclusion that minorities collectively as well as individually have the right to remedy; its first operative paragraph, refers to "victims, either individually or collectively." Another indication regarding the categories of victims is the repeated reference in Sub-Commission resolution 1989/14 to "gross violations of human rights and fundamental freedoms." The resolution mentions in its first preambular paragraph "individuals, groups and communities." According to Theo van Boven, under most international legal instruments dealing with individual rights, the violation of any one provision may entail a right to an appropriate remedy, while instruments concerned with the rights of minorities to compensation focus on gross violations of human rights and fundamental freedoms. Van Boven's interpretation is suggested in the first preambular paragraph of Sub-Commission resolution 1989/14 which refers to "substantial damages and acute sufferings." In this regard the notion of "victims," spelled out in paragraph 18 of the *Declaration of Basic Principles of Justice for Victims of Crime and Abuse of Power*, should be taken into account. The paragraph reads in part:

> Victims means persons who, individually or collectively, have suffered harm, including physical or mental injury, emotional suffering, economic loss or substantial impairment of their fundamental rights through acts of omissions that...constitute violations... of internationally recognized norms relating to human rights.

The Permanent Court of International Justice establishes the basic principles governing remedy, which may be applied to situations of gross violations of human rights, and indicates the purpose of granting any other special rights:

> The essential principle contained in the actual notion of an illegal act — a principle which seems to be established by international practice and in particular by the decisions of arbitral tribunals — is that reparation must, as far as possible, wipe out all consequences of the illegal act and re-establish the situation which would, in all probability, have existed if that act had not been committed. Restitution in kind [special rights] or, if this is not possible, payment of a sum corresponding to the value which a restitution in kind would bear; the award, if need be, of damages for loss sustained which would not be covered by restitution in kind or payment in place of it — such are the principles which should serve to determine the amount of compensation due for an act contrary to international law.[22]

U.S. Domestic Law and the Right to Remedy

American jurisprudence, like that of most states, recognizes the right of victims to remedy. It has generally acknowledged that individuals may be entitled to compensation for the effects of actions wrongfully undertaken even before those they harmed were born. Furthermore, such acknowledgment may have occurred not only for individuals, but also on a collective basis. When the U.S. Congress exercised its authority under Section 2 of the Thirteenth Amendment and Section 5 of the Fourteenth Amendment — Amendments whose original intent is often said to have been for the protection of formerly-enslaved African-Americans — it has done so to protect groups or classes of persons, not to serve individual interests. The Congress was addressing the institution and legacy of slavery as an ancient wrong and redressing grievances of those presently affected by establishing modern civil rights.[23]

U.S. recognition of the collective or minority right to remedy is reflected in the U.S. payment of reparations to the Sioux of South Dakota (1985), the Seminoles of Florida (1985), the

Ottawas of Michigan (1986) and Japanese Americans (1990). These U.S. actions are similar to the recognition of the minority or collective right existing in the international community, where we note the payment of reparations to the Jewish people and to the State of Israel by Germany in 1952, to Japanese Canadians by Canada in 1988, and to Holocaust survivors by Austria in 1990.[24]

U.S. domestic law itself confirms that official U.S. policies of enslavement and segregation may have been in violation of international law, insofar as the *Third Restatement of the Foreign Relations Law of the United States* declares that a state violates international law if, as a matter of State policy, it practices, encourages or condones:

> ...(b) slavery or slave trade...(d) systematic racial discrimination... (g) a consistent pattern of gross violations of internationally recognized human rights.[25]

The Right to Remedy and American National Minorities

Up to this point, we have denoted the international-legal and democratic basis for the obligation of multi-national states to ensure effective democratic participation of national minorities and fulfillment of minority rights by instituting democratic pluralism. We have also called attention to the international-legal obligation of states to provide remedy for damages to victims suffering from abuse of their internationally protected human rights. We have further indicated the extent to which, both in domestic law and in policy, the U.S. may have recognized the right to remedy of collective victims of human rights abuse.

It remains to be suggested that, in the case of American national minorities, the international legal notions of minority rights and of the right to remedy are mutually re-enforcing. The remedy for the past gross violations of their human rights would be the establishment of minority rights (democratic pluralism) and the abandonment of present U.S. policies of forced assimilation, which constitute a continuing attack on national minorities' culture and separate identity.

For some American national minorities, such as African-Americans, whose ancestors were victims of gross violations, the passage of time has no attenuating effect on damages suggered, but on the contrary has increased post-traumatic stress, deteriorated social, material, and other conditions. Appropriate remedy may require all necessary special rights as well as compensation and rehabilitation measures. Insofar as the effects of past and ongoing gross violation and resulting damages can be demonstrated as the cause of present and on-going developmental problems, it would be difficult to produce an acceptable argument for statutory limitations since that would amount to the denial of the fundamental human right to a remedy for past injustices. The *Convention on the Non-Applicability of Statutory Limitations to War Crimes and Crimes Against Humanity*, indicates international law's recognition that some crimes are so grave as to demand retribution "irrespective of date of commission." [26] Enslavement and segregation would fall within the framework of crimes against humanity. As noted by UN Special Rapporteur Theo van Boven:

> It is sometimes contended that as a result of passage of time the need for reparations is outdated and therefore no longer pertinent. As is borne out in this study, the application of statutory limitations often deprives victims of gross violations of human rights of the reparations that are due to them. The principle should prevail that claims relating to reparations for gross violations of human rights shall not be subject to a statute of limitations. In this connection, it should be taken into account that the effects of gross violations of human rights are linked to the most serious crimes to which, according to authoritative legal opinion, statutory limitations shall not apply.[27]

In order to adequately compensate American national minorities for human rights violations which have occurred in almost unprecedented magnitude and with on-going effect over a period of three centuries,[28] all internationally accepted modes of remedy (restitution, compensation and satisfaction) may be required.

1) With regard to restitution, we suggest that only the institution of a form of minority rights/democratic pluralism could hope to restore to minorities like the African-Americans the capacity for cultural and socio-economic self-development which was damaged or prevented by U.S. official policies of slavery, segregation and forced assimilation (ethnocide). Insofar as the damages suffered by the American national minorities were to their collective existence, as well as to the individuals belonging to them, it seems appropriate that restitution should seek to restore the dignity of that collective identity which, by gross human rights violation in law and in fact, the U.S. government has sought to suppress.

2) Concerning the right to compensation, cash payments to the American national minorities could also be most effectively

projected through the framework of minority rights, for instance as an initial subsidization for an African-American development bank, as a share of taxes, as regular transfer payments to support the operational and development program of an African-American Council which would have jurisdiction over the operation, policies and delivery of such community services as social welfare, criminal justice and economic development. Such awards would avoid the complexities and difficulties surrounding the notion of compensation on an individual level to presently living persons (who should be eligible, how much paid to each, etc.),[29] complexities which to date have served only to reinforce arguments that reparations to African-Americans cannot be undertaken. Cash payments within the context of minority rights, however, entail the utilization of funds for development purposes by the minority as a whole, and should be processed by a democratically established African-American controlled political assembly.

3) As far as satisfaction is concerned, the African-American national minority might reasonably expect and demand an official apology, similar to that recently extended to Japanese Americans for their interment during the Second World War, or to Native Hawaiians for action by U.S. navy and marines leading to the overthrow of Queen Liluikalani.[30] The value of such an apology cannot be understated, and has been well expressed by Jose Zalaquett, who served on the Chilean National Commission on Truth and Conciliation:

> ... society cannot simply block out a chapter of its history; it cannot deny the facts of its past, however differently these may be interpreted. Inevitably, the void would be filled with lies or with conflicting, confusing versions ... The truth also brings a measure of healthy social catharsis...[31]

---

1 This conclusion is suggested by a review of the continuing situation in the Americas of Native and African-American minorities. In every state, except perhaps Canada, these minorities are found in politico-social and economic inferiority due to historical exploitation, etc. and are not empowered by the democratic systems to call attention to their special situation and needs.

2 See Y.N. Kly, *The Anti-Social Contract,* 1987.

3 Harold Cruise, *The Crisis of the Negro Intellectual,* 1967.

4 C.J. Woodson, *The Miseducation of the Negro,* 1990.

5 Derrick Bell, *And We Are Not Yet Saved,* 1989.

6 Andrew Hacker, *Two Nations: Black and White, Separate, Hostile, Unequal,* 1992.

7 A wide range of statistics is available in Perry A. Plooskie and James Williams, eds., *The Negro Almanac: A Reference Work on the African-American,* 5th edition, 1989.

8 Ethnocide, or involuntary or non-cognitive assimilation, as opposed to integration within the state as a politico-legally recognized entity.

9 See Cynthia Enloe, "Internal Colonialism, Federalism and Alternative State Development Strategies," *Publius: The Journal of Federalism,* Vol. vii, Fall 1977, p. 150.

10 Witness the situation of NAACP leader Ben Chavis, whose firing was widely interpreted by the African-American community as due to his willingness to recognize Min. Louis Farrakhan as a bona fide leader among others in the African-American community.

11 Y.N. Kly, *International Law and the Black Minority in the U.S.,* Third Edition, 1990.

12 Y.N. Kly, *supra,* note 2.

13 Witness UN assistance to indigenous peoples, to the electoral process in El Salvador, Cambodia, etc.

14 See the recent Human Rights Committee General Comment on Article 27 of the *International Covenant on Civil and Political Rights*, widely recognized as the "minorities article," UN Doc. CCPR/C/ 21/Rev.1/Add.5).

15 Richard Falk, "The Struggle of Indigenous Peoples and the Promise of National Political Communities," in Ruth Thompson, ed., *The Rights of Indigenous Peoples in International Law,* 1987, p. 6. Richard Falk writes: "We need to understand the extent to which there exists in all parts of the world now, an awareness that one of the great current problems of world order, is the plight of what I would call entrapped nations, nations that are entrapped within the structure and framework of the sovereign state. An enormous juristic fraud has been perpetrated on modern political consciousness by confusing national identity with the power political reality of state sovereignty. The whole idea of what it means to be a national has been converted through a formal juristic device into a legal status that the same confers which, for the majority of people living in the world, does not correspond with their ethnic, psychological and political reality. Their sense of what it means to belong to a collectivity, however one describes it, whether in tribal terms or in national terms, is often at odds with a network of imposed obligations owed to the sovereign state. Rather than a sense of loyalty associated with the natural sentiment of nationality, there exists a condition of political alienation in a variety of forms."

16 See Arendt Lijphart, *Democracy in Pluralist Societies: A Comparative Exploration,* 1977. We feel that consociated democracy should be viewed as a more specific type of pluralist democracy.

17 A number of both universal and regional human rights instruments contain express provisions relating to the right to an "effective remedy" by competent national tribunals for acts violating human rights (see article 8 of the *Universal Declaration of Human Rights*.) The notion of an "effective remedy" is also included in article 2(3)(a)

of the *International Covenant on Civil and Political Rights* and in article 6 of the *Declaration on the Elimination of All Forms of Racial Discrimination*. Some human rights instruments refer to a more particular "right to be compensated in accordance with the law" (Article 10, *American Convention on Human Rights)* or the "right to an adequate compensation" (Article 21(2), *African Charter on Human and Peoples' Rights.)* Even more specific are the provisions of Article 9(5) of the *International Covenant on Civil and Political Rights*, and of Article 5(5) of the *European Convention for the Protection of Human Rights and Fundamental Freedoms*, which refer to the "enforceable right to compensation." Similarly, Article 14(1) the *Convention Against Torture and Other Cruel, Inhuman or Degrading Treatment or Punishment* contains a provision providing for the torture victim a redress and "an enforceable right to fair and adequate compensation, including the means for as full rehabilitation as possible." In Article 14(6) of the *International Covenant on Civil and Political Rights* and Article 11 of the *Declaration on the Protection of All Persons from Being Subjected to Torture and Other Cruel, Inhuman or Degrading Treatment or Punishment*, a specific provision is contained indicating that compensation is due in accordance with law or with national law. Equally, provisions relating to "reparation" or "satisfaction" of damages are contained in the *International Convention on the Elimination of All Forms of Racial Discrimination*, Article 6, which provides for the right to seek "just and adequate reparation or satisfaction for any damage suffered." The ILO Convention concerning Indigenous and Tribal Peoples in Independent Countries also refers to "fair compensation for damages" (Article 15(2)), to "compensation in money" and "under appropriate guarantees," (Article 16(4)); and to full compensation "for any loss or injury" (Article 16(5)). The *American Convention on Human Rights*, to which the U.S. is a party, speaks of "compensatory damages" (Article 68) and provides that the consequences of the measure or situation that constituted the breach of the right or freedom "be remedied" and that "fair compensation be paid to the injured party" (Article 63(1)). The *Convention on the Rights of the Child* contains a provision to the effect that States Parties shall take all appropriate measures to promote "physical and psychological recovery and social reintegration of a child victim..." (Article 39).

18 Theo van Boven, Special Rapporteur, *Study concerning the right to restitution, compensation and rehabilitation for victims of gross violations of human rights and fundamental freedoms*, July 2, 1993, UN. Doc. E/CN.4/Sub.2/1993/8, p. 56.

19 P.C.I.J. Collection of Judgments, Series A, No. 17, p. 29.

20 Theo van Boven, *supra*. note 19, p. 16.

21 *Id.*, p. 8.

22 P.C.I.J. Collection of Judgments, *supra*. note 18, p. 47.

23 See Gregory Kellam Scott, "Present Remedies and Ancient Wrongs: In Search of a New Civil Rights Jurisprudence," in George

Shepherd, Jr. and David Penna, eds., *Racial Discrimination and the Underclass,* 1990.

24 Dorothy Benton-Lewis, "Black Reparations Now!" cited in S.A. Reid, "Account Past Due," *Atlanta Journal-Constitution*, Section G1,3, October 24, 1993.

25 Section 702 of The Third Restatement of the Foreign Relations Law of the United States (1987).

26 Article 1, *Convention on the Non-Applicability of Statutory Limitations to War Crimes and Crimes Against Humanity*, November 26, 1968, in *A Comprehensive Handbook of the United Nations*, Vol. II, 1979.

27 Theo van Boven, *supra.* note 18, at 54.

28 See Civil Rights Congress staff, ed. William L. Patterson,*We Charge Genocide: The Historic Petition to the United Nations for relief from a Crime of the United States Government Against the Negro People*.

29 See Boris Bittker, *The Case for Black Reparations,*1973 for a discussion of the complexities involved in the notion of extending compensation on an individual basis.

30 The U.S. House on November 1st approved by voice vote a resolution providing a formal apology to native Hawaiians for the U.S. role in the 19th century overthrow of an independent Hawaiian monarchy. The coup paved the way for U.S. annexation of the Hawaiian islands in 1898. The Congressional resolution acknowledged U.S. complicity in the coup and called for "reconciliation between the U.S. and the native Hawaiian people." Cited in *Facts on File,* 1993.

31 As cited in Theo van Boven, *supra* note 18, p. 53.

International Law and Reparations*

Theo van Boven

8 ... No agreed definition exists of the term "gross violations of human rights."

9 [U]seful guidance may be found in the work of the International Law Commission regarding the draft Code of Crimes Against the Peace and Security of Mankind. Relevant among the draft articles provisionally adopted by the Commission on first reading are for present purposes those articles which pertain to genocide (art. 19), apartheid (art. 20) and systematic or mass violations of human rights (art. 21). In the latter category are listed by the International Law Commission: murder; torture; establishing or maintaining over persons a status of slavery servitude or forced labor; persecution on social, political, racial, religious or cultural grounds in a systematic manner or on a mass scale; deportation or forcible transfer of population.

10 Guidance may also be drawn from common article 3 of the Geneva Conventions of 12 August 1949, containing minimum humanitarian standards which have to be respected "at any time and in any place whatsoever" and which categorically prohibits the following acts: (a) violence to life and person, in particular murder of all kinds, mutilation, cruel treatment and torture; (b) taking of hostages; (c) outrages upon personal dignity, in particular humiliating and degrading treatment; (d) the passing of sentences and the carrying out of executions without previous judgment pronounced by a regularly constituted court, affording all the judicial guarantees which are recognized as indispensable by civilized peoples.

* Selected excerpts from Theo van Boven, "Study concerning the right to restitution, compensation and rehabilitation for victims of gross violations of human rights and fundamental freedoms, Final Report," UN Doc. E/CN.4/Sub.2/1993/8.

11 While the above-cited categories of gross violations of human rights were taken from an existing or emerging body of international criminal law and from the law of basic humanitarian standards applicable in international and non-international armed conflicts, similar categories were drawn up from the perspective of State responsibility for violations of human rights based on customary international law. Thus, according to the Third Restatement of the Foreign Relations Law of the United States (Section 702), "A state violates international law if, as a matter of State policy, it practices, encourages or condones: (a) genocide; (b) slavery or slave trade; (c) the murder or causing the disappearance of individuals; (d) torture or other cruel, inhuman or degrading treatment or punishment; (e) prolonged arbitrary detention; (f) systematic racial discrimination; (g) a consistent pattern of gross violations of internationally recognized human rights."

12 It should be noted that virtually all examples of gross violations of human rights cited in the previous paragraphs and taken from different sources are equally covered by human rights treaties and give rise also on that basis to State responsibility on the part of the offending State party and to the obligation to provide reparations to the victims of those gross violations. Given also the indivisibility and interdependence of all human rights, gross and systematic violations of the type of human rights cited above frequently affect other human rights as well, including economic, social and cultural rights. Equally, systemic practices and policies of religious intolerance and discrimination may give rise to just entitlements to reparation on the part of the victims.

13 The scope of the present study would be unduly circumscribed if the notion of "gross violations of human rights and fundamental freedoms" would be understood in a fixed and exhaustive sense... Therefore it is submitted that, while under international law the violation of any human right gives rise to a right to reparation for the victim, particular attention is paid to gross violations of human rights and fundamental freedoms which include at least the following: genocide, slavery and slavery-like practices; summary or arbitrary executions; torture and cruel, inhuman or degrading treatment or punishment; enforced disappearance; arbitrary and prolonged detention; deportation or forcible transfer of population; and

systematic discrimination, in particular based on race or gender.

Individuals and collectivities as victims

14 It cannot be denied that both individuals and collectivities are often victimized as a result of gross violations of human rights. Most of the gross violations listed in the previous paragraph inherently affect rights of individuals and rights of collectivities. This was also assumed in Sub-Commission resolution 1989/13 which provided some useful guidelines with respect to the question of who is entitled to reparation. In this regard, the resolution mentions in its first preambular paragraph "individuals, groups and communities." In the next part of this section, which will deal with some special issues of interest and attention, the individual and collective aspects of victimized persons and groups are in many instances closely interrelated. This coincidence of individual and collective aspects is particularly manifest with regard to the rights of indigenous peoples. Against this background it is therefore necessary that, in addition to individual means of reparation, adequate provision be made to entitle groups or victims or victimized communities to present collective claims for damages and to receive collective reparation accordingly.

16 ... [T]he parameters of the present study are shaped by the notion of serious damages and grave injuries to human dignity, to the physical and moral integrity of the human person and to the very existence of groups, communities and peoples, which result in legitimate claims to reparation on the part of those who are victimized.

24 The Working Group on Contemporary Forms of Slavery also referred to the need for moral compensation* for *victims of the slave trade and other early forms of slavery.* This problem was also touched upon by two African members of the Sub-Commission in connection with the issue of compensation to the African descendants of the victims of gross violations of human rights by colonial Powers.[1] In

*At the 1994 meeting of the Sub-Commission, an intervention by IHRAAM representatives challenged the notion that moral compensation provides sufficient remedy to victims of the slave trade, in light of the ongoing damages suffered by the communities concerned.

this respect the Special Rapporteur would draw attention to the report of the Secretary-General on the international dimensions of the right to development as a human right in which a series of ethical aspects of the right to development were listed, among these a moral duty of reparation to make up for past exploitation by the colonial Powers and some others. The Secretary-General noted that acceptance of such a moral duty is by no means universal.[2] Perhaps more to the point on this issue are some recommendations included in the study on the achievements made and obstacles encountered during the Decades to Combat Racism and Racial Discrimination, prepared by Special Rapporteur Mr. A. Eide.[3] In the section of recommendations relating to situations originating in slavery, the following are pertinent in the present context:

(a) Research should be carried out in the countries concerned to determine the degree to which descendants of persons held as slaves continue to suffer from social handicaps or deprivations (recommendation 17);

(b) Effective affirmation action should be carried out until such time as members of these groups experience no further handicaps or deprivations. Such affirmative action should not be construed to constitute discrimination against members of the dominant society (recommendation 18).

While it would be difficult and complex to construe and uphold a legal duty to pay compensation to the descendants of the victims of the slave trade and other early forms of slavery, the present Special Rapporteur agrees that effective affirmative action is called for in appropriate cases as a moral duty. In addition, an accurate record of the history of slavery, including an account of the acts and the activities of the perpetrators and their accomplices and of the sufferings of the victims, should receive wide dissemination through the media, in history books and in educational materials...

IX PROPOSED BASIC PRINCIPLES AND GUIDELINES

137 The Special Rapporteur hereby submits the following proposals concerning reparation to victims of gross violations of human rights.

General Principles

1 Under international law, the violation of any human right gives rise to a right of reparation for the victim. Particular attention must be paid to gross violations of human rights and fundamental freedoms, which include at least the following: genocide; slavery and slavery-like practices; summary or arbitrary executions; torture and cruel, inhuman or degrading treatment or punishment; enforced disappearance; arbitrary and prolonged detention; deportation or forcible transfer of population; and systematic discrimination, in particular based on race or gender.

2 Every State has a duty to make reparation in case of a breach of the obligation under international law to respect and to ensure respect for human rights and fundamental freedoms. The obligation to ensure respect for human rights includes the duty to prevent violations, the duty to investigate violations, the duty to take appropriate action against the violators, and the duty to afford remedies to victims. States shall ensure that no person who may be responsible for gross violations of human rights shall have immunity from liability for their actions.

3 Reparation for human rights violations has the purpose of relieving the suffering of and affording justice to victims by removing or redressing to the extent possible the consequences of the wrongful acts and by preventing and deterring violations.

4 Reparation should respond to the needs and wishes of the victims. It shall be proportionate to the gravity of the violations and the resulting harm and shall include: restitution, compensation, rehabilitation, satisfaction and guarantees of non-repetition.

5 Reparation for certain gross violations of human rights that amount to crimes under international law includes a duty to prosecute and punish perpetrators. Impunity is in conflict with this principle.

6 Reparation may be claimed by the direct victims and, where appropriate, the immediate family, dependents or other persons having a special relationship to the direct victims.

7 In addition to providing reparation to individuals, States shall make adequate provision for groups of victims to bring collective claims and to obtain collective reparation. Special measures should be taken for the purpose of affording opportunities for self-development and advancement to groups who, as a result of human rights violations, were denied such opportunities.

Forms of Reparations

8 *Restitution* shall be provided to re-establish, to the extent possible, the situation that existed for the victim prior to the violations of human rights. Restitution requires, *inter alia*,restoration of liberty, citizenship or residence, employment or property.

9 *Compensation* shall be provided for any economically assessable damage resulting from human rights violations, such as:

(a) Physical or mental harm;

(b) Pain, suffering and emotional distress;

(c) Lost opportunities, including education;

(d) Loss of earnings and earning capacity;

(e) Reasonable medical and other expenses of rehabilitation;

(f) Harm to property or business, including lost profits;

(g) Harm to reputation or dignity;

(h) Reasonable costs and fees of legal or expert assistance to obtain a remedy.

10 *Rehabilitation* shall be provided, to include legal, medical, psychological and other care and services, as well as measures to restore the dignity and reputation of the victims.

11 *Satisfaction* and *guarantees of non-repetition* shall be provided, including:

(a) Cessation of continuing violations;

(b) Verification of the facts and full and public disclosure of the truth;

(c) A declaratory judgment in favor of the victim;

(d) Apology, including public acknowledgment of the facts and acceptance of responsibility;

(e) Bringing to justice the persons responsible for the violations;

(f) Commemorations and paying tribute to the victims;

(g) Inclusion of an accurate record of human rights violations in educational curricula and materials;

(h) Preventing the recurrence of violations by such means as:

(i) Ensuring effective civilian control of military and security forces;

(ii) Restricting the jurisdiction of military tribunals;

(iii) Strengthening the independence of the judiciary;

(iv) Protecting the legal profession and human rights workers;

(v) Providing human rights training to all sectors of society, in particular to military and security forces and to law enforcement officials.

Procedures and Mechanisms

12 Every State shall maintain prompt and effective disciplinary, administrative, civil and criminal procedures, with universal jurisdiction for human rights violations that constitute crimes under international law.

13 The legal system, especially in civil, administrative and procedural matters, must be adapted so as to ensure that the right to reparation is readily accessible, not unreasonable impaired and takes into account the potential vulnerability of the victims.

14 Every State shall make known, through the media and other appropriate mechanisms, the available procedures for reparations.

15 Statutes of limitations shall not apply in respect to periods during which no effective remedies exist for human rights violations. Claims relating to reparations for gross violations of human rights shall not be subject to a statute of limitations.

16 No one may be coerced to waive claims for reparations.

17 Every State shall make readily available all evidence in its possession concerning human rights violations.

18 Administrative or judicial tribunals responsible for affording reparations should take into account that records or other tangible evidence may be limited or unavailable. In the absence of other evidence, reparations should be based on the testimony of victims, family members, medical and mental health professionals.

19 Every state shall protect victims, their relatives and friends, and witnesses from intimidation and reprisals.

20 Decisions relating to reparations for victims of violations of human rights shall be implemented in a diligent and prompt manner. In this respect follow-up, appeal or review procedures should be devised.

---

1 E/CN.4/Sub.2/1992/SR.27, paragraph 46 (Mrs. Mbonu) and E/CN.4/Sub.2/1992/SR.31, paragraphs 1-2 (Mrs. Ksentini).

2 E/CN...4/1334, paragraphs 52-54.

3 E/CN.4/Sub.2/1989/8 and Add.1.

Arthur M. Schlesinger's
The Disuniting of America: Reflections on a Multicultural Society
A Critique

Y.N. Kly

The nearly universal acceptance, in the late 20th century, of the inherent right of the world's peoples to democracy, points toward a further deepening of the democratic process in the 21st century, as emergent minorities seek the development of pluralistic democratic systems in order to fully exercise their right to exist and be different in equal status with the majority. In the interim, however, we are witness to what may be an unavoidable period of adjustment, even in developed countries, as majorities and minorities grapple with the notion of the need for changes to the status quo.

In the United States, as an instance, controversy rages as to how to handle, on the one hand, the increasingly vocal aspirations of the national minorities for affirmation of their cultural identities, and how to solve, on the other, the increasing social malaise resulting from centuries-long systemically-enforced inequality which now threatens to spill out from minority communities and engulf the whole of the nation. The response on the level of state policy has been disheartening: the stiffening of criminal justice legislation, and the building of more penitentiaries.

Yet somehow even more disquieting is the response from scholars representing the dominant intellectual traditions in America. How has it been possible for mainstream American scholars to avow that state unity without changing existing politico-legal structures as they relate to minorities is for the benefit of all, when the extreme suffering of U.S. national minorities under existing structures, and the consequences which flow from this suffering — increased crime, increased urban blight, increased fear and paranoia throughout the nation propelling the entire social agenda rightward — should be plain to even the least informed of scholarly observers? Can it really be due simply to machiavellian propagandism on the part of all those who officially or unofficially represent and favor the dominant group in intellectual channels and elsewhere? Or is it more plausible to suggest that another factor enters in: an actual blindness, shall we say a psychologically-induced inability (denial syndrome) to admit the need *to try something else*, insofar as change might threaten not only relative material benefits but also — perhaps even worse for some intellectuals — the much-cherished and most invideous of all notions, that of *superiority on the moral, intellectual and cultural levels.*

Minorities are by definition always a politico-economically weaker segment of a state's population. Thus, where their devaluation is institutionalized as a historical normality, often even the most intelligent of scholars from the dominant group can be found double-talking or talking down on issues as they concern minorities, particularly when minority perspectives challenge views so habitual and visceral as to approach patterns of transcendent belief. We address this Preface to a particular instance of this phenomena, which typifies many of the arguments against minority rights which international legal scholars have come to anticipate from beneficiaries of the status quo in majoritarian states. It should help us to look beyond the buttress of scholarship and glimpse what may be psychological roadblocks lying at the heart of the minority-majority problematic.

Resistance to minority rights, we feel it fair to say, forms the *raison d' être* of the recent book, *The Disuniting of America: Reflections on a Multi-cultural Society*[1] by Arthur M. Schlesinger, Jr., an eminent American scholar situated in the mainstream of the American intellectual tradition. While Schlesinger seeks to present his work as a generalized comment on the contemporary "ethnic upsurge," the term functions as encoded language (in a manner similar to "the inner city" or "the underclass") whose subliminal meaning is generally well-understood within the American public at large. What "ethnic upsurge" really refers to is the contemporary assertion of American national minorities' ethnic consciousness which has accompanied their realization that the gains promised by the Civil Rights era have proved largely illusory.

The impetus for *The Disuniting of America* is the attachment of a major Anglo-American scholar to the emotion-laden American myth — the emergence in America of a new race of man, product of a cultural melting pot, and uniquely empowered in a land of individual freedom and equal economic opportunity. Schlesinger's attachment to the myth seems so strong as to completely overshadow well-known historical reality, prompting him to equate minority demands for equal status and input into what their children are being taught through the American educational system with an attempt to destroy the American dream.

The glorious American tradition is established through a recitation of opinions, either Schlesinger's own or that of other authors (which acquire no greater credibility simply by providing a chorus). Quoting Lawrence Fuchs, Schlesinger asserts that "No nation in history has proved as successful as the U.S. in managing ethnic diversity. No nation had ever made diversity itself a source of national identity and unity."[2] Most scholars give that honor to states like Switzerland. Even the British during the efforts to resolve the Northern Ireland dilemma appear to have given little consideration to the U.S. model.[3] Schlesinger muses that "ethnic interpretation... reverses the historical theory of America as one people — the theory that managed to keep American society whole."[4] (This, and not the Civil War, the conquest of the Indian and Chicanos, the enslavement of the Africans, the coerced acceptance of Anglo-Saxon culture by non-English immigrants, etc.)[5] He writes: "At the beginning, America was seen as a severing of roots, a liberation from the stifling past, an entry into a new life, an interweaving of the separate ethnic strands into a new national design"[6] (in which, incidentally, all European ethnies came to speak English and to purvey English values and institutions). And so on.

Revisionist history has punched holes through these idealizations of American national identity. At this point in historical discourse, it is no longer possible to deny such realities. But why ignore or deny realities, if you can state them, even elaborate them, and then reach conclusions as if nothing of the kind had been said? Schlesinger freely elaborates the extent to which the notion of the "new American man," like most national myths, was promulgated by self-interested parties with a view to self-justification and national self-aggrandizement.[7] He acknowledges how it served the purpose of luring succeeding European generations to swell a much-needed labor force[8] and thereby numerically ensured the process of land expropriation from the Indians and enslavement of Africans. Then, concluding a text that admits that the American dream of the "new man" has never truly reflected America's reality and certainly has never been extended to include the national minorities, Schlesinger circles back to the idealizations from which he began, appealing to the glorious notion of "individuals of all nations ... melted into a new race of man" as "still our best hope." He does this without having substantiated whether this is, could or should be the case in relation to its benefits for non-European minorities — or indeed, without the slightest apprehension that the "our" to whom he refers might not be of universal dimension. Could it truly include the African-American national minority which Schlesinger notes was thought by most 'white' Americans through most of American history to be unassimilable,[9] and whom all statistics show to have remained unassimilated, despite the apparent *volte face* of official United States policy with *Brown v. Board of Education*, etc.?

What can be so upsetting about national minorities wishing to assert their cultural identity, to have it taught to their children in a manner different than it has been taught to them through the majority's education system and historiography, particularly if "the cruelty with which white Americans have dealt with black Americans has been compounded by the callousness with which white historians have dealt with black history."[10] Rather than assisting the national minorities to redress this callousness, Schlesinger devotes his weighty scholarship to attacking the theoretical foundations of one strain of their efforts to respond: Afrocentrism. He finds it important to assert that those who promote anti-western Afrocentric notions (in an effort to counter the damaging and Eurocentric effects of an admittedly Anglo-Saxon-dominated intellectual tradition) nonetheless are forced to appeal to western ideal of equality for the moral authority to do so. Does he mean to imply, in Eurocentric fashion, that non-European traditions have no such moral notions? Should appealing to the western ideal of equality be viewed as concommitant to acknowledging the moral superiority of the west -- and thereby the right to dominance of the Euro-majority?

In any event, can the Anglo-American tradition be accurately described as *being* the western tradition? While Anglo-Americans are definitely a part of the west, there may also be some Anglo-American traditions that are not considered western traditions. Most states in Europe attempted to forbid slavery institutions on their territories though profiting from this practice in the territory of the Americas. Should chattle slavery and the socio-pathological racial orientation it gave birth to in the Anglo-American culture (the superiority of the "white" man's culture, as opposed to the superiority of German, French or English culture) be considered a western tradition? Should U.S. treatment of its minorities be viewed as completely in line with the western minority rights tradition or in some respects, significantly at odds with it?

While which tradition national minorities challenge, and which they appeal to for moral authority may be of theoretical interest, we suggest that it might be more useful to focus on what they are trying to do: to deepen the majority's notion of equality. They are trying to change this notion of equality from the right "to be regarded as the same" and thereby receive the same treatment, to the right to be different and equal, with treatment appropriate to equal status.[11] Historically, the majoritarian notion, while admitting diversity, in reality is simply saying that this diversity won't be held against you — as opposed to celebrated and/or provided for in official policy. Such an equality is so shallow as to be almost purely formal, disregarding all of those factors which distinguish human beings from one another, and yet are highly operative in affecting their social, economic, cultural and political life. What is not admitted by Schlesinger or accepted in the majoritarian tradition is the full profundity of the notion of equality — which includes the *right to be equal but different, the right of a group to enjoy, celebrate, understand and promulgate its difference as well as its sameness.* Clearly, this equality — which places the individual within the fullness of a historical and contemporary problematic, which unavoidably has collective dimensions — is the equality which national minorities have in mind when they turn to the American creed of equality in diversity, hoping to extend and deepen its heretofore shallow and formal meaning. In order to be implemented in actuality, such an equality requires more than lip-service to abstract notions; it may require concrete empowerment through changing policies and politico-legal structures.

Similar to scholars from dominant groups in most multinational states, Mr. Schlesinger tells us that the minority has no interest in its past identity or in a present separate identity. He refers to a *Washington Post* poll to substantiate this, embellished by less contemporary opinion derived from the period when institutional, legal and systemic forces employed by the society could be assumed to have made the minority afraid of expressing its true feelings.[12] As every politician knows, polls can be accurate or totally misleadingt. Notably,in contrast to the *Washington Post* poll, the International Human Rights Association of American Minorities (IHRAAM) conducted its own poll in 1993 on whether African-Americans wanted self-determination among registered voters in predominantly African-American political enclaves. Ninety percent of those polled responded "Yes." This poll was formulated and conducted by Dr. Farid Muhammad and students at East-West University in Chicago (see Appendix III).

What do the minorities want? Insofar as there is no democratic procedure available for establishing this, again we view a situation common within most dominant groups in multinational states that do not respect minority rights — the refusal to believe that the minorities have the right or the ability to define themselves or speak for themselves, followed by the effort, when it has become impossible to deny that the minority has a different cultural identity, to control the minority's definition of that identity, thereby in essence allowing it no identity other than that acceptable to the majority ethny.

Since arguments against the internationally accepted notion of cultural pluralism — which after all is promoted by the Council of Europe and the Conference on Security and Cooperation in Europe, major bodies formulating the European (western) approach to minority rights — run counter to the world current, Schlesinger seeks to sidestep the issue, while attacking its manifestation in actuality. Stating that "Cultural pluralism is not the issue..." (which most assuredly it is), he searches for ground on which to redefine the issue, and believes he finds one: "The issue is *the kind of history* that ... Afrocentric ideologues propose for American children. The issue is the teaching of *bad* history under whatever ethnic banner."[13] Once again we find an appeal to an abstract idealization — this time, the cult of "excellence" — to counter the intrusion in actuality of a national minority's demands for cultural rights.

It might be asked: is it reasonable to expect that minority history, seeking to correct the majority's long history of prejudices —heretofore passing as objective scholarship — should itself emerge in all sectors in perfections of scholarship or indeed, of disengagement? Should the minorities be held to a standard to which the dominant ethny is seldom held before they are allowed to speak, write or teach? Do they have a right to make mistakes, take wrong paths, learn, enquire and develop, just as other cultures have done, without being overseen or reined short *by others* the moment they take a path the others may find unacceptable? Does the majority ethny have the right to protest teaching of minority perspectives on the historical record?

One might wonder why an attack against bad history, which abounds in America, should be directed with such passion against a minority perspective in particular, to the extent of calling forth an entire book by a senior historian from the majority ethny. What can one say of the objectivity of such a scholar who in turn resorts to name-calling and inflammatory language, by discussing the issues in such terms as: "*The militants of ethnicity* now contend that a main objective of public education should be the protection, strengthening, celebration and perpetuation of ethnic origins and identities;"[14] or "*ethnic ideologues*" who have "set themselves against the old American ideal of assimilation," calling on the republic to "think in terms not of individual but of group identity and to move the polity from individual rights to group rights"[15] thereby filling "the air with *recrimination and rancor*."[16]

Schlesinger's articulation of the reason American national minorities seek to assert their ethnic presence in the American educational system is little short of insulting. He refers to it as "essentially therapeutic," "so that minorities can feel good about themselves," "so that minorities can have positive role models." However, these minority demands are simply to teach what they feel is a correct viewpoint, and are in accord with the constitutional-legal provisions enacted by states in Europe and elsewhere to provide for cultural pluralism. Control over education is the jurisdiction most commonly ceded to minorities, a right recognized even earlier than the 1935 Permanent Court of International Justice decision on Albanian schools.[17] Next to religious rights, language rights of national minorities (witness Schlesinger's critique of bilingualism) have been among the first to be recognized in both the western tradition, and in international law in general.

The search for group and minority rights is an international phenomena affecting all multinational states, and has been found by the UN and most multicultural states to be required to ensure internal social peace, economic development and democratic state unity. However, typical of scholars from dominant ethnicities in multi-national states who protest what to them may be an unwelcome intrusion of a minority ethnicity's legitimate desire to seek to maintain and develop its unique culture, Schlesinger presents the issue as a cultish notion contrived by selfish American minorities who have no concern about threatening the well-being of a heretofore successfully unified body politic by their trivial search for "roots".

Historically, minorities have responded negatively to such wilfull majoritarian misinterpretation of their needs. A typical minority response might be: "It's not role models (tokens) sprinkled throughout the education system that we want. We want to control what is taught to our children in the public schools in our communities. What gets taught there is ours to work out, and we'll work it out and improve on it over time, just like every dominant group has done. We appreciate your concern at protecting us from ignorance, but isn't there enough ignorance in *your* community for you to worry about?"

It is unlikely that Schlesinger is ignorant of the European tradition of minority rights, any more than he is ignorant of revisionist American history. Rather, his knowledge surfaces selectively, then vanishes, equally so. Asserting that the U.S.'s northern neighbor, Canada, couldn't make a multi-ethnic state work, he blames its use of multicultural and multinational policies (in the European (western) tradition)[18]for the threat posed by the Quebecois to Canadian political unity. However, he omits to mention that the Quebecois' bitterest accusation concerning remaining in the Canadian federation concerned the extent to which Canadian policies approached the American model by inadequately recognizing and protecting the "French fact" in Quebec. Significantly, the book and slogan most effectively used in French Canada to stir emotions against Canadian federalism was entitled *The White Negroes of America (Les Negres blanc d' Amerique* by Pierre Vallières). During the 1960's, to promote the Quebec case for political independence, posters referring to the white negroes of America were being posted by the thousands in universities, public facilities, street rallies, etc. It was no doubt the most popular and provocative slogan of the early French-Canadian natonalist awakening. Interestingly, the English-Canadian response to the French charges that they were being treated like American negroes seemed to take a page from the American book: "Speak white," they said. Had the American model also fostered the idea that the language of the new white race created in North America was only English and that any group speaking Spanish or French was somehow not as "white" as groups speaking English?

Rather than discussing the issue of group rights within the framework of the western and international tradition of minority rights, Schlesinger reverts to the framework of segregation (apartheid), which is neither the same as nor even similar to group rights, but rather an internationally-recognized violation of human rights. He accuses minority rights advocates of trying to return to segregation although, within the minority rights context, viewing minority communities which have been politico-legally and socio-economically empowered *within* multi-national states structures as segregated makes as much sense as viewing North Carolina as being segregated from South Carolina, or New Yorkers as segregated from Bostonians, etc. Segregation, in its most objective sense, means the forced physical separation of a minority which nonetheless remained subjected to the unified and centralized political, cultural, educational and social domination of a majority ethny or nation, wherein biological race, not culture or cultural preference, is the only criteria for the separation, Clearly, this is not the same as a political, cultural, educational empowerment (minority rights) within an integrated non-racist multinational state system. In such a system, minority institutions are open to anyone regardless of biological race, who shares or wishes to share the minority's cultural viewpoint, and majority institutions are similarly open. Of course, there would also be common public institutions, etc. where control would be equitably shared by all groups.

It is an irony that American intellectuals, who once heralded the right to exist of submerged or oppressed minorities in the former Soviet Union, should now converge in a common prognostication of peril such as that by Schlesinger against the "cult of ethnicity," or that by Daniel Patrick Moynihan, whose recent work, *Pandemonium*[19] compares proponents of ethnic self-determination to the lesser demons seeking to dwell with Satan in Pandemonium, certain that he had their best interests at heart. It is easy to adopt the posture of being above ethnic preoccupations when it is not one's own ethnicity that is in question, not one's own that is to be denied, erased, despised, denigrated, or destroyed. All very well to rail against ethnicity — when one is certain, once this nonsense about ethnicity subsides and we go back to "all just getting along," that one will still be able to speak one's language in public institutions, see one's children being taught one's culture and view of history in public schools, and be assured that one's community will continue to dominate the major institutions of the state. However, proponents of majoritarianism might well consider an opposite but equally ominous metaphor concerning the suppression of ethnicity — that of Pharoah's oppression of the Israeli minority, of his blindness and hardness of heart (refusal to negotiate), which led to blight and devastation throughout Egypt, and spurred on rather than prevented the Exodus.

From our perspective, the central problem raised by a work such as *The Disuniting of America*, simply put, is bad communication: double talk, double think. Does it result from "bad faith," from clinging to dominance, from the refusal to come down off the perch of cultural superiority? Or the insistence on comparing "my idealizations vs. your practice"? Is it the compulsion, despite the capacity to see through a myth, to go back and find other ways of asserting it once again? In books like *The Disuniting of America*, the scholarly error, if you will, involves the selective application of knowledge to support positions to which one is emotionally attached, the offering of one's wishful thinking in the guise of "objective scholarship" rather than presenting it as advocacy. If such efforts cannot be recognized, particularly by their authors, as advocacy in behalf of, in this case, the dominant group position, then a socio-cultural fixation may appear involving a personal dedication to the status quo, a fear of losing something that is extremely dear, giving birth to a sense of duty to use intellect to preserve the privilege, advantages and sense of moral sanctity that ancestors may have fought for and died to provide.

Arthur M. Schlesinger, Jr.'s book should be read by all who are looking for the reasons why some minorities find it preferable or necessary to seek political independence or engage in violent national liberation struggles. His careless and playful analysis and emotion-baiting symbolism only serves to bedazzle the problematic so that the use of force and socio-economic coercion against minority rights can continue to be popularly acceptable. In fact, Mr. Schlesinger's reasoning so closely resembles that of apologists for all other states desirous of avoiding the implementation of minority rights, particularly those where there exists a historical and well-known systemic and institutional discrimination against minorities, that it leads us to question whether the ideas expressed by such scholars represent a common ideological shield for maintenance of minority domination and exploitation, developed in face of a common foreboding of the widely-heralded ethnic upheavals to come?

Establishing and maintaining state unity through ethnocide and mythology may appear successful as long as the overwhelming monopoly of force rests in the hands of the dominant ethny that controls the apparatus of the state, and international intervention can be avoided. Once, however, for whatever reason, this overwhelming monopoly of available politico-economic and military force is dissipated, the state concerned and the international system usually end up with incredibly bitter and unmanageable violent conflicts.

Perhaps the most damaging aspect in relation to the human rights movement worldwide of works such as Mr. Schlesinger's is the suggestion that America will be able to gloss over the longstanding problem posed by the unassimilable national minorities entrapped within it by re-immersing itself in its historic idealizations rather than examining this problem in an objective and practical manner, which should include looking outward towards Europe or the UN for new concepts and assistance. Those who would have America turn inwards to its own unique traditions heavily influenced by slavery and minority domination, and in so doing swing the entire world behind it, may well find that what is being turned towards represents, not the best, but some of the most eggregious elements in the western tradition.

---

1 Arthur M. Schlesinger, Jr., *The Disuniting of America: Reflections on a Multi-cultural Society,* 1991.

2 *Id.*, p. 131.
3 See "Patterns of Future Government," Her Majesty's Stationery Office, Northern Ireland Office, 1975.
4 *Id.*, p. 16.
5 See any texts on the era of Theodore Roosevelt or the notion of "manifest destiny."
6 *Id.*, p. 23.
7 *Id.*, p. 48.
8 *Id.*, p. 35.
9 *Id*,. p. 58.
10 *Id.*
11 Equal status is different from equality in that it focuses on providing a group with proportionally equal political, economic and socio-cultural autonomy so that it has the tools required to pursue its development independently or in interdependents with the majority group, nation, or ethny.
12 *Id.*, pp. 85-89.
13 *Id.*, p. 75. Italics added.
14 *Id.*, p. 17.
15 *Id.*, p. 130.
16 Italics added to all quotations above.
17 Advisory Opinion of 6 April 1935 on *Minority Schools in Albania*, P.C.I.J., Ser. A/B, No. 64, 17.
18 *Supra*, pp. 11, 13.
19 Daniel Patrick Moynihan, *Pandemonium*, 1993. The metaphor is derived from John Milton's "Paradise Lost."

Using the UN to Advance Minority Concerns

The IHRAAM Petition under ECOSOC Resolution 1503 (XLVIII) 1993

In its continuing efforts to expand the scope and effectiveness of its human rights instrumentation and processes, the UN provides a steadily increasing number of channels where human rights NGOs and minorities might raise their concerns and advance their interests. Notable among these is ECOSOC's grievance procedure, Resolution 1503 (XLVIII), concerning the gross violaton of human rights. Should a communication be approved, the Sub-Commission has the power to launch a thorough study of the human rights situation concerned, and to report and recommend thereon to ECOSOC. Given the extreme sensitivity of issues raised under the 1503 procedure, the UN has only been able to institute it by guaranteeing strictest confidentiality to submissions received thereunder. This limitation placed on the 1503 process must, however, be understood within the context of the subtleties and effective diplomacy occurring at the international level. Even should a communication fail to be accepted by the Sub-Commission, this does not mean that a complex process of bargaining and exchange between the UN and the state concerned may not have taken place.

The first IHRAAM Petition was submitted in reference to the much-publicized beating of Los Angeles motorist Rodney King, as an instance of an ongoing situation of gross human rights violations against African-Americans. While the U.S. was able to avoid Sub-Commission condemnation (by only one vote), the federal government shortly thereafter instituted new more successful processes against the police officers concerned in the King beating, and a few months later, the U.S. Senate ratified the International Covenant on Civil and Political Rights.

Following submission of the second IHRAAM Petition (below), the UN Special Rapporteur on Contemporary Forms of Racial Discrimination scheduled the U.S. as the first country on his tour of investigation, and met with IHRAAM and numerous other

THE IHRAAM DIRECTORATE seated on the podium of the Dag Hammarskjold Library, United Nations Headquarters, New York during delivery of an IHRAAM-facilitated Briefing on Minority Rights delivered by UN Human Rights Center Director, Elsa Stamatopoulou-Robbins, on November 8, 1991. (Left to right): Dr. Farid I. Muhammad, Dr. Y. N. Kly, Thlau-Goo-Yailth-Thlee, and Dr. Yvonne King.

African-American groups. In addition, the U.S. is now scheduled to ratifiy the International Convention on the Elimination of All Forms of Racial Discrimination.

While it is not claimed that the IHRAAM Petition effected these actions, it seems reasonable to conclude that its international interventions numbered among the numerous forces which influenced U.S. actions, which themselves should lead to an ever deepening U.S. responsiveness to UN human rights standards. To say that a single petition submitted by a single NGO was a force in causing the UN to publicly and specifically launch an inquiry into discrimination in a country with the power and status of the U.S. may seem beyond expectation. However, should the effort of a single NGO be picked up and magnified by the support of another major state, such a UN inquiry may result.

PETITION FOR UN ASSISTANCE
UNDER RESOLUTION 1503 (XLVIII)*

Mr. Boutros Boutros-Ghali
Secretary-General of the United Nations
Palais des Nations
United Nations
CH-1211 Geneva
Switzerland

In response to a request by Ashanti Chimurenga of Amnesty International concerning the case of Gary Graham, which concerns U.S. application of the death penalty to an African-American child, in violation of international standards forbidding the execution of juvenile offenders, a policy nonetheless applied in the U.S. with such demonstrable effect as to indicate prejudicial intent towards African-Americans, and thus forming a part of the ongoing and persistent pattern of gross violations of the human rights of the African-Americans. This Petition views such celebrated instances as those relating to Rodney King, Lani Guinier, and most recently Gary Graham, as resulting from the continuing necessity to maintain the inequitable situation resulting from a history of systemic gross violations (enslavement, segregation, forced assimilation, etc.)

*Submitted by the International Human Rights Association of American Minorities (IHRAAM), 20 November, 1993

Whereas recognition of the inherent dignity, equality and inalienable rights of all members of the human family, including the fundamental right of members of minorities to exist in equal status with the majority, is the foundation of freedom, justice and peace in the world;

Whereas slavery, apartheid, forced assimilation and those measures required for their enforcement, such as torture, murder, lynching, ethnocide, etc. are internationally recognized as violating the most basic premises of human rights; and whereas nations which practice, encourage or condone activities such as genocide, ethnocide, ethnic cleansing, systematic racial discrimination, etc. are in violation of international law;[1]

Whereas both the historical oppression and resulting present inequality and circumstances of the African-Americans (descendants of the formerly enslaved Africans in the U.S.) are well known;

Keeping in mind that Articles 1 and 55 of the *UN Charter* specifically refer to the principle of self-determination; that one of the basic purposes of the UN, according to Article 1(2) is to "develop friendly relations among nations based on respect for the principle of equal rights and self-determination of peoples;"[2] that Article 55 explicitly ties the principle of self-determination to respect for human rights and fundamental freedoms for all or part of its people;[3] that the principle of self-determination is implicated in chapters XI, XII and XIII of the Charter;[4] that in the years since 1945, the principle has found its way into both the International Covenants (Article 27 of the ICCPR as it relates to minorities, and Article 1 as it relates to peoples),[5] the *Declaration on the Granting of Independence to Colonial Countries and Peoples*,[6] the *Declaration of Principle of International Law Concerning Friendly Relations*[7] and the decisions of the International Court of Justice in its numerous advisory opinions in relation to minority rights as these rights involved both external and internal self-determination,[8] just as it has been upheld by the UN General Assembly in relation to numerous recently emerging eastern European minorities; and that, although long applied only in the colonial context,[9] it is now in the post-colonial age being applied to minorities as well as some secessionist movements, to the extent that today legal scholars and the UN itself have agreed that the principle of internal self-determination applies outside of the colonial context, though within strict limits;[10]

Recognizing that the legal acceptability of self-determination outside of the colonial context also means making a distinction between external and internal self-determination; that is, excluding the right to secession and limiting self-determination to minority rights as it has been interpreted under Article 27 of the ICCPR and evolved in customary international law;

Keeping in mind that Articles 1 and 55 of the Charter commit the UN to the promotion of universal respect for human rights and basic freedoms, while Article 56 gives member nations an obligation to act, jointly or separately, to achieve the purposes set out in Article 55 — that is, Article 56 creates a duty to act to promote respect for rights and freedoms; and that when the core human rights rooted in the principle of autonomy[11] are grossly, systematically and persistently violated, UN intervention to end that violation is morally and legally permissible, since the principle of autonomy implies that government is only justifiable if it and its policies are an expression of the self-determination of peoples;[12]

Recognizing that of such violations, only those that are (1) gross, (2) systematic, and (3) persistent may be sufficiently severe as to justify UN involvement; and that violations are systematic if they are part of a consistent pattern, or a matter of state policy[13] (systematic violations include both overt governmental actions and covert but institutionalized practices, the effect of which is to regularly prevent the exercise of core rights, and are more than occasional, or of short duration {e.g. U.S. slavery, segregation, systemic racial discrimination resulting in ethnocide or forced assimilation});[14]

Understanding that to be a people, a group of persons must not only subjectively see themselves as a single people, but also objectively be seen, through speech and action, to be participating in or be able to participate in the creation or recreation of their own distinct social world;[15] that the concentration of all the power of a multi-national state in the hands of a single group thereby effectively preventing other constituent groups from realizing their own social space; and that any government or the agents and institutions of any government that prevent a minority or people from achieving its right to equal status with the majority, in fact or in law, may be regarded in the eyes of that people, and by international law, as acting illegitimately;[16]

Recognizing that international standards prohibit the imposition of death sentences, particularly on children, and that treaties and instruments containing such a prohibition include most importantly the Second Protocol of the *International Covenant on Civil and Political Rights* (ICCPR), and can be discerned as well from Article 6(5) of the ICCPR; Article 4(5) of the *American Convention on Human Rights*; Article 3, Resolution 1984/50 of ECOSOC; and Protocols I and II to the Geneva Conventions of 12 August 1949.

Therefore, insofar as gross, systematic and persistent denial of human rights is a violation of international law calling forth the right to international assistance, the Petitioners herein request that the UN employ all measures at its disposal, including those to be indicated herein, to exert pressure upon the U.S. government to cease its violations of the human rights of African-Americans, and to seek to resolve the long-standing grievances and inequities resulting from such historic and on-going policies, which includes extending to the African-Americans minority rights or internal self-determination, if such is required to achieve equal status with the majority.

Dear Mr. Boutros-Ghali:

IHRAAM, on behalf of its members and all descendants of enslaved Africans in America, takes this opportunity to congratulate and thank the Working Group of the Sub-Commission and those members who voted to accept for consideration the IHRAAM Petition of 30 April 1992 concerning Los Angeles motorist Rodney King, as exemplifying an individual instance of continuing human rights abuse resulting from past gross systemic violations of human rights of African-Americans in the U.S.. Although the IHRAAM Petition of 30 April 1992 was narrowly defeated in the Sub-Commission, IHRAAM was delighted to see that, so shortly after the show of international concern by the Working Group and many members of the Sub-Commission, the U.S. saw fit to ratify the *International Covenant on Civil and Political Rights* (ICCPR), to bring a new Ambassador to the UN, to find new legal grounds to retry the police involved in the cruel and callous

* There were over 200 pages in the 12 appendices accompanying the IHRAAM Petition. Due to space limitations, they cannot be reprinted here.

beating of the African-American motorist, Rodney King, and to effectively prosecute the Detroit police (see Appendix A*) for the murder of an African-American, Malice Green.

While direct linkage cannot be proved, most African-American organizations contacted by IHRAAM feel that the concern shown by the Sub-Commission was instrumental in securing a fair verdict in the King and Green trials, which thus avoided new rounds of violence, loss of life, and property damage. If this is true, then the U.S. government and all Americans should be thankful to the Sub-Commission for responding seriously to the slogan of the Los Angeles rioters: "No justice, no peace."

However, while it is likely that national and international opinion probably encouraged U.S. Judge John Davies to convict the officers in the King trial, the minimal sentence of 30 months that Judge Davies imposed upon them, his refusal to impose any fines (where $250,000.00 in fines had been pending), and his assignment of part of the blame to the victim, Mr. King, for the treatment that he endured, all indicate that the historic difficulty of African-Americans in obtaining justice through U.S. courts persists. (See Derrick Bell for a listing of major cases in which African-American interest was surrendered to that of the Anglo-American majority, Appendix B; also see Aviam Soifer* and Kathleen M. Sullivan for restrictions placed upon justiciable discrimination by recent rulings in U.S. Courts, Appendix C. As this Petition contends, however, African-Americans are victimized not only by laws and judicial decisions where their situation is specifically addressed or where discrimination is at issue, but also by those laws of an apparently general nature, whose true effect or intent can only be demonstrated through an historical examination of their enforcement record to see which groups such laws disproportionately affect.)

Dear Mr. Secretary-General,

The history of Africans in America began with the capture and forced emigration of African populations to America. During the "middle voyage" to America and the enslavement which awaited survivors, millions met their deaths, while in their homelands in Africa, the social fabric of entire civilizations was rent and destroyed. The African population did not ask to come to America; their arrival was purely involuntary and against their will. Their labor was exploited; all attempts were made to

* See Aviam Soifer, "Non-Discrimination in U.S. Courts: A Non-Solution?" abridged herein.

reduce them to cattle. Although African-Americans' rejection of this effort eventually succeeded, it took many years of struggle, many years of enduring torture and murder, etc. At the beginning, the Anglo-American majority attempted to regard the African population as property and less than human, and although legally instituted, this too failed. Not only did the U.S. government wish to place the bodies of Africans at the unlimited disposal of Anglo-Americans; the U.S. government wished to place their minds and cultures at its disposal. These efforts too met with failure. Thus later attempts were limited to efforts to destroy their social habits, and the long and rich traditions which they carried with them from the land of their birth. The U.S. was most successful in relation to the majority population in labeling these culturally different habits and practices as manifestations of heathenism and barbarism, and attempting to ruthlessly and rigorously suppress them. For example, any African caught practicing Islam was mercilessly tortured, killed, or forced to run away or go into hiding. The U.S. historical policy of enslavement is well known and documented (see Appendix D).

Subsequent to the Civil War, American citizenship was conferred upon the descendants of the enslaved Africans without any pretense of democratic consultation. After a relatively short period of Reconstruction, they were forced into a system of "separate but equal" segregation, which they rejected as being neither equal nor separately (self-)administered. During this period, they struggled against unequal distribution of wealth and discriminatory Jim Crow laws. The official recognition of difference by the Anglo-American majority during the official period of segregation or apartheid provided a theoretical cornerstone of the "separate but equal" argument without according minority rights or providing for the right to be different in a truly egalitarian sense. The official policy of "separate but equal," while unofficially permitting a significant degree of socio-cultural equality, in reality served as a societal opiate to avoid African-American revolt and secure co-operation; it did not provide for any significant economic or political autonomy, equality or self-determination.

The U.S. official policy of forced assimilation (referred to in the U.S. as "integration") in actuality began during the enslavement period with the concerted efforts to stamp out any official recognition of the African cultural heritage in America, particularly as it related to languages and religions. The process of acculturation to the dominant culture in the areas of language and religion, accompanied by extreme coercion and violence, proved largely successful to the extent that it produced a new African people: the African-Americans.

The separate but equal period which followed Reconstruction, however ill-conceived, nonetheless permitted, or was unable to prevent, the welding of separate African traditions into what became a distinct and recognizable African-American culture, demonstrable in lifestyle, music, cuisine, dress, language, dance, religious practice, socio-political organization and a wide range of distinct cultural differences which distinguish the African-American people from the majority population.

Forced assimilation entered its final stage in the 1960's, following the massive struggle by the African-American community as they became aware that the separate but equal system was not intended or capable of providing equality but was intended to enforce subordination and oppression. This period saw the dismantling of the separate but equal system and a further official incorporation of the African-Americans into the body politic of the American majority. Once again, there was no consultation with the population concerned. The popular slogans seeking "freedom" and "equality" were not discussed within the framework of their practical implications for a pluralistic democracy in a multi-national state (e.g. in a range of constitutional-legal options which might have permitted the African-American minority varying degrees of self-administration under terms of political and socio-economic equality). The abolition of separate legal systems pertaining to African-Americans, and their replacement by official policies of civil rights and non-discrimination, were never presented to the African-American people in terms of whether they wished to destroy their African-American identity and assimilate into the Anglo-American majority. Their recent widespread self-designation as "African-Americans," as well as other similar indicators, demonstrates that African-Americans, if asked, would respond with a resounding *"No!"*

The U.S. Courts, in line with the U.S. government, continue to promote forced assimilation (ethnocide) through the concept that all minority needs and rights can be subsumed within the concept of non-discrimination and equality (or sameness) before the law — this despite the fact that historical evidence strongly contradicts such a notion, and judicial enforcement of non-discrimination has become formal and de-contextualized, disallowing appropriate consideration for historical injustices and present special needs. Indeed, the courts have further restricted satisfaction by requiring "intent to discriminate," and refusing consideration to those who are not "immediate victims" (see Soifer and Sullivan, Appendix C).

However, the inadequacy of such policies is clearly demonstrable by the fact that African-Americans have neither been successfully assimilated nor have they achieved equality. This can be discerned from any statistical survey of indices related to political and socio-economic well-being. The inequality of the African-American community is today a fixture of life in the U.S. (see Appendix E). A few examples here will suffice:

* "The U.S. Imprisons Black Men at 4 Times S. Africa's Rate" (headline, *L.A. Times*, Jan. 5, 1991)
* "White Families Wealth Put at 10 times Blacks" (headline, *L.A. Times*, Jan. 11, 1991)
* "If the United States were divided into three countries based on race, the white population would rank No.1, ahead of Japan, while black Americans would fall to 31st spot, alongside Trinidad and Tobago." UN 1993 Human Development Report cited in *The Globe & Mail*, May 18, 1993.

Individual manifestations of the general phenomenon of gross violations of human rights — the excessive use of police force against Los Angeles motorist, Rodney King; the dumping of Lani Guinier, the African-American community's choice for the position of Assistant Attorney General for Civil Rights, whose nomination was withdrawn by President Clinton in response to charges that her modest "modified at-large voting" proposal would in effect constitute affirmative action on behalf of the African-American minority[18] (see Appendix F); or the application of the death sentence against juvenile offender Gary Graham, a subject of the present Petition — can only be viewed as the tip of the iceberg, the result of a prolonged official policy of systemic discrimination which in law and in fact subjugates the African-American minority to majority control and domination. As before mentioned, this iceberg is made up of a consistent, persistent and systematic pattern of past gross violations of the human rights of African-Americans by means of enslavement, torture, murder, lynching (see Appendix G), political intimidation, harassment (see Appendix H), and forced cultural assimilation (ethnocide), with neither apology nor compensation for these past gross violations whose ramifications continue into the present (see Appendix E).

Insofar as African-Americans' relation to the U.S. system has been involuntary and without consultation throughout its history, insofar as the majoritarian nature of the U.S. democracy has acted to thwart the expression of their needs through the electoral process, and insofar as the judicial system and the government itself has acted against affirmative action (see Appendix C), the African-American national minority has been unable to effectively exercise the control over their individual lives and that of their community that is so prominent and favorable a feature of pluralistic democratic systems in multi-national states and is called for by the right to equal status development in international law. No people can develop themselves without political and economic empowerment.

Mr. Secretary-General,

As the IHRAAM Petition of April 30, 1992 indicated and historical evidence substantiates (see Appendix E), the rectification of profound damages caused by past and present U.S. systemic discrimination against and gross violation of the human rights of African-Americans cannot occur until African-Americans are able to exercise their minority rights. All statistical evidence indicates that a policy of non-discrimination alone is insufficient to permit the African-American minority to achieve equal status with the majority, but rather, under the guise of aiding them, serves to continue their victimization. While a multi-national state may argue that treating all people (majority as well as formerly enslaved minorities) the same, legally and institutionally, regardless of their different histories and circumstances, somehow leads to a new society in which oppressed or formerly enslaved minorities, at some time in the future, will achieve equal-status, sameness or equality with the majority, this line of reasoning more frequently serves merely to justify or mask majority domination, and often exploitation, of national or ethnic minorities. Even the most superficial analysis reveals that treating such minorities as if they were the same as the majority in a majority-ruled multi-national society does not permit minority needs to be legitimately known or expressed, let alone addressed. Practically every multi-national society since the dawn of written history tried some version of this notion without succeeding, usually with the implicit intention of maintaining the domination of the minority group. That is why every UN study on minorities, such as those of Cruz, Capotorti, Eide, Calley, Daes, etc. discovered that non-discrimination may not be enough, and special measures or special rights are often required by Article 2:2 in conjunction with Article 27 of the ICCPR to achieve equal status for national minorities.

In relation to this issue, Karel Vasak suggested in *The International Dimension of Human Rights* that without self-determination (internal or external), all other rights become meaningless. Similarly, unless African-Americans are accorded appropriate forms of internal self-determination, it may not be possible for them to experience their human rights. Further, without appropriate enablement provided over time to financially facilitate the development of the required minority policies and institutions, the right to internal self-determination may be impossible to implement.

Mr. Secretary General,

In light of the foregoing, this Petition would now like to add the problematic caused by the U.S. policy of applying the death penalty to minors contrary to recognized standards of international law, and to raise, most specifically, the question of its application to Mr. Gary Graham, as an example of the continuing gross violations of the human rights of African-Americans.

Mr. Gary Graham is a 30-year old African-American who has been confined to death row in Texas for a crime which he was alleged to have committed at the age of 17, and of which overwhelming evidence appears to demonstrate, he is innocent. Mr. Graham's case has sparked a worldwide campaign to stop his execution, supported by such notables as Bishop Desmond Tutu, Vaclev Havel, Danny Glover and Harry Belafonte, among others. On Sunday, August 1, 1993, the *Washington Post* ran an article in support of Gary Graham, titled "The Executioner's Wrong: Texas Will Execute Gary Graham for a Murder He Almost Certainly Didn't Commit." (Documentation concerning the Gary Graham case, including a copy of the Memorandum in Support of Petition for Recommendation of Reprieve of Execution by Gary Graham's Texas attorneys is in Appendix I.)

Subsequent efforts to bring new evidence into court have been blocked by a procedural rule in Texas which limits the time available for introduction of newly-discovered evidence in a criminal case to thirty days after the sentence is entered.

However, Prof. Richard J. Wilson of the Washington College of Law of American University in Washington, D.C. proceeded to petition the Inter-American Commission in this regard, requesting it to take precautionary measures under Article 29 of its Regulations to prevent the death of Gary Graham. In response, at its 84th period of Sessions, the Inter-American Commission took precautionary measures as requested, resolving to:

1. Call upon the United States to take the necessary

measures to ensure that Mr. Graham is afforded a hearing before the Board of Pardons and Paroles in Texas.

2. Request that the Governor of Texas and the United States Government ensure that the sentence of death be not carried out in relation to Mr. Gary Graham for humanitarian reasons and to avoid irreparable damage.

3. Note that these measures are without prejudice to the final decision in this case.

Documentation pertinent to the petition to the Inter-American Commission is in Appendix J.

Mr. Secretary-General,

As petitioners under Resolution 1503 (XLVIII) concerning the gross violations of human rights, IHRAAM requests that the United Nations view the case of Gary Graham within the context of the larger issues to which it pertains: a) the general U.S. policy of application of the death penalty to minors in contravention of international standards, and b) its application in a prejudicial and disproportionate manner in relation to African-Americans. Due to systemic discrimination resulting from the past gross violations of their human rights, African-Americans are disproportionately represented in U.S. prisons, on death row, etc. (see Appendix K).

Concerning the execution of juveniles, the international standards are clear. As reported by Amnesty International, there is widespread adherence to such standards in practice. As of 1991, the USA was one of only seven countries worldwide known to have executed juvenile offenders in the last decade. (See Appendix L for documentation on international standards.)

The United States Government has not ratified Optional Protocols I and II, although it has ratified the International Covenant on Civil and Political Rights (ICCPR) and the Fourth Geneva Convention of 12 August 1949. In its ratification of the ICCPR, the Senate's advice and consent was subject to the following reservation: "(2) That the United States reserves the right, subject to its Constitutional constraints, to impose capital punishment on any person (other than a pregnant woman) duly convicted under existing or future laws permitting the imposition of capital punishment, including such punishment for crimes committed by persons below eighteen years of age."

It is obvious that such a reservation, if taken seriously,

defeats the purpose of many international instruments designed to end the death penalty, to protect children, as well as to prevent ethnocide or genocide, and in the case of African-Americans, to prevent the continuation of gross violations. One expert commentator, William A. Schabas, contends that the U.S. reservation "emasculates article 6 and is therefore incompatible with the nature and purpose of the Covenant" (see *The Abolition of the Death Penalty in International Law*, pp. 92-93, 1993). The Inter-American Court has declared (Advisory Opinion OC3/83 of September 8, 1983, *Restrictions to the Death Penalty (Arts. 4/2 and 4/4 American Convention on Human Rights)* that a reservation designed to suspend any non-derogable fundamental right is incompatible with the Convention.

Mr. Secretary-General,

The prejudicial and disproportionate application of the death penalty to African-American juveniles is of particular interest to this Petition on gross human rights violations of African-Americans, insofar as these U.S. laws can be seen to be directed against African-Americans — if not by intent in their drafting, then at minimum by effect, as illustrated by the historical record of their enforcement. As noted by Amnesty International:

> According to data published by Professor Victor Streib in 1987, [*Death Penalty for Juveniles*, Indiana University Press, 1987] 69% of all executed juvenile offenders since 1600 whose race was known were black and only 25% were white. (A further 3% were American Indians, 2% were Mexican-American and 1% were Chinese.) Streib found that racial disparities became even more marked after 1900 when the proportion of black children executed rose to 75%. He also noted that all 43 rape cases resulting in the execution of juveniles up to 1964 involved black offenders. In contrast, according to Streib's data, only 9% of the victims in the cases of executed juvenile offenders were black and this fell to only 4% between 1900 and 1986. (Streib's data did not include the last recorded execution, of Dalton Prejean in May 1990.) Racial disparities based on the race of offender alone have fallen considerably under present statutes, although some 49% of the 31 juvenile offenders on death row as of July 1991 were black. [It should be noted that African-Americans are only 15% of the American population.] Seventy-five percent had been convicted of murdering white victims. All four juvenile offenders executed since 1985 (of whom three were white and one was black) had been convicted of crimes against white victims.

As further cited by Amnesty International:

> According to recently published data, a total of 92 juvenile offenders were sentenced to death in the USA between January 1974 and 1 May 1991. Of these, 49 (53%) were black, 36 (39%) were white, three (3%) were Hispanic and the race of four unknown... As of 1 May 1991, 57 of the 92 inmates had had their death sentences reversed on appeal; most were re-sentenced to life imprisonment... As of 1 May 1991, 31 juvenile offenders were under sentence of death for murder in 12 US states. All were males. Fifteen (48%) were black, a further 15 were white and one was Hispanic. 74% of the victims in these cases were white...

Not only are blacks discriminated against by their disproportionate numbers among the executed; correspondingly, crimes against whites appear to receive proportionate to disproportionately greater legal response. This therefore raises the issue as to whether these laws — and the U.S.'s reluctance to dispense with them, even to the extent of inserting a reservation in its ratification of the ICCPR — represent an instrument of U.S. official policy for the control of the African-American minority, in contradiction of international standards and in gross violation of the human rights of African-Americans (and all juvenile offenders), hence forming yet another part of the historic and persistent U.S. pattern of gross violation of human rights of the African-American minority.

IHRAAM calls attention to this latest provocation of international law — the enforcement of the death penalty against children, which will mean, disproportionately, African-American children — and to the violation of the rights of Gary Graham in particular, as another example of continuing gross violations of the human rights of African-Americans by the U.S. government.

Mr. Secretary-General,

The U.S. government should not be given the tacit approval of the UN to continue to ignore past gross violations without compensation, nor to continue present gross violations against its national minorities. Surely, Mr. Secretary General, it is not your position nor that of the UN, while situated in New York within eyesight of more than one million obviously oppressed national minority members, to ignore their desperate plight — and at the same time assist U.S. human rights efforts in other countries. Surely Mr. Secretary General, your position and that of the UN cannot be that in the U.S., only "white Americans" have internationally protected human rights, and that what is done to African-Americans does not count. IHRAAM is sure that this is not your position, nor that of the UN.

The African-American national minority is now emerging from the period of political domestication. It is only normal that it now begins, in addition to looking towards the majority government, to look towards the UN and the international community for technical, political and economic assistance. The UN cannot continue to ignore the oppression of national minorities in its host country, and still maintain its human rights credibility in the world.

Therefore:

In the name of the African-American people, who are in full possession of their inherent human rights, and in light of the foregoing delineation of historic and ongoing gross violations of the human rights of African-Americans by U.S. policy in fact and in law, IHRAAM calls upon the United Nations and the world community to provide active assistance in the resolution of the long-standing human rights grievances of African-Americans.

While we have argued herein that, insofar as minority rights are not present in the U.S. constitution or law, any such resolution may require the extension of minority rights to the African-American people, as these measures alone will enable it to achieve equal status with the majority population and to recover from the historic damages which it has endured, IHRAAM believes that no progress towards any resolution whatsoever can be achieved without the active intervention of a third party, such as the UN Sub-Commission, whose willingness to provide the political, legal and conceptual leverage, the fora and the legal framework required by the oppressed formerly enslaved minority might convince the U.S. government to open a sincere dialogue on the historical grievances of the African-American minority, and modalities for their resolution.

IHRAAM calls upon the UN to act as a third party in setting up a situation wherein such a dialogue can occur. The African-American people do not believe that an honest, truly useful and equitable solution can be achieved without a significant degree of UN assistance. African-American history is filled with attempts at trying to achieve a sincere dialogue with the majority government. All attempts to achieve domestic remedy have failed. In 400 years, African-Americans have not even come close to achieving equal-status relations with the Anglo-American majority ethny which controls and runs the U.S. government as it sees fit, claims and distributes socio-economic resources as it sees fit, and ignores the human rights of African-Americans when it sees fit, etc.

UN assistance can be accomplished by observers being sent to the U.S., by a UN inquiry, by a special rapporteur's investigation, by the opening of a forum at the UN wherein any and all sectors of the African-American community and the U.S. government will be able, without fear of retaliation, to express their grievances on the issues of minority rights and past and ongoing gross violations of African-Americans' human rights, and seek UN assistance in defining and resolving the crisis in this relation which has proved so destructive, not just to African-Americans, but to America as a whole. *In this endeavor, the UN can expect the full cooperation and assistance of IHRAAM and the vast majority of African-American groups and individuals.*

Dear Mr. Secretary General,

African-Americans demand only those remedies that have been afforded to all other peoples or minorities, including the Native peoples and minorities of most developed countries. If the U.S. government is sincere about dealing honestly and candidly with the human rights problems of its African-American population, then it should not object to this time-honored process of third party (UN) assistance.

IHRAAM salutes you, Mr. Secretary General, and looks forward to cooperation with the UN and the U.S. government to facilitate the success of an appropriate forum.

We await the UN response.

Sincerely,

Dr. Y. N. Kly
for the IHRAAM Directorate

YNK:dc

---

1 This is not to deny that the "realm of rights" (to borrow a phrase from Judith Jarvis Thompson) is dynamic rather than static. Judith J. Thompson, *The Realm of Rights*, (1990). Rather, the "list" of

accepted rights is likely to grow and shrink over time, as attitudes are altered, balances of power shift, and the number and identities of those given a voice in the international legal forum change. Thus, human rights remains primarily a matter of customary international law, subject to all the forces affecting custom. For a useful discussion, see Theodor Meron, *Human Rights and Humanitarian Norms as Customary Law,* ch. 2 (1989). For a useful caution against the proliferation of rights in international legal discourse, see Philip Alston, "Conjuring Up New Human Rights: A Proposal for Quality Control," 78 *American Journal of International Law* 607 (1984).

2 UN Charter, art. 1.

3 UN Charter, art. 55.

4 See UN Charter, arts. 73-91. Article 73 in particular obliges states administering non-self-governing territories "to develop self-government, to take due account of the political aspirations of the peoples, and to assist them in the progressive development of their free political institutions..."

5 G.A. Res. 2200, UN GAOR, 21st Sess., Supp. No. 16, at 49 UN Doc. A/6316 (1967). Article 1 of the Covenant provides: "All peoples have the right of self-determination. By virtue of that right they freely determine their political status and freely pursue their economic, social and cultural development." The same wording is repeated in Article 1 of the International Covenant on Civil and Political Rights, G.A. Res. 2200, UN GAOR, 21st Sess., Supp. No. 16, at 52, UN Doc.A/6316 (1966).

6 G.A. Res. 1514, UN GAOR, 15th Sess., Supp. No. 16, at 66, UN Doc. A/4684 (1961).

7 *Declaration on Principles of International Law Concerning Friendly Relations and Co-operation among States in Accordance with the Charter of the United Nations.* G.A.Res. 2625, UN GAOR, 25th Sess., Supp. No. 28, at 121, UN Doc. A/8028 (1971) ("all peoples have the right freely to determine, without external interference, their political status and pursue their economic, social and cultural development, and every state has the duty to respect this right in accordance with the provisions of the Charter"). See C. Don Johnson, Note, "Toward Self-Determination — A Reappraisal as Reflected in the Declaration on Friendly Relations," 3 GA, *Journal of International and Comparative Law* 145 (1973). The principle is also contained in the *Declaration on the Establishment of a New International Economic Order*, G.A. Res. 3201, UN GAOR, 6th Special Sess., Supp. No. 1, UN Doc.A/9559 (1974).

8 Advisory Opinion on Legal Consequences for States of the Continued Presence of South Africa in Namibia (South West Africa) Notwithstanding Security Council Resolution 276 (1970), 1971 I.C.J. 16; Western Sahara (Advisory Opinion), 1975 I.C.J. 12. Also see Advisory Opinion of 6 April 1935 on *Minority Schools in Albania,* P.C.I.J., Ser. A/B, No. 64, 17.

9 As Professor Nanda has pointed out, "self-determination, at least in the specific context of colonialism, has acquired the status of an established rule of customary international law." Ved P. Nanda,

"Self-Determination Under International Law: Validity of Claims to Secede," 13 *Case Western Reserve Journal of International Law* 259 (1981). See also Ofuatey-Kodjoe, *The Principle of Self-Determination in International Law* 147 (1977).

10 See, e.g. Agolo Auna-Osolo, "A Retrospective Analysis of United Nations Activity in the Congo and its Significance for Contemporary Africa," 8 *Vand Journal of Transnational Law* 451 (1975); Lung-Chu Chen & W. Michael Reisman, "Who Owns Taiwan: A Search for International Title," 81 *Yale Law Journal* 599 (1972); John A. Collins, Note, "Self-Determination in International Law: The Palestinians," 12 *Case Western Reserve Journal of International Law* 137 (1980).

11 See generally Nanda, *supra* note 9 at 263-66.

12 A minority right can be viewed as essentially a protective fence built around a minority which allows it to develop its own distinct social world. It is grossly violated only if the easement becomes so large as to encompass the entire property — i.e., the fence is completely gone, the protective space around the minority invaded, its sense of its distinctive identity is forcibly dissipated, and it is placed under adverse rule, with no ability to choose the use to which the belongings of the minority (cultural, institutional, property, etc.) are put.

13 A similar conclusion is reached in Myers S. McDougal et al, *Human Rights and World Public Order: The Basic Policies of an International Law of Human Rights*, 239, (1960).

14 See *Restatement (Third) of Foreign Relations Law of the United States*, ss. 702, comment m.

15 To say people must be able to participate in the constitution of their social world is to assert that political action must be possible, not necessarily that all people take advantage of the occasions to speak and act. In a passive sense, people constitute their social world no matter how oppressive their surroundings. See Anthony Giddens, *The Constitution of Society* (1984). The principle of autonomy, however, requires more than this minimal involvement. It requires active participation through speech and action in construction and remodeling the economic, political and cultural structures. See Hannah Arendt, *The Human Conditions* (1958).

16 The social contract tradition in political theory forcefully argues this point. See, e.g. John Locke, *Two Treatises of Government* (Peter Laslett ed., 1988), Jean-Jacques Rousseau, *The Social Contract* (G.D.H. Cole ed., 1950), etc.

17 See Kevin Ryan, "Rights, Intervention and Self-Determination," *Denver Journal of International Law & Policy*, Vol. 20:1, p. 69.

18 Ms. Guinier was well received in the African-American community, whose leadership felt that her views might provide ideas and concepts that are crucial to enabling African-Americans to resolve many of their socio-political and economic problems. Ms. Guinier felt that a system of "modified at-large voting" would provide a more broadly democratic electoral system in general, and might assist the African-American population in gaining more effective

representation, by introducing a mechanism which would allow voters across a community to participate in electoral alliances rooted in any number of factors, not just race, but, as Guinier says, on like minds, not like bodies. Ms. Guinier's writings represent "an eloquent plea against electoral quotas, against measuring black electoral success in terms of the number of minority officials holding office" (*The Nation*, May 31, 1993) — a significant compromise, insofar as proportional representation is popularly used by states to enable minorities to achieve equal status and self-determination. Despite Guinier's modest suggestion, which was not even offered within the conceptual framework of minority rights *per se*, President Clinton has been forced to withdraw her nomination by powerful coalitions which fear that her proposal "amounts to affirmative action [special measures] for electoral and legislative outcomes — and suggests she might back job and other quotas" (*Business Week*, May 31, 1993). For supporting documentation, see Appendix F.

This occurred after the U.S. had become a party to the International Covenant on Civil and Political Rights, which most scholars and the Human Rights Committee have interpreted to support more than the humble proposal made by Ms. Guinier. Affirmative action is provided for explicitly by Article 2:2 and implicitly by Article 27 (special measures, as interpreted by most international legal scholars) of the ICCPR, as well as by Articles 1:4 and 2:2 of the Convention on the Elimination of All Forms of Racial Discrimination (CERD). The willingness of the highest executive authority in the United States to respond to putative fears of affirmative action rather than uphold it in accordance with his international-legal obligations under the ICCPR constitutes yet another indication of U.S. policymakers' historic tendency to block initiatives arising from the African-American community to address their political and socio-economic interest, in the interest of powerful sectors of the dominant majority (see Y. N. Kly, *International Law and the Black Minority in the U.S.*, 1985). Indeed, it is a refusal to permit African-Americans to experience a democratic process in the choice of their leaders and/or their community policies, if these leaders or policies do not accord with the interest of the Anglo-American majority — even if the majority's interest involves enslavement or apartheid (segregation) for the African-American, as it admittedly has in the past, or absorption into the American "underclass" through the processes of forced assimilation, which is primarily the U.S. policy regarding African-Americans in the present. Following this historical pattern, certainly the day after tomorrow for African-Americans will be the same as the day before yesterday.

Appendix I
Minority Rights in State Practice

The following examples of state practice have been selected from a wide array of possibilities, not in order to recommend any one instance in particular, but rather to indicate the diversity of constitutional-legal measures and approaches to state provision of minority protection.

The Basques in Spain
(Euzkadi)

The 1978 Constitution of Spain established the principle of regional autonomy in general, and specifically for four historic ethnic regions: Basque Country, Catalonia, Galicia and Andalusia.

While some jurisdictions might not pertain to more dispersed minorities, the Autonomy Statute of the Basques is of particular interest insofar as its extensive and comparatively specific elaboration of minority jurisdiction permits a cursory view of the range of sectors in which a minority might be empowered.

from the 1978 Constitution of Spain

Article 143

(1) In the exercise of the right of self-government recognized in Article 2 of the Constitution, bordering provinces with common historic, cultural and economic characteristics, island territories and provinces with historic regional status may accede to self-government and form Autonomous Communities in conformity with the provisions contained in this Title and in the respective Statutes.

(2) The right to initiate the process towards self-government lies with all the Provincial Councils concerned or with the corresponding inter-island body and with two-thirds of the municipalities whose populations represent at least the majority of the electorate of each province or island...

from the Autonomy Statute of the Basque Country Organic Law 3/1979 of 18 December 1979

Title I - Concerning the Jurisdiction of the Basque Country
Article 10
The Autonomous Community of the Basque Country has sole jurisdiction in the following matters:

(1) Delimitation of municipal territory, without prejudice to the powers corresponding to the Historic Territories in accordance with Article 37 of this Statute.

(2) Organization, regime and functioning of its institutions of self-government in accordance with the rules of this Statute.

(3) Internal electoral legislation affecting the Basque Parliament, "Juntas Generales" and Provincial Councils ("Disputaciones Forales"), in the terms laid down in this Statute and without prejudice to the powers vested in the Historic Territories, in accordance with the provisions of Article 37 herein.

(4) Local Government and Statute for the Public Officials of the Basque Country and of its Local Administration, without prejudice to the provisions of Article 149.1.18 of the Constitution.

(5) Preservation, modification and development of the Traditional, Regional Law and Special Civil Law, whether written or common law, belonging to the Historic Territories which make up the Basque Country, and the establishment of the territorial area of their applicability.

(6) Procedural rules and rules concerning administrative and economic-administrative procedure arising from the special features of the substantive law and the peculiar organization of the Basque Country.

(7) Public domain and property in the possession of the Autonomous Community, and public servitudes in matters under its jurisdiction.

(8) Woodland and forestry resources and services, livestock tracks and pastures without prejudice to the provisions of Article 149.1.23 of the Constitution.

(9) Agriculture and livestock farming, in accordance with the general planning of the economy.

(10) Fishing in inland waters, the shellfish industry and aquiculture, hunting and river and lake fishing.

(11) Hydraulic projects, canals and irrigation schemes when the waters flow, in their entirety, within the Basque Country; installations for the production, distribution and transport of energy, provided that such transport does not leave the territory and that its use does not affect any other province or Autonomous Community; mineral, thermal and subterranean waters. All this without prejudice to the provisions of Article 149.1.25 of the Constitution.

(12) Social welfare work.

(13) Foundations and Associations of an educational, cultural, artistic, charitable, welfare or similar nature in so far as their activities are carried out mainly in the Basque Country.

(14) Organization, regime and functioning of institutions and establishments for the protection and guardianship of juveniles, prisons and social rehabilitation centers, in conformity with the general legislation on civil, penal and penitentiary matters.

(15) Pharmaceutical control in accordance with the provisions of Article 149.1.16 of the Constitution, and hygiene, taking into account the provisions of Article 18 of this Statute.

(16) Scientific and technical research in co-ordination with the State.

(17) Culture, without prejudice to the provision of Article 149.2 of the Constitution.

(18) Institutions concerned with the promotion and teaching of Fine Arts. The Handicraft industry.
(19) Historical, artistic, monumental, archeological and scientific heritage. The Autonomous Community shall comply with the rules and obligations to be established by the State for the protection of this heritage from export and spoliation.
(20) Archives, Libraries and Museums not in state ownership.
(21) Agricultural and Property Chambers, Fishermen's Guilds, Chambers of Commerce, Industry and Shipping, without prejudice to the jurisdiction of the State in matters of foreign trade.
(22) Professional Associations and exercise of the degree professions, without prejudice to the stipulations of Articles 36 and 139 of the Constitution. Appointment of notaries public in accordance with State Laws.
(23) Co-operatives, Mutual Benefit Societies not belonging to the Social Security and other co-operative associations, in conformity with the general legislation on commerce.
(24) The Basque Country's own public sector, in so far as it is not affected by other rules in this Statute.
(25) Promotion, economic development and planning of economic activity in the Basque Country in accordance with the general planning of the Economy.
(26) Institutions of corporate, public and territorial credit and Saving Banks, within the framework of the guidelines issued by the State concerning the control of credit and banks and in accordance with general monetary policy.
(27) Internal trade, without prejudice to the general price policy, and free circulation of goods in the State territory and legislation on protection of competition. Local markets and fairs. Control of origin of goods and advertising in collaboration with the State.
(28) Protection of consumers and users in the terms of the previous paragraph.
(29) Establishment and regulation of Commodity Exchanges and other centers for dealings in commodities and securities in conformity with the commercial legislation.
(30) Industry, excluding the installation, expansion and transfer of industries subject to special rules for reasons of safety, military or health interest and those needing specific legislation for such functions, and those requiring prior contracts for the transfer of foreign technology. In the restructuring of industrial sectors, the Basque Country is responsible for the development and implementation of the plans established by the State.
(31) Planning of inland territory and coastline, town planning and housing.
(32) Railways, transport by land, sea, river and cable, ports, heliports, airports and the Meteorological Service of the Basque Country, without prejudice to the provisions of Article 149.1.20 of the Constitution. Hiring centers and loading terminals for transport matters.
(33) Public Works not legally classified as being of general interest or whose execution does not legally affect other territories.
(34) As regards roads and thoroughfares, in addition to the powers contained in paragraph 5, n.° 1 of Article 148 of the Constitution, the Provincial Councils of the Historic Territories shall retain in their entirety the legal regime and powers they already possess or which, as the case may be, they are to recover in accordance with Article 3 of this Statute.
(35) Casinos, gaming and betting, except for the national system of wagers for sporting charities.
(36) Tourism and sport. Leisure and entertainment.
(37) Basque Country statistics for its own purposes and jurisdiction.
(38) Public performances.
(39) Community development. Condition of women. Policy regarding children, youth and old people.

Article 42
The revenue of the General Treasury of the Basque Country shall consist of:

(a) The sums paid in by the Provincial Councils, as the expression of the contribution of the Historic Territories to the Basque Country's budget expenditure. A Law of the Basque Parliament shall establish criteria for equitable distribution and the procedure whereby, in accordance with such criteria, the contributions to be made by each Historic Territory shall be agreed upon and paid.

(b) The proceeds of the Autonomous Community's own taxes that may be established by the Basque Parliament, in accordance with the provisions of Article 157 of the Constitution and as stipulated in the Organic Law on the financing of the Autonomous Communities.

(c) Transfers from the Inter-Territorial Clearing Fund and other allocations to be charged to the General State Budgets.

(d) Revenues accruing from its own property and private law income.

(e) The yield from credit operations and public debt issues.

(f) Any other income which may be established by virtue of the stipulations of the Constitution or of this Statute.

Article 43

(1) The rights and property of the State or other public agencies attached to services and functions assumed by the Autonomous Community shall be included in the latter's own resources.

(2) The Basque Parliament shall decide to which of the agencies of the Basque Country ownership or use of such property and rights is to be transferred.

(3) A Law of the Basque Parliament shall regulate the administration, defence and preservation of the Heritage of the Basque Country.

Article 44
The General Budgets of the Autonomous Community shall contain the revenue and expenditure of general public activity, and shall be drawn up by the A Basque Government and approved by the Basque Parliament in accordance with the rules it shall itself establish.

Article 45

(1) The Autonomous Community of the Basque Country may issue public debt to finance investment expenditure.

(2) The size and characteristics of issues shall be established in accordance with the general planning of credit policy, and in CO-ordination with the State.

(3) Bonds issued shall be considered for all purposes as public funds.

Nationalities in China

A noteworthy aspect of the 1982 Chinese Constitution is its effort to establish equal status between the various ethnicities in China, avoiding the notion of majority and minority by use of the term "nationalities," and explicitly militating against the dangers of "big nation chauvinism." Also of interest is the fact that autonomy is

provided to nationalities on a variety of levels: autonomous regions, autonomous prefectures and autonomous counties, thereby providing for varying concentrations of groups in the overall population distribution.

from the Constitution of China (1982)

Preamble

...The people of all nationalities in China have jointly created a splendid culture and glorious revolutionary tradition

... The People's Republic of China is a unitary multinational state built up jointly by the people of all nationalities. Socialist relations of equality, unity and mutual assistance have been established among them and will continue to be strengthened. In the struggle to safeguard the unity of the nationalities, it is necessary to combat big-nation chauvinism, mainly Han chauvinism. The state does its utmost to promote the common prosperity of all nationalities in the country.

...The people of all China's nationalities, all state organs, and armed forces, all political parties and public organization and all enterprises and undertakings in the country must take the Constitution as the basic norm of conduct and they have the duty to uphold the dignity of the Constitution and ensure its implementation.

Article 4

All nationalities in the People's Republic of China are equal. The state protects the lawful rights and interests of the minority nationalities and upholds and develops the relationship of equality, unity and mutual assistance among all of China's nationalities. Discrimination against or oppression of any nationality, and acts which undermine the unity between them are prohibited; big-nationality chauvinism and local-nationality chauvinism must be opposed.

Regional autonomy is practised in areas where people of minority nationalities live in compact communities; in these areas organs of self-government are established for the exercise of the right of autonomy. All the national autonomous areas are inalienable parts of the People's Republic of China.

The people of all nationalities have the freedom to use and develop their own spoken and written languages, and to preserve or reform their own ways and customs.

Article 63

Minority nationalities are entitled to appropriate representation on the Standing Committee of the National People's Congress.

Article 98

Organs of self-government are established in autonomous regions, autonomous prefectures and autonomous counties...

Article 102

The people's congresses of nationality townships may, within the limits of their authority as prescribed by law, take specific measures suited to the characteristics of the nationalities concerned.

Section VI
The Organs of Self-Government of National Autonomous Areas

Article 114
The organs of self-government of national autonomous areas are the people's congresses and people's governments of autonomous regions, autonomous prefectures and autonomous counties...

Article 115
In addition to the deputies of the nationality or nationalities exercising regional autonomy in given administrative areas, the other nationalities inhabiting the same are entitled to appropriate representation in people's congresses of autonomous regions, autonomous prefectures and autonomous counties, and the number of deputies of the nationalities concerned is specified by statutes governing the exercise of autonomy in the national autonomous areas.

Article 116
The chairman of autonomous regions, heads of autonomous prefectures and heads of autonomous counties shall be persons of the nationality or nationalities exercising regional autonomy in those areas.

Article 117
The organs of self-government of autonomous regions, autonomous prefectures and autonomous counties exercise the right of national autonomy within the limits of their authority as prescribed by the Constitution, the law of regional national autonomy and the other laws; and at the same time they exercise the functions and powers of local organs of state as specified in Section V of Chapter Three of the Constitution.

Article 118
People's congresses of national autonomous areas have the power to draw up statutes governing the exercise of autonomy as well as separate regulations, in the light of the political, economic and cultural characteristics of the nationality or nationalities in a given area. The statutes governing the exercise of autonomy and the separate regulations drawn up by autonomous regions shall be submitted to the Standing Committee of the National People's Congress for approval before they become effective. The statutes governing the exercise of autonomy and the separate regulations drawn up by autonomous prefectures and autonomous counties shall be submitted to the standing committees of the people's congresses of provinces or autonomous regions for approval before they become effective, and they should be reported to the Standing Committee of the National People's Congress for record.

Article 119
The organs of self-government of national autonomous areas have autonomous powers in administering the finances of their areas. All revenues accruing to the national autonomous areas under the financial system of state shall be used according to the arrangements made independently by the organs of self-government of those areas.

Article 120
The organs of self-government of national autonomous areas independently administer the economic construction of their areas under the guidance of the state plans.
In developing natural resources and building enterprises in the national autonomous areas, the state should give due consideration to the interests of those national autonomous areas.

Article 121
The organs of self-government of national autonomous areas independently administer the education, science, culture, public health and physical culture in their respective areas, take charge of and protect the national cultural heritage, develop the good cultures of the nationalities and help them to flourish.

Article 122
The organs of self-government of national autonomous areas may, in accordance with the military system of the state and the actual local needs, and with the approval of the State Council, organize their local public security forces for the maintenance of public order.

Article 123
In performing their functions, the organs of self-government of national autonomous areas employ the spoken and written language or languages commonly used by the nationality or nationalities in a given area, according to the statutes governing the exercise of autonomy in the given national autonomous area.

Article 124
The state safeguards the right of national autonomy of the organs of self-government of national autonomous areas in the implementation of the laws and policies of the state according to the actual local situation; it gives financial, material and technical assistance to minority nationalities to accelerate their economic and cultural development.
The state helps the national autonomous areas to train large numbers of cadres, specialized personnel and skilled workers from among the nationality or nationalities in the given area.

The Sami People of Norway

The constitutional-legal institutionalization of politico-legal rights for the Sami people, including establishment of a Sami Assembly, is of particular interest insofar as it concerns a minority population which is dispersed throughout state territory. The Sami Act establishes, inter alia, *that the business of the Sami Assembly is any matter which affects the Sami, as determined by the Sami themselves, and that public bodies must consult with the Assembly prior to making decisions on matters coming within its scope. Economic control over some Sami activities has been transferred from Norwegian government ministries to the Sami Assembly. Affirmative action is part of official government policy, and is implemented by legal, financial and organizational measures. The following is abridged from a paper, originally titled "A Presentation of Norway's Policy Towards the Sami People," presented by the government of Norway to the Conference on Security and Cooperation in Europe Seminar: "Case Studies on*

National Minorities Issues: Positive Results," 1992. Not included: Amendments to Act No. 24 of 13 June 1969 concerning primary and lower secondary education.

A new article 110a was inserted into the Constitution on 27 May 1988:

"It is the responsibility of the authorities of the State to create conditions enabling the Sami people to preserve and develop its language, culture and way of life."

Act No. 56 of 12 June 1987 relating to the Sami Assembly ("Sametinget") and other Sami Legal Matters (the Sami Act) entered into force on 24 February 1989. The first election to the Sami Assembly was held in September 1989, and the Sami Assembly was formally inaugurated by the King of Norway on 9 October 1989. For the purpose of the Sami Assembly, Norway is divided into 13 constituencies, each of which has three representatives. The representatives are chosen by direct ballot by and among the Sami people who are registered in the Sami electoral register. All persons who regard themselves as belonging to the Sami population and who use Sami as their language at home, or who have a parent or grandparent who does or has done so, are entitled to be included in the Sami electoral register.

The Sami Act was amended by Act. No. 78 of 21 December 1990, whereby Sami-speaking people were given the right to use their language in contact with the local and regional authorities. A translation of the Act is enclosed as *Appendix 1*. The Act entered into force on 1 January 1992. It sets out the following language rights.

Six municipalities in the counties of Finnmark and Troms, where the Sami language has a strong position, form an administrative area for the Sami language. Special rules apply in this area. It is estimated that around 7,500 people are Sami-speaking in the whole area.

Local public bodies in the administrative area are obliged to answer in Sami when members of the public contact them in the Sami language, orally or in writing. Regional public bodies whose geographical area of competence covers the whole or part of the administrative area shall also reply in Sami when they receive written applications from members of the public. The King may extend these duties to public bodies outside the administrative area. Employees in public bodies to which the rules apply have the right to paid leave in order to learn Sami if the body needs such knowledge. It is not required that all the employees of a particular body master Sami, and the body may use interpreters if appropriate.

Official announcements that are directed especially towards the population in the administrative area shall appear both in Sami and in Norwegian. Acts and regulations that particularly concern the Sami population shall be translated into Sami. Official forms to be used in contact with public bodies in the administrative area shall be available in Sami and Norwegian.

The municipal councils are given the authority to decide that Sami shall be equal to Norwegian in the whole or parts of their administrations. This applies only to internal administration.

In addition to these general rights, extended rights to use the Sami language have been established in the legal system, the health and welfare sectors and vis-à-vis the church (sections 3-4, 3-5 and 3-6 of the Act).

Everyone shall have the right to learn Sami. Act No. 24 of 13 June 1969 relating to Primary and Lower Secondary Education was amended by Act. No. 78 of 21 December 1990 Act to enhance protection of this right. Children in

Sami districts are entitled to an education in or on the Sami language, and the municipal council may make such education compulsory. Outside Sami districts, children with a Sami background may receive instruction in Sami, and if there are at least three Sami-speaking pupils in a school, they may demand such education.

A Sami college of higher education was established in 1989. The college has about 80 students, most of whom are studying to be teachers.

Today, the Norwegian Broadcasting Corporation transmits through the Sami Radio in Karasjok for more than 300 hours a year. Sami Radio also produces television programs concerning Sami issues.

The Minister of Cultural Affairs is planning to establish a Sami Cultural Council on the basis of the existing Committee on Sami Cultural Affairs. If such a body is established, it will most likely be linked to the Sami Assembly.

On 20 June 1990 Norway ratified ILO Convention No. 169 concerning indigenous and tribal peoples in independent countries.

In the autumn of 1990, the Minister of Local Government appointed an interministerial working group to examine the possibilities of transferring duties and authority to the Sami Assembly. The working group submitted its recommendation in the spring of 1991, and it was circulated to a large number of institutions and agencies, including the Sami Assembly, for comments.

Several of the recommendations of the working group have already been implemented. These concern the administration of budgets for Sami culture and language which have been transferred from the central administration to the Sami Assembly.

Some of the allocations to Sami economic activities have also been transferred from the relevant ministries to the Sami Assembly. This has been done in order to strengthen the role and influence of the Sami Assembly.

Affirmative action for the benefit of the Sami people is part of official policy, and such measures have been implemented in many fields. In addition to legal measures, the Government also employs financial and organizational measures to implement this policy. Approximately NOK 200 million is allocated each year in direct state support for various Sami activities, institutions, etc.

1987
12 June. Act No. 56

ACT CONCERNING THE SAMI ASSEMBLY AND OTHER SAMI LEGAL MATTERS (SAMI ACT).

Passed by the Odelsting on 29 May 1987 and by the Lagting on 3 June 1987. Proposed by the Royal Ministry of Justice and Police.

Chapter 1. General provisions.

§ 1-1. *The purpose of the Act.*

The purpose of the Act is to make it possible for the Sami people in Norway to safeguard and develop their language, culture and way of life.

§ 1-2. *The Sami Assembly*

The Sami people are to have their own Sami Assembly elected by and among the Sami population all over this country.

§ 1-3. *The annual report of the Sami Assembly.*

The annual report of the Sami Assembly is to be sent to the King.

§ 1-4. *The financial liability of the State.*

The particular expenses falling upon county municipalities and municipalities in connection with elections to the Sami Assembly are to be covered by the State.

The King may issue regulations concerning the way in which the provision of the first paragraph is to be put into effect.

Chapter 2. The Sami Assembly.

§ 2-1. *The business and powers of the Sami Assembly.*

The business of the Sami Assembly is any matter which in the view of the Assembly particularly affects the Sami people.

The Sami Assembly may on its own initiative raise and pnounce an opinion on any matter coming within the scope of its business. It may also on its own initiative bring a matter before public authorities and private institutions, etc.

The Sami Assembly has the power of decision when this follows from other provisions in the Act or is otherwise laid down.

§ 2-2. *Seeking the view of the Sami Assembly.*

Other public bodies should give the Sami Assembly the opportunity to express an opinion before they make decisions on matters coming within the scope of the business of the Sami Assembly.

§ 2-3. *Method of election, time of election and term of office.*

Election to the Sami Assembly is by direct ballot.

Proportional representation is to be the method of election when more than one list of candidates is approved in a constituency. In other cases election is by majority vote.

Elections are to be held on the same day as elections to the Storting.

The Sami Assembly is elected for a term of four years. The term of office is reckoned from the first of October in the election year.

§ 2-4. *Constituencies and distribution of seats.*

At elections to the Sami Assembly three members with alternates are to be elected from each of the following constituencies *{listed in original paper, ed.}*

§ 2-5. *The right to vote.*

All persons having the right to vote in municipal elections in the constituency and who on polling day are included in the Sami electoral register (cf § 2-6) have the right to vote at elections to the Sami Assembly.

§ 2-6. *Sami electoral register*

All persons who provide a declaration to the effect that they consider themselves to be Sami, and who either

a) have Sami as the language of the home

b) have or have had a parent or grandparent with Sami as the language of the home

may demand to be included in a separate register of Sami electors in their municipality of residence.

§ 2-7. *Eligibility and right to propose candidates.*

All persons who are included in the Sami electoral register in the constituency are entitled to stand for election to the Sami Assembly. Those standing for election must also be included in the population register as being resident in the constituency on polling day. Administrative staff of the Sami Assembly are not however entitled to stand for election.

All persons who are included in the Sami electoral register in the constituency have the right to propose candidates in the constituency. A proposal for a list of candidates must be signed by at least 15 Sami with the right of proposal.

§ 2-8. *Obligation to accept election and grounds for exemption.*

All those who are entitled to stand for election to the Sami Assembly are under an obligation to accept election unless they are exempted in accordance with the rules contained in the second paragraph.

The right to claim exemption from election may be exercised by all those who:

a. have reached the age of sixty by the end of the election year, or

b. have served as members of the Sami Assembly during the last four years, or

c. prove to the constituency Sami electoral board that they will not be able to fulfill their obligations as members of the Sami Assembly without undue difficulty.

§ 2-9. *Exemption and retirement during the Assembly's term of office.*

Members of the Sami Assembly who are unable to fulfill the obligations of their office without undue difficulty may on application be relieved of their office by the Sami Assembly for a specified period of time or for the rest of its term of office.

Members who lose the right to vote in accordance with § 53 of the Norwegian Constitution, or who join the administrative staff of the Sami Assembly, retire from the Sami Assembly for the rest of its term of office.

§ 2-10. *Electoral authority.*

The Sami Assembly is the highest electoral authority at elections to the Sami Assembly.

§ 2-11. *Additional electoral provisions.*

The Kind may issue additional provisions concerning elections to the Sami Assembly.

§ 2-12. *The Administration of the Sami Assembly*

The Sami Assembly is to have its own administration. Administrative staff are to be appointed by the Sami Assembly.

§ 2-13. *Languages of negotiation.*

At meetings of the Sami Assembly all persons have the right to speak Sami or Norwegian in accordance with their own wish.

§ 2-14. *Rules of procedure.*

The Sami Assembly issues regulations concerning the summoning and order of business of the Sami Assembly.

Chapter 3. Transitional rules and commencement of functions.

§ 3-1. *Transitional rules.*

The Sami Assembly is a further development of the Norwegian Sami Council. The Sami Assembly is to assume all the functions, rights and obligations of the Norwegian Sami Council.

The King may issue rules concerning the summoning and order of business of the Sami Assembly. These rules shall apply until the Sami Assembly has established its rules of procedure in accordance with § 2-14.

§ 3-2. *Commencement.*

This Act comes into force on the date decided by the King.

Act concerning amendments to Act No. 56 of 12 June 1987 (Sami Act), to Act No. 24 of 13 June 1969 (Primary and Lower Secondary Education Act), and to Act No. 5 of 13 August 1915 (Courts Act)

I

In Act No. 56 of 12 June 1987 concerning the Sami Assembly and other Sami legal matters (Sami Act) the following provisions shall read thus:

§ 1-5. *The Sami language*

Sami and Norwegian are equal languages. They shall be languages with equal status pursuant to the provisions of Chapter 3.

Chapter 3. The Sami language

§ 3-1. *Definitions*

In this Chapter the following definitions shall apply:

1. The administrative area for the Sami language means the municipalities of Karasjok, Kautokeino, Nesseby, Porsanger, Tana and Kåfjord.
2. Public body means any state or municipal body
3. Local public body in the administrative area means any municipal, county or state body serving an area which includes a municipality or a part of a municipality in the administrative area for the Sami language.
4. Regional public body in the administrative area means any county or state body serving an area which wholly or partly includes several of the municipalities in the administrative area for the Sami language but which is nevertheless not nationwide.

§ 3-2. *Translation of rules. Announcements and forms*

Acts and Regulations of particular interest to the whole or parts of the Sami population shall be translated into Sami.

Announcements from public bodies which are particularly addressed to the whole or parts of the population in the administrative area shall be made in both Sami and Norwegian.

Forms for use with respect to a local or regional public body in the administrative area shall be available in both Sami and Norwegian. The King will issue more detailed rules concerning the implementation of this provision.

§ 3-3. *Right to a reply in Sami.*

Any person who contacts a local public body in the administrative area in Sami has a right to a reply in Sami. However this does not apply to oral approaches to public servants carrying out duties outside the office of the body concerned.

Any person who contacts a regional public body in the administrative area in writing in Sami has a right to a written reply in Sami. The King may in special cases make exceptions for particular regional public bodies.

§ 3-4. *Extended right to use Sami in the legal system*

To courts with jurisdictions which wholly or partly include the administrative area the following rules concerning the use of Sami additionally apply:

1. Any person has the right to submit processual writs with annexes, written evidence or other written submissions in Sami. If the court is to transmit the submission to an opposite party, it makes provision for translation into Norwegian. Translation may be dispensed with if the opposite party consents.

2. Any person has the right to contact the court orally in Sami provided the legal procedure legislation allows for oral instead of written submission. If the court is under an obligation to take down the submission in writing, the person putting forward the submission may demand that it be taken down in Sami. Such a demand does not waive any time limit. The second and third sentences of 83-4(1) apply correspondingly.
3. Any person has the right to speak Sami in court. If any person who does not speak Sami is to participate in the proceedings, use is made of an interpreter appointed or approved by the court.
4. When a party makes application for this, the presiding judge may decide that the language of the proceedings shall be Sami. The second sentence of § 3-4(3) applies correspondingly.
5. If the language of the proceedings is Sami, the presiding judge may decide that the court record shall also be kept in Sami. The court makes provision for translation into Norwegian.
6. The court makes provision for court records that are written in Norwegian to be translated into Sami when a party so demands. Such a demand does not waive any time limit.

To the police and prosecuting authority serving an area which wholly or partly includes the administrative area, the following rules concerning the use of Sami additionally apply:

1. Any person has the right to speak Sami during interrogation at the office of the body concerned.
2. Any person has the right to use Sami when submitting an oral report and a notice of appeal.

To the Prison Service's institutions in Troms and Finnmark the following rules concerning the use of Sami additionally apply:

1. §-5 applies correspondingly to inmates.
2. Inmates have the rignt to use Sami to one another and to their family.
3. Inmates have the right to use Sami for oral notice of appeal to the prison authority.

§ 3-5. *Extended right to use Sami in the health and welfare sectors.*

Any person wishing to use Sami to safeguard his or her interests vis-à-vis local and regional public health and welfare sectors.

Any person wishing to use Sami to safeguard his or her interests vis-à-vis local and regional public health and welfare institutions in the administrative area has the right to be dealt with in Sami.

SS 3-6. *Individual ministration by the Church*

Any person has the right to individual ministration by the Church in Sami in the parishes of the Church of Norway in the administrative area.

SS 3-7. *The right to leave for educational purposes*

Employees of a local or regional public body in the administrative area have a right to leave with pay in order to acquire knowledge of Sami when the body has a need for such knowledge. This right may be made conditional upon the employee's undertaking to work for the body for a certain time after such educational provision. The King will issue more detailed rules concerning the implementation of these provisions.

SS 3-8. *The right to be taught in Sami*

Any person has the right to be taught Sami. The King may issue more detailed rules concerning the implementation of this provision.

The rules contained in and issued pursuant to the Primary and Lower Secondary Education Act and the Upper Secondary Education Act apply to instruction in and through the medium of Sami in primary and lower secondary schools and in upper secondary schools.

SS 3-9. *Sami in the municipal administration*

The municipal council may decide that Sami shall have equal status with Norwegian in the whole or parts of the municipal administration.

SS 3-10. *Extension of the scope of the provisions.*

The King may determine that the provisions of this Chapter which are limited to local or regional public bodies in the administrative area shall also wholly or partly apply to other public bodies or to private legal persons when they make decisions on behalf of the state or a municipality.

§ 3-11. *Appeal*

If a public body does not follow the provisions of this Chapter, the person whom the case directly concerns may appeal to the body which is immediately above the body the appeal concerns. The county governor is the appellate authority when the appeal concerns municipal or county bodies.

Nationwide Sami organizations and nationwide public bodies with tasks of particular relevance for the whole or parts of the Sami population also have the right of appeal in such cases. The same applies in cases in which no single person is individually affected.

§ 3-12 *Sami Language Council*

A Sami Language Council is to be established. The Sami Assembly appoints the members of the council and determines who shall be the president and vice-president of the council.

The King will issue more detailed rules concerning the composition, organization, term of office, tasks, etc. of the council.

Constitution of the Mi'kmaq Commonwealth

The Mi'kmaq Constitutional Text was commissioned by the Native Council of Nova Scotia (NCNS) and drafted with the advice of one of the foremost authorities on the constitutions of the world, the late Albert P. Blaustein, Professor of Law Emeritus at Rutgers University School of Law, Camden, New Jersey. While the Constitution has not yet been approved by the Mi'kmaq people or recognized by the Canadian government, the Mi'kmaq have recently been accorded jurisdiction over education by the Canadian government (see* Globe & Mail *article opposite) in line

with the steadily evolving Canadian effort to extend self-government to its aboriginal peoples. The NCNS has proposed the Constitution to the Mi'kmaq people in the hope that this "concept of Mi'kmaq self-government will not only contribute to the debate about aboriginal rights but will stimulate the search for a new mutually beneficial relationship between the Mi'kmaq and Canada." Following are selected articles.*

from the Constitution of the Mi'kmaq Commonwealth

Preamble

We the Mi'kmaq, a sovereign people under the Creator of all life and all that is around us, who have maintained sovereign nationhood since time immemorial, in the exercise of our inherent sovereignty and inalienable right of self-determination, do hereby give unto ourselves and our posterity this Constitution to establish a Commonwealth, to achieve genuine social dignity, to protect our rights and liberties, to promote our aspirations, to assert our principles, to affirm our ecocentric convictions avowing respect for all plant and animal life, and to proclaim our identity and ideals to all other nations of the world.

Chapter 1 Constitutional Principles

Article 1 The Mi'kmaq Commonwealth is the sovereignty of the Mi'kmaq, wherever they may be domiciled.

Article 2 The Mi'kmaq ascribe to multi-citizenship. Every Mi'kmaq is simultaneously a citizen of the Mi'kmaq Commonwealth and a citizen of Canada and is entitled to all of the rights and privileges appertaining to such citizenship.

Article 4 Unless otherwise provided in this Constitution, any agreement between the Mi'kmaq Commonwealth and other sovereignties, including other Indian Nations, shall have the form and the substance of an international treaty.

Article 5 Unless otherwise provided by treaty, the lands of the Mi'kmaq Commonwealth shall not be subject to taxation either by the Government of Canada or its provinces, nor shall there be any restrictions on the establishment of private businesses on Mi'kmaq lands save those of the Mi'kmaq Commonwealth.

Article 6 (1) The Mi'kmaq Commonwealth is established to serve the needs and aspirations of the Mi'kmaq people. Its fundamental purpose shall be to guarantee, protect and actively promote the social dignity of the Mi'kmaq people, both as individuals and as a Nation.
(2) All citizens are entitled to equal legal treatment and protection and to equal opportunity. The Mi'kmaq Commonwealth shall promote and develop institutions, programs and services, and shall solicit such development of programs in Canada, to ensure the

* Dwight A. Dorey, *Aboriginal Self-Government for the Mi'Kmaq People of Nova Scotia: Essential Features of a Workable Model," Native Council of Nova Scotia, Truro, N.S., 1994, p. 54.*

N.S. Micmac gain control of education

Historic deal gives natives power to create curriculum

BY RUDY PLATIEL
Native Affairs Reporter

TORONTO — An accord hailed as a historic step forward in native self-government that gives complete control of education to Nova Scotia's Micmac was signed yesterday by federal Indian Affairs Minister Ron Irwin and 13 Nova Scotia chiefs.

Chief Noel Doucette of the Chapel Island First Nations, chairman of the Mi'kmaq Educational Authority, said the agreement gives the Micmac complete jurisdiction over the education of their children and is something he has been seeking for 25 years.

The accord pledges both sides to negotiate a final agreement on the transfer by next June that would give Nova Scotia Micmac the right to pass laws affecting the education of their children, Mr. Doucette said in a telephone interview.

While the Micmac would probably retain much of Nova Scotia's teaching standards and school curriculum, the transfer will allow them to create areas of special emphasis on their language and culture, he said.

Mr. Irwin said the accord is the first one in Canada's history to turn complete control of education over to natives throughout a province and is another example of recognizing the inherent right of self-government.

A great deal of progress has already been made in native education by turning over administration to Indians, and "I thought it was time to move jurisdiction."

Mr. Irwin said the transfer will mean that Micmac education officials will be able to negotiate directly with school boards, the province and universities on such things as subject matter and tuition.

"I think that it will keep more aboriginal people in school because they have a proprietary interest in the process," the minister said.

Harvey McCue, executive director of the Mi'kmaq Educational Authority, said that in addition to the ability to pass laws, there will be accountability for the education of Micmac children, of which 2,200 are currently in schools throughout the province.

"Parents or leaders will be able to identify who or what group is responsible for any difficulties," Mr. McCue said.

"Right now there is no accountability. Legally, the Minister of Indian Affairs is accountable . . . and that is substantively unlike the provincial system where you have either a superintendent or a board chairman or a minister of education who is responsible."

Mr. Irwin said he expects the Micmac agreement to become a model for others across Canada.

If he had tried to go to natives with a national proposal, aboriginal leaders would have been suspicious, Mr. Irwin said.

"By going to a specific province or specific group and saying, 'What do you want to do?' and them telling me, I am finding that from their success more [groups] want to buy in," Mr. Irwin said.

"Already New Brunswick first nations want to do the same thing, and Saskatchewan also wants to do it. I am finding that by having a successful experience, the experience can be moved easier."

One of the big stumbling blocks in the past has been the issue of financing. But Mr. Irwin said he has also changed that approach.

"Traditionally you would sit down at a table and the second or third question would be about the money," he said. The result is that negotiations would often bog down without getting to the other fundamentals.

Now, he said, he focuses discussion on what aboriginal leaders want to achieve in restructuring, and assigns discussion of financing to separate talks with lower-level government and aboriginal representatives.

That puts negotiating on financing where it is traditionally done between Ottawa and the provinces, Mr. Irwin said.

The Globe and Mail,

Saturday, November 5, 1994

achievement of the social dignity of the Mi'kmaq and the removal of the political, economic and social obstacles and barriers which impair the full equality of opportunity and the equal social treatment and economic self-sufficiency of the Mi'kmaq.

Article 11 Nothing in this Constitution shall authorize or be interpreted as consent to the termination of any trust or other responsibility of the Canadian or Provincial Governments to the Mi'kmaq.

Chapter II Territory and Jurisdiction

Article 12 (1) The sovereign powers, authority and jurisdiction of the Mi'kmaq Commonwealth shall extend to all of its traditional territory.

Article 13 Under the conditions to be determined by law, the sovereign powers, authority and jurisdiction of the Mi'kmaq Commonwealth over the Mi'kmaq may extend beyond its geographical boundaries.

Chapter III Citizenship

Article 17 The criteria for Mi'kmaq citizenship shall include parentage, location of birth, length of residence, self-identification, adoption, affiliation and community acceptance.

Article 19 No provision on citizenship in this Constitution or in the law shall have the effect of depriving or impairing any right or privilege of a descendant of a Mi'kmaq citizen toward the Canadian Government or any of its provinces based on awards made for the benefit of the Mi'kmaq or other cause.

Chapter IV: Fundamental Rights and Duties

Article 22 The citizens of the Mi'kmaq Commonwealth, as aboriginals, shall possess and enjoy inherent aboriginal rights wherever they may be throughout Canada, limited only by laws enacted by other Indian Nations.

Article 23 The citizens of the Mi'kmaq Commonwealth shall possess and enjoy equal opportunity to participate in the activities and share in access to the economic resources of the Mi'kmaq Commonwealth.

Article 26 Nothing contained in this Constitution shall affect the rights of Mi'kmaq citizens as citizens of Canada or as citizens of their respective provinces.

Chapter VI: Assembly of Delegates

Article 32 The Assembly of Delegates shall be the legislative arm of the Mi'kmaq Commonwealth. It shall be a unicameral body, with one Delegate from each of the constituencies of the Mi'kmaq Commonwealth, elected for three years.

Article 33 A Constituency Commission shall be appointed to establish the constituencies of the Mi'kmaq Commonwealth. One-third of its membership shall be appointed by the Grand Council of the Mi'kmaq, one-third by the President of the Mi'kmaq Commonwealth and one-third by the President of the Assembly of Delegates... The constituencies for the first elections under this Constitution shall be established by a six-member Temporary Constituency Commission, with two members appointed by the Grand Council of the Mi'kmaq, two members appointed by the _____ and two members appointed by the _____.

Article 34 The members of the Assembly of Delegates shall make their own procedural rules and regulations in conformance with the principles of this Constitution. They shall elect their own President of the Assembly and such other officers as they deem proper. They shall appoint committees, employ advisors, clerks and security personnel and provide for the maintenance of records. They shall meet at least four times a year in sessions of not less than seven working days at times and at places to be determined by the membership.

Article 35 The Assembly of Delegates shall have all of the legislative powers of the Mi'kmaq Commonwealth and shall, pursuant to this Constitution, have the power, duty and responsibility to provide laws, ordinances and resolutions:

1) To govern the conduct of Mi'kmaq citizens;

2) To regulate the land and resources of the Mi'kmaq Commonwealth, including (a) the right to acquire lands and resources; (b) the right to prevent the sale, disposition, lease, use or encumbrance of Mi'kmaq lands and resources when injurious to the interests of the Mi'kmaq Commonwealth; (c) the right to otherwise enter into agreement to lease or grant the use of Mi'kmaq lands and resources to private persons and public bodies; and (d) the right to provide for the proper use and development of Mi'kmaq lands and resources and to prevent their misuse;

3) To manage, protect, preserve and regulate hunting, fishing and fowling rights in the Mi'kmaq Commonwealth;

4) To monitor all activities which might have an environmental impact and to take action to ensure proper environmental protection;

5) to lay and collect taxes and assessment, both directly and indirectly through fiscal agreements with the Canadian and Provincial Governments and with other Indian Nations andorganizations, including the authority to enter into agreements with other governments on taxes and royalties on the use and exploitation of Mi'kmaq Commonwealth lands and resources;

6) To amend, approve and adopt annual budgets and to authorize the expenditure of funds in accordance with those budgets;

7) To regulate finance and economic development and trade, both within Canada and with foreign nations and international organizations;

8) To regular inheritance of personal property and interests in lands;

9) To provide for the maintenance of law and order, the administration of justice and the preservation of Mi'kmaq customary law by establishing judicial tribunals, law enforcement agencies and criminal and civil laws necessary to the governance of the Mi'kmaq Commonwealth;

10) To provide for educational, cultural and social institutions and other measures for the preservation of the Mi'kmaq language, culture and traditions;

11) To promote, protect and provide for the social well-being of the

Mi'kmaq with measures (a) on domestic affairs to strengthen the family unit and the traditions of the extended family; (b) on adoption and the appointment of guardians for minors and incapacitated persons; (c) on public health generally and especially for the health and care of elders; and (d) on housing;

12) To approve by a majority vote of all of its Delegates the appointments made by the President of the Mi'kmaq Commonwealth;

13) To retain professional and technical advisors;

14) To establish a Constitutional Advisory Council to recommend constitutional changes and amendments for Canada, for the Canadian provinces and for the Mi'kmaq Commonwealth and to counsel and advise other Canadian Indian nations on the drafting of their own constitutions;

15) To enact laws, ordinances and regulations necessary and proper to carry out the foregoing powers and such other legislative responsibilities incumbent upon the Assembly of Delegates pursuant to this Constitution.

Article 36 In order to assist in the implementation of this Constitution, the treaties entered into and the legislation enacted pursuant thereto, the Assembly of Delegates shall establish by law the following autonomous Administrative Commissions, whose members shall be appointed by the President of the Mi'kmaq Commonwealth and confirmed by the Grand Council of the Mi'kmaq and the Assembly of Delegates;

a) Elections Commission

b) Budget and Audit Commission

c) Public Service Commission

d) Police Commission

e) Ombudsman Office

f) Environment Commission

g) Fish, Game and Fowling Commission

h) Business, Trade and Commerce Commission

i) Gambling Commission

j) Other commissions necessary to carry out the objectives and goals of this Constitution.

Chapter VII Executive-Administrative Branch

Article 37 The President of the Mi'kmaq Commonwealth shall be the head of state of the Mi'kmaq Commonwealth and shall serve as its official representative. The President shall oversee, implement and execute all laws, ordinances and resolutions enacted by the Assembly of Delegates.

Article 41 The President of the Mi'kmaq Commonwealth shall appoint a foreign minister, an attorney-general, a minister of finance and such other cabinet officers as the Assembly of Delegates shall authorize.

Article 42 Ambassadors, high commissioners, chargés d'affaires, consuls, trade commissioners and other diplomatic officers shall be appointed by the President of the Mi'kmaq Commonwealth, in conjunction with the Grand Council, to represent the Mi'kmaq Nation in embassies and consulates to be established in Canada, in the Canadian provinces, in the other Indian Nations within the borders of Canada and in nations beyond the Canadian borders. Diplomatic representatives shall also be designated to Métis and Inuit organizations. The President shall also send representatives to conferences and meetings of the United Nations and other international organizations dealing with issues relating to human rights, aboriginal rights and minority rights.

Chapter IX Ratification and Amendments

Article 49 This Constitution shall come into effect following ratification by the electorate of the Mi'kmaq Commonwealth in a referendum called for that purpose. The referendum shall be under the supervision of the Temporary Constituencies Commission.

Appendix II
Minority Rights: Selected International Texts

UNESCO Convention Against Discrimination in Education (1960)

Article 2

When permitted in a State, the following situations shall not be deemed to constitute discrimination, within the meaning of Article 1 of this convention:

(b) The establishment or maintenance, for religious or linguistic reasons, of separate educational systems or institutions offering an education which is in keeping with the wishes of the pupil's parents or legal guardians, if participation in such systems or attendance at such institutions is optional and if the education provided conforms to such standards as may be laid down or approved by the competent authorities, in particular for education of the same level;

Article 5

1 The States parties to this convention agree that:

(c) It is essential to recognize the right of members of national minorities to carry on their own educational activities, including the maintenance of schools and, depending on the educational policy of each State, the use or the teaching of their own language, provided however:

(i) That this right is not exercised in a manner which prevents the members of these minorities from understanding the culture and language of the community as a whole and from participating in its activities, or which prejudices national sovereignty;

(ii) That the standard of education is not lower than the general standard laid down or approved by the competent authorities; and

(iii) That attendance at such schools is optional.

International Convention on the Elimination of All Forms of Racial Discrimination (1966)

Article 1

1 In this Convention, the term 'racial discrimination' shall mean any distinction, exclusion, restriction or preference based on race, colour, descent, or national or ethnic origin which has the purpose of nullifying or impairing the recognition, enjoyment or exercise, on an equal footing, of human rights and fundamental freedoms in the political, economic, social, cultural or any other field of public life.

4 Special measures taken for the sole purpose of securing adequate advancement of certain racial or ethnic groups or individuals requiring such protection as may be necessary in order to ensure such groups or individuals equal enjoyment or

exercise of human rights and fundamental freedoms shall not be deemed racial discrimination, provided, however, that such measures do not, as a consequence, lead to the maintenance of separate rights for different racial groups and that they shall not be continued after the objectives for which they were taken have been achieved.

Article 2

2 States Parties shall, when the circumstances so warrant, take, in the social, economic, cultural and other fields, special and concrete measures to ensure the adequate development and protection of certain racial groups or individuals belonging to them, for the purpose of guaranteeing them the full and equal enjoyment of human rights and fundamental freedoms. These measures shall in no case entail as a consequence the maintenance of unequal or separate rights for different racial groups after the objectives for which they were taken have been achieved.

International Covenant on Civil and Political Rights (1966)

Article 27

In those states in which ethnic, religious or linguistic minorities exist, persons belonging to such minorities shall not be denied the right, in community with the other members of their group, to enjoy their own culture, to profess and practice their own religion, or to use their own language.

UNESCO Declaration on Race and Racial Prejudice (1978)

Extracts

The General Conference of the United Nations Educational, Scientific and Cultural Organization, meeting in Paris at its twentieth session, on 27 November 1978 adopted unanimously and by acclamation the following Declaration:

Preamble

The General Conference of the United Nations Educational, Scientific and Cultural Organization, meeting at Paris at its twentieth session, from 24 October to 28 November 1978,

Whereas it is stated in the Preamble to the Constitution of Unesco, adopted on 16 November 1945, that the great and terrible war which has now ended was a war made possible by the denial of the democratic principles of the dignity, equality and mutual respect of men, and by the propagation, in their place, through ignorance and prejudice, of the doctrine of the inequality of men and races, and whereas, according to Article I of the said Constitution, the purpose of Unesco 'is to contribute to peace and security by promoting collaboration among the nations through education, science and culture in order to further universal respect for justice, for the rule of law and for the human rights and fundamental freedoms which are affirmed for the peoples of the world, without distinction of race, sex, language or religion, by the Charter of the United Nations',

Recognizing that, more than three decades after the founding of Unesco, these principles are just as significant as they were when they were embodied in its Constitution,

Mindful of the process of decolonization and other historical changes which have led most of the peoples formerly under foreign rule to recover their sovereignty, making the international community a universal and diversified whole and creating new opportunities of eradicating the scourge of racism and of putting an end to its odious manifestations in all aspects of social and political life, both nationally and internationally,

Convinced that the essential unity of the human race and consequently the fundamental equality of all human beings and all peoples, recognized in the loftiest expressions of philosophy, morality and religion, reflect an ideal towards which ethics and science are converging today,

Convinced that all peoples and all human groups, whatever their composition or ethnic origin, contribute according to their own genius to the progress of the civilizations and cultures which, in their plurality and as a result of their interpenetration, constitute the common heritage of mankind,

Confirming its attachment to the principles proclaimed in the *United Nations Charter* and the *Universal Declaration of Human Rights* and its determination to promote the implementation of the International Covenants on Human Rights as well as the *Declaration on the Establishment of a New International Economic Order*,

Determined also to promote the implementation of the United Nations Declaration and the *International Convention on the Elimination of all Forms of Racial Discrimination*,

Noting the *International Convention on the Prevention and Punishment of the Crime of Genocide*, the *International Convention on the Suppression and Punishment of the Crime of Apartheid* and the *Convention on the Non-Applicability of Statutory Limitations to War Crimes and Crimes against Humanity*,

Recalling also the international instruments already adopted by Unesco, including in particular the *Convention and Recommendation against Discrimination in Education*, the *Recommendation concerning the Status of Teachers*, the *Declaration of the Principles of International Cultural Cooperation*, the *Recommendation concerning Education for International Understanding, Cooperation and Peace and Education relating to Human Rights and Fundamental Freedoms*, the *Recommendation on the Status of Scientific Researchers*, and the Recommendation on participation by the people at large in cultural life and their contribution to it,

Bearing in mind the four statements on the race question adopted by experts convened by Unesco,

Reaffirming its desire to play a vigorous and constructive part in the implementation of the program of the Decade for Action to Combat Racism and Racial Discrimination, as defined by the General Assembly of the United Nations at its twenty-eighth session,

Noting with the gravest concern that racism, racial discrimination, colonialism and apartheid continue to afflict the world in ever-changing forms, as a result both of the continuation of legislative provisions and government and administrative practices contrary to the principles of human rights and also of the continued existence of political and social structures, and of relationships and attitudes, characterized by injustice and contempt for human beings and leading to the exclusion, humiliation and exploitation, or to the forced assimilation, of the members of disadvantaged groups,

Expressing its indignation at these offenses against human dignity, *deploring* the obstacles they place in the way of mutual understanding between peoples and *alarmed* at the danger of their seriously disturbing international peace and security,

Adopts and solemnly proclaims this Declaration on Race and Racial Prejudice:

Article 1

1. All human beings belong to a single species and are descended from a common stock. They are born equal in dignity and rights and all form an integral part of humanity.

2. All individuals and groups have the right to be different, to consider themselves as different and to be regarded as such. However, the diversity of life styles and the right to be different may not, in any circumstances, serve as a pretext for racial prejudice; they may not justify either in law or in fact any discriminatory practice whatsoever, nor provide a ground for the policy of apartheid, which is the extreme form of racism.
3. Identity of origin in no way affects the fact that human beings can and may live differently, nor does it preclude the existence of differences based on cultural, environmental and historical diversity nor the right to maintain cultural identity.
4. All people of the world possess equal faculties for attaining the highest level in intellectual, technical, social, economic, cultural and political development.
5. The differences between the achievements of the different peoples are entirely attributable to geographical, historical, political, economic, social and cultural factors. Such differences can in no case serve as a pretext for any rank-ordered classification of nations or peoples.

Article 2

1. Any theory which involves the claim that racial or ethnic groups are inherently superior or inferior, thus implying that some would be entitled to dominate or eliminate others, presumed to be inferior, or which bases value judgments on racial differentiation, has no scientific foundation and is contrary to the moral and ethical principles of humanity.
2. Racism includes racist ideologies, prejudiced attitudes, discriminatory behavior, structural arrangements and institutionalized practices resulting in racial inequality as well as the fallacious notion that discriminatory relations between groups are morally and scientifically justifiable; it is reflected in discriminatory provisions in legislation or regulations and discriminatory practices as well as in anti-social beliefs and acts; it hinders the development of its victims, perverts those who practice it, divides nations internally, impedes international co-operation and gives rise to political tensions between peoples; it is contrary to the fundamental principles of international law and, consequently, seriously disturbs international peace and security.
3. Racial prejudice, historically linked with inequalities in power, reinforced by economic and social differences between individuals and groups, and still seeking today to justify such inequalities, is totally without justification.

Article 3

Any distinction, exclusion, restriction or preference based on race, color, ethnic or national origin or religious intolerance motivated by racist considerations, which destroys or compromises the sovereign equality of States and the right of peoples to self-determination, or which limits in an arbitrary or discriminatory manner the right of every human being and group to full development is incompatible with the requirements of an international order which is just and guarantees respect for human rights; the right to full development implies equal access to the means of personal and collective advancement and fulfillment in a climate of respect for the values of civilizations and cultures, both national and world-wide.

Article 4

1. Any restriction on the complete self-fulfillment of human beings and free communication between them which is based on racial or ethnic considerations is contrary to the principle of equality in dignity and rights; it cannot be admitted.
2. One of the most serious violations of this principle is represented by apartheid which, like genocide, is a crime against humanity, and gravely disturbs international peace and security.
3. Other policies and practices of racial segregation and discrimination constitute crimes against the conscience and dignity of mankind and may lead to political tensions and gravely endanger international peace and security.

Article 5

1. Culture, as a product of all human beings and a common heritage of mankind,

and education in its broadest sense, offer men and women increasingly effective means of adaptation, enabling them not only to affirm that they are born equal in dignity and rights, but also to recognize that they should respect the right of all groups to their own cultural identity and the development of their distinctive cultural life within the national and international context, it being understood that it rests with each group to decide in complete freedom on the maintenance and, if appropriate, the adaptation or enrichment of the values which it regards as essential to its identity.

2. States, in accordance with their constitutional principles and procedures, as well as all other competent authorities and the entire teaching profession, have a responsibility to see that the educational resources of all countries are used to combat racism, more especially by ensuring that curricula and textbooks include scientific and ethical considerations concerning human unity and diversity and that no invidious distinctions are made with regard to any people; by training teachers to achieve these ends; by making the resources of the educational system available to all groups of the population without racial restriction or discrimination; and by taking appropriate steps to remedy the handicaps from which certain racial or ethnic groups suffer with regard to their level of education and standard of living and in particular to prevent such handicaps from being passed on to children.
3. The mass media and those who control or serve them, as well as all organized groups within national communities, are urged — with due regard to the principles embodied in the *Universal Declaration of Human Rights*, particularly the principle of freedom of expression — to promote understanding, tolerance and friendship among individuals and groups and to contribute to the eradication of racism, racial discrimination and racial prejudice, in particular by refraining from presenting a stereotyped, partial, unilateral or tendentious picture of individuals and of various human groups. Communication between racial and ethnic groups must be a reciprocal process, enabling them to express themselves and to be fully heard without let or hindrance. The mass media should therefore be freely receptive to ideas of individuals and groups which facilitate such communication.

Article 6

1. The State has prime responsibility for ensuring human rights and fundamental freedoms on an entirely equal footing in dignity and rights for all individuals and all groups.
2. So far as its competence extends and in accordance with its constitutional principles and procedures, the State should take all appropriate steps, *inter alia* by legislation, particularly in the spheres of education, culture and communication, to prevent, prohibit and eradicate racism, racist propaganda, racial segregation and apartheid and to encourage the dissemination of knowledge and the findings of appropriate research in natural and social sciences on the causes and prevention of racial prejudice and racist attitudes, with due regard to the principles embodied in the *Universal Declaration of Human Rights* and in the *International Covenant on Civil and Political Rights*.
3. Since laws proscribing racial discrimination are not in themselves sufficient, it is also incumbent on States to supplement them by administrative machinery for the systematic investigation of instances of racial discrimination, by a comprehensive framework of legal remedies against acts of racial discrimination, by broadly based education and research programs designed to combat racial prejudice and racial discrimination and by programs of positive political, social, educational and cultural measures calculated to promote genuine mutual respect among groups. Where circumstances warrant, special programs should be undertaken to promote the advancement of disadvantaged groups and, in the case of nationals, to ensure their effective participation in the decision-making processes of the community.

Article 7

In addition to political, economic and social measures, law is one of the principal means of ensuring equality in dignity and rights among individuals, and of curbing any propaganda, any form of organization or any practice which is based on ideas or theories referring to the alleged superiority of racial or ethnic groups or which seeks to justify or encourage racial hatred and discrimination in any form. States should adopt such legislation as is appropriate to this end and see that it is given effect and applied by all their services, with due regard to the principles embodied in the *Universal Declaration of Human Rights*. Such legislation should form part of a political, economic and social framework conducive to its implementation. Individuals and other legal entities, both public and private, must conform with such legislation and use all appropriate means to help the population as a whole to understand and apply it.

Article 8

1. Individuals, being entitled to an economic, social, cultural and legal order, on the national and international planes, such as to allow them to exercise all their capabilities on a basis of entire equality of rights and opportunities, have corresponding duties towards their fellows, towards the society in which they live and towards the international community. They are accordingly under an obligation to promote harmony among the peoples, to combat racism and racial prejudice and to assist by every means available to them in eradicating racial discrimination in all its forms.
2. In the field of racial prejudice and racist attitudes and practices, specialists in natural and social sciences and cultural studies, as well as scientific organizations and associations, are called upon to undertake objective research on a wide interdisciplinary basis; all States should encourage them to this end.
3. It is, in particular, incumbent upon such specialists to ensure, by all means available to them, that their research findings are not misinterpreted, and also that they assist the public in understanding such findings.

Article 9

1. The principle of the equality in dignity and rights of all human beings and all peoples, irrespective of race, color and origin, is a generally accepted and recognized principle of international law. Consequently any form of racial discrimination practiced by a State constitutes a violation of international law giving rise to its international responsibility.
2. Special measures must be taken to ensure equality in dignity and rights for individuals and groups wherever necessary, while ensuring that they are not such as to appear racially discriminatory. In this respect, particular attention should be paid to racial or ethnic groups which are socially or economically disadvantaged, so as to afford them, on a completely equal footing and without discrimination or restriction, the protection of the laws and regulations and the advantages of the social measures in force, in particular in regard to housing, employment and health; to respect the authenticity of their culture and values; and to facilitate their social and occupational advancement, especially through education.
3. Population groups of foreign origin, particularly migrant workers and their families who contribute to the development of the host country, should benefit from appropriate measures designed to afford them security and respect for their dignity and cultural values and to facilitate their adaptation to the host environment and their professional advancement with a view to their subsequent reintegration in their country of origin and their contribution to its development; steps should be taken to make it possible for their children to be taught their mother tongue.
4. Existing disequilibria in international economic relations contribute to the exacerbation of racism and racial prejudice; all States should consequently endeavor to contribute to the restructuring of the international economy on a more equitable basis.

Article 10

International organizations, whether universal or regional, governmental or non-governmental, are called upon to co-operate and assist, so far as their respective fields of competence and means allow, in the full and complete implementation of the principles set out in this Declaration, thus contributing to the legitimate struggle of all men, born equal in dignity and rights, against the tyranny and oppression of racism, racial segregation, apartheid and genocide, so that all the peoples of the world may be forever delivered from these scourges.

Declaration on the Rights of Persons Belonging to National or Ethnic, Religious and Linguistic Minorities (1992)

The General Assembly,

Reaffirming that one of the basic aims of the United Nations, as proclaimed in its Charter, is to promote and encourage respect for human rights and for fundamental freedoms for all, without distinction as to race, sex, language or religion,

Reaffirming faith in fundamental human rights, in the dignity and worth of the human person, in the equal rights of men and women and of nations large and small,

Desiring to promote the realization of principles contained in the *Charter of the United Nations*, the *Universal Declaration of Human Rights*, the *Convention on the Prevention and Punishment of the Crime of Genocide*, the *International Convention on the Elimination of All Forms of Racial Discrimination*, the *International Covenant on Civil and Plitical Rights*, the *International Covenant on Economic, Social and Cultural Rights*, the *Declaration on the Elimination of All Forms of Intolerance and of Discrimination Based on Religion or Belief*, and the *Convention on the Rights of the Child*, as well as other relevant international instruments that have been adopted at the universal or regional level and those concluded between individual States Members of the United Nations,

Inspired by the provisions of article 27 of the *International Covenant on Civil and Political Rights* concerning the rights of perosns belonging to ethnic, religious or linguistic minorities,

Considering that the promotion and protection of the rights of persons belonging to national or ethnic, religious and linguistic minorities contribute to the political and social stability of States in which they live,

Emphasizing that the constant promotion and realization of the rights of persons belonging to national or ethnic, religious and linguistic minorities, as an integral part of the development of society as a whole and within a democratic framework based on the rule of law, would contribute to the strengthening of friendship and cooperation among peoples and States,

Considering that the United Nations has an important role to play regarding the protection of minorities,

Bearing in mind the work done so far within the United Nations system, in particular the Commission on Human Rights, the Sub-Commission on Prevention of Discrimination and Protection of Minorities as well as the bodies established pursuant to the International Covenants on Human Rights and other relevant international human rights instruments on promoting and protecting the rights of persons belonging to national or ethnic, religious and linguistic minorities,

Taking into account the important work which is carried out by intergovernmental and non-governmental organizations in protecting minorities and in promoting the rights of persons belonging to national or ethnic, religious and linguistic minorities,

Recognizing the need to ensure even more effective implementation of international instruments with regard to the rights of persons belonging to national or ethnic, religious and linguistic minorities,

Proclaims this *Declaration on the Rights of Persons Belonging to National or Ethnic, Religious and Linguistic Minorities*:

Article 1

1. States shall protect the existence and the national or ethnic, cultural, religious and linguistic identity of minorities within their respective territories, and shall encourage conditions for the promotion of that identity.
2. States shall adopt appropriate legislative and other measures to achieve those ends.

Article 2

1. Persons belonging to national or ethnic, religious and linguistic minorities (hereinafter referred to as persons belonging to minorities) have the right to enjoy their own culture, to profess and practise their own religion, and to use their own language, in private and in public, freely and without interference or any form of discrimination.
2. Persons belonging to minorities have the right to participate effectively in cultural, religious, social, economic and public life.
3. Persons belonging to minorities have the right to participate effectively in decisions on the national and, where appropriate, regional level concerning the minority to which they belong or the regions in which they live, in a manner not incompatible with national legislation.
4. Persons belonging to minorities have the right to establish and maintain their own associations.
5. Persons belonging to minorities have the right to establish and maintain, without any discrimination, free and peaceful contacts with other members of their group, with persons belonging to other minorities, as well as contacts across frontiers with citizens of other States to whom they are related by national or ethnic, religious or linguistic ties.

Article 3

1. Persons belonging to minorities may exercise their rights including those as set forth in this Declaration individually as well as in community with other members of their group, without any discrimination.
2. No disadvantage shall result for any person belonging to a minority as the consequence of the exercise or non-exercise of the rights as set forth in this Declaration.

Article 4

1. States shall take measures where required to ensure that persons belonging to minorities may execise fully and effectively all their human rights and fundamental freedoms without any discrimination and in full equality before the law.
2. States shall take measures to create favourable conditions to enable persons belonging to minorities to express their characteristics and to develop their culture, language, religion, traditions and customs, except where specific practices are in violation of national law and contrary to international standards.
3. States should take appropriate measures so that, wherever possible, persons belonging to minorities have adequate opportunities to learn their mother tongue or to have instruction in their mother tongue.
4. States should, where appropriate, take measures in the field of education, in

order to encourage knowledge of the history, traditions, language and culture of the minorities existing within their territory. Persons belonging to minorities should have adequate opportunities to gain knowledge of the society as a whole.

5. States should consider appropriate measures so that persons belonging to minorities may participate fully in the economic progress and development in their country.

Article 5

1. National policies and programmes shall be planned and implemented with due regard for the legitimate interests of persons belonging to minorities.
2. Programmes of cooperation and assistance among States should be planned and implemented with due regard for the legitimate interests of persons belonging to minorities.

Article 6

States should cooperate on questions relating to persons belonging to minorities, including exchange of information and experiences, in order to promote mutual understanding and confidence.

Article 7

States should cooperate in order to promote respect for the rights as set forth in this Declaration.

Article 8

1. Nothing in this Declaration shall prevent the fulfilment of international obligations of States in relation to persons belonging to minorities. In particular, States shall fulfil in good faith the obligations and commitments they have assumed under international treaties and agreements to which they are parties.
2. The exercise of the rights as set forth in this Declaration shall not prejudice the enjoyment by all persons of universally recognized human rights and fundamental freedoms.
3. Measures taken by States in order to ensure the effective enjoyment of the rights as set forth in this Declaration shall not *prima facie* be considered contrary to the principle of equality contained in the *Universal Declaration of Human Rights*.
4. Nothing in this Declaration may be construed as permitting any activity contrary to the purposes and principles of the United Nations, including sovereign equality, territorial integrity and political independence of States.

Article 9

The organs and specialized agencies of the United Nations system shall contribute to the full realization of the rights and principles as set forth in this Declaration, within their respective fields of competence.

Appendix III
A Chicago Survey on Self-Determination

Dr. Farid I. Muhammad

The International Human Rights Association of American Minorities (IHRAAM), an NGO in consultative status with the Economic and Social Council of the United Nations, conducted an extensive phone survey of registered voters throughout the city of Chicago. A systematic sample of 507 registered voters revealed that 89% believed that "problems of racial inequality exist in American society," while 50% of those voters agreeing with this statement believed such inequality exists to a "significant degree." Survey data were gathered during November, 1993 in preparation for a report to the UN Human Rights Committee.

The purpose of the study was to determine American voters' awareness of the U.S. ratification of the UN International Covenant on Civil and Political Rights (ICCPR), and their attitudes toward the issue of "self-determination" for African-American citizens. Since its ratification of the ICCPR on September 8, 1992, the U.S. has submitted its obligatory Five-Year Plan to the UN Human Rights Committee. This report proposes steps to be taken by the U.S. to comply with international human rights law and related requirements.

Though it was found that 73% of all voters were not aware of the UN's ICCPR and the U.S. ratification, 58% did believe "that African-Americans have the right to self-determination." When asked if they believe "that the U.S. Constitution and present U.S. civil rights legislation adequately protect African-American citizens and insure them fair and equal treatment," 40% of all voters said "yes," 27% were "uncertain" and 33% responded "no." Voters were also asked if they "believe that Special Measures, which are consistent with the rule of international law, should be extended to African-Americans in their attempt to achieve true and equal status with the majority ethnic group in the U.S." Fifty-three (53%) of all voters responded "yes" to this item, while 36% were "uncertain" and 11 said "no."

Results further indicated that 52% of Chicago voters "believe that African-Americans have the right to independently elect State and National Councils to help manage and represent their collective interests." In responding to this same question, 72% of all African-American voters said "yes," while only 39% of Anglo-American voters were similarly inclined. Eight voter variables were analyzed to determine which were most significantly related to voter attitudes on these issues. It was found that registered voters in southern wards of Chicago were significantly more in favor of self-determination for African-Americans than were voters in either the central or nothern sectors of the city. Additionally, the voter variables of race, social class and education were found to be the best correlates with and predictors of voter attitudes concerning this issue.

In short, African-American voters living in typically "working class" communities which are already geographically and demographically isolated, tended to be significantly in favor of exercising "self-determination." Exclusive of the variables of race and social class, the study also revealed that Chicago voters who completed high school, college or graduate study were significantly more in favor of self-determination for African-Americans than were voters who had an 8th grade education or less. Female voters also tended to be slightly more in favor than were male voters.

IHRAAM has submitted its findings to Secretary-General Boutros Boutros-Ghali and the UN Human Rights Committee as an extension of an earlier report. Among its recommendations to the UN, IHRAAM suggests there be a wider dissemination of UN human rights information, as requested by 70% of voters surveyed. IHRAAM also encouraged continued and expanded study of human rights issues as they relate to American national minorities.

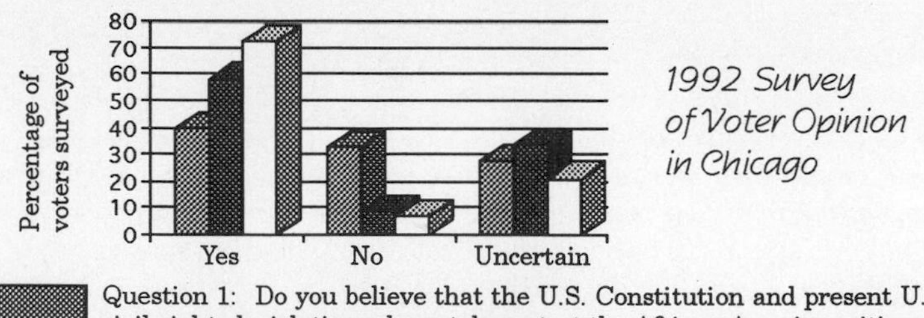

1992 Survey of Voter Opinion in Chicago

Question 1: Do you believe that the U.S. Constitution and present U.S. civil rights legislation adequately protect the African-American citizenry and ensure them fair and equal treatment?

Question 2: Do you believe that African-Americans have the right to self-determination?

Question 3: Do you believe that African-Americans have the right to independently elect state and national councils to help manage and represent their collective interests?